THE FREEDMEN'S BUREAU IN VIRGINIA:

NAMES OF DESTITUTE FREEDMEN DEPENDENT UPON THE GOVERNMENT IN THE MILITARY DISTRICTS OF VIRGINIA

EXTRACTED AND COMPILED BY
ELIZABETH CANN KAMBOURIAN

HERITAGE BOOKS
2009

HERITAGE BOOKS
AN IMPRINT OF HERITAGE BOOKS, INC.

Books, CDs, and more—Worldwide

For our listing of thousands of titles see our website at
www.HeritageBooks.com

Published 2009 by
HERITAGE BOOKS, INC.
Publishing Division
100 Railroad Ave. #104
Westminster, Maryland 21157

Copyright © 1997 Elizabeth Cann Kambourian

All rights reserved. No part of this book may be reproduced or transmitted in any form or by any means, electronic or mechanical, including photocopying, recording or by any information storage and retrieval system without written permission from the author, except for the inclusion of brief quotations in a review.

International Standard Book Numbers
Paperbound: 978-0-7884-0774-1
Clothbound: 978-0-7884-7623-5

This book is dedicated to my children:

Daphne K. Dandridge

Melissa K. Kidd

Haig B. Kambourian, 3rd

Christopher Lee Cann

TABLE OF CONTENTS

Destitute Freedmen in Fauquier, Prince William,
Stafford and King George Counties 1

Destitute Freedmen in Norfolk County 2

Destitute Freedmen in Nansemond & Southampton
Counties 10

Indigent Freedmen in Northampton County,
Eastern Shore 10

Destitute Freedmen in Accomac County 11

Destitute Freedmen in Princess Anne County . . 12
    On the Gregory Farm 14
    On the Hopkins Farm 18, 21
    On the Sylvester Farm 18
    On the Bilisoly and Lindsay Farms 19
    On the Taylor Farm 20

Destitute Freedmen in Halifax County 22

Destitute Freedmen in Greensville and
Dinwiddie Counties 28

Destitute Freedmen in Cumberland County 29

Destitute Freedmen in Chesterfield County . . . 30

Destitute Freedmen at City Point 31

Destitute Freedmen in Charlotte County 34

Destitute Freedmen in Buckingham and
Brunswick Counties 35

Destitute Freedmen in Lunenburg County 36

Destitute Freedmen in Mecklenburg County . . . 37

Destitute Freedmen in Nottoway County 39

Destitute Freedmen in the City of Petersburg . 40

Destitute Freedmen in Powhatan County 44

Destitute Freedmen in Prince Edward County . . 44

Destitute Freedmen in Prince George County . . 49

Destitute Freedmen in Surry County 54

Destitute Freedmen at Howard's Grove Hospital,
City of Richmond 55

Destitute Freedmen in the City of Richmond . . 59

Destitute Freedmen in Henrico County 60

Destitute Freedmen and Orphans
in Goochland County 62

Destitute Freedmen in Greene County 63

Destitute Freedmen in Fluvanna County 64

Destitute Freedmen in the Town of Fredericksburg 67

Destitute Freedmen in Spotsylvania County . . . 69

Destitute Freedmen in Frederick County 71

Destitute Freedmen in Jefferson County
(now West Virginia) 71

Destitute Freedmen in Hospital at Lynchburg,
Amherst Co. VA 73

Destitute Freedmen in Hospital at Amherst
Courthouse, VA   73

Destitute Freedmen in Hospital at Lovington,
Nelson Co. VA   74

Destitute Freedmen in Hospital at Appomattox
Courthouse, VA   74

Destitute Freedmen in Hospital at Liberty,
Bedford Co. VA   74

Names of Persons Dependent on the Government
Rationed at Fort Monroe, VA   76

Indigent Freedmen at the Downey Farm,
Princess Anne County 107

Destitute Freedmen at the Yorktown Commissary,
York Co. VA 112

Former Slave Owners Listed with
Their Freed Slaves 115

Free Born Persons at Fort Monroe,
Hampton, VA 178

Free Born Persons at the Downey Farm in
Princess Anne Co. VA 180

COUNTY MAPS

Virginia and West Virginia   ix

North Carolina x

Maryland   xi

The Freedmen's Bureau in Virginia

The Bureau of Refugees, Freedmen and Abandoned Lands was created by an act of Congress in March 1865, in response to the need in the former Confederate States for an agency to oversee the affairs of the newly freed slaves. The passing of the legislation marked the end of several years of ad hoc programs and joint ventures intended to help the freedmen. These early attempts had been undertaken by the occupying Union Army, the Department of the Treasury, the War Department, and northern benevolent societies.

When the Civil War broke out in 1861, President Lincoln had no policy for dealing with runaway slaves who would come under the control of the U.S. Army as it occupied territory in the south. Union military bases throughout the south dealt with their incoming black refugees in a variety of ways. At first, the runaways were declared "contraband", ie., property of the enemy that could potentially be used to further the war effort against the United States. Many were put to work building fortifications. Others were put to work on abandoned plantations to produce crops, which would be sent to market to supplement the U.S. Treasury. Northern abolitionist and benevolent societies soon sent teachers and volunteers to help the transitional blacks, who were now free of their old masters, but still under the close watch of the U.S. Army as "contraband".

When the war ended and civil order had to be restored in the south, the need for a more structured organization became a necessity. There had been some four million slaves freed in the south, who now made up a huge unemployed class of people with no means of support. Many of those needing assistance were uneducated, lone women with dependent children, and the elderly and infirm.

The Bureau of Refugees, Freedmen and Abandoned Lands' most critical job at the outset was to keep these indigent persons alive. The newly freed slaves had to be fed, housed, educated, and put to work. The local districts of the Bureau distributed food, medical supplies, clothing and some housing.

Next in importance was putting the vast labor pool to work in a region where the socio-economic structure had collapsed. With the economy in ruins, the quickest way to get the old plantations back into production, and pay the freedmen a regular wage, was under the system of labor contracts. This plan allowed freedmen and their families, often as a unit, to make a contract with local plantation owners, or with the managers of confiscated "government farms". Sometimes black workers found themselves in the employ of their former owners - either earning a specific wage, or a portion of the crop at the end of the growing season.

Soon, however, abuses in the contract system flared up. There were white land owners who refused to pay the wages or crop share according to agreement. Some of the freedmen refused to work, and attempted to evade the terms of the contracts. It became clear that a higher authority would be needed to oversee the contract system - to protect the blacks from being cheated, and to see that the whites received the labor force for which they had contracted. Most of all, the U.S. government wanted to see the economy restored. They wanted southern plantations back in production, the former slaves gainfully employed and not dependent on the government for their sustenance.

The Freedmen's Bureau took over the contract system - writing the contracts or approving those presented to them by the contracting parties. Most importantly, the Bureau enforced the terms of the contracts on both the white and black signers.

At the close of the war, the civil authority in the south was in the same disordered condition as the economy. The local courts were not dispensing justice, and still favored whites who came before them. Freedmen found that they were being cheated out of their property, harassed, and assaulted, with little or no recourse to the law. The Freedmen's Courts were set up as a temporary measure to handle complaints and lawsuits of freedmen until the civil authority could be brought into line in the southern military districts.

Another aspect of the Freedmen's Bureau was the investigation of bounty claims made by former "colored troops". Those blacks, free born and slave, who had joined the Union armed forces were owned certain bounties for their service. Many were illiterate, and when they became ensnared in bureaucratic red tape after the war, free-lance "agents" offered to help them claim their bounties - often cheating the black veteran in the bargain. The Bureau soon took over the duty of resolving the uncollected or disputed claims for the freedmen.

The Assistant Superintendent of the Freedmen's Bureau in Virginia was responsible for collecting reports from the various military districts in the state. Each local jurisdiction (county or town) made monthly reports to their District leader, who then made his own report, which was forwarded to the Headquarters in Washington, D.C.

These local and District reports contained information about social and economic conditions, relations between the races, crimes and court activity. Reports were also sent of the accounts of recruited soldiers, and the bounties they were due. The localities and Districts also sent accounts of food, housing and medical treatment dispensed to the indigent - both black and white, many of which contained the names of those persons who had received assistance. It is these reports, letters and accounts which make up the bulk of the Bureau of Refugees, Freedmen, and Abandoned Lands' records for the Commonwealth of Virginia.

In the 67 rolls of microfilm in the Library of Virginia, there are several which contain a goldmine of names of newly freed slaves. These lists appear in reports on destitute freedmen, military bounty claims, and outrages committed against freedmen.

This work is taken from reel 57, concerning destitute freedmen. These records are reports and correspondence to and from Virginia localities. Many contain lists of former slaves and free blacks who received rations and medical help from the Freemen's Bureau in Virginia. The personal information recorded about the recipients varied from locality to locality. However, all reporting jurisdictions gave the former (or "pre-war") residence of the freedmen.

Some of the persons in this record lived outside of Virginia before the war. County maps of Virginia (including the counties now comprising West Virginia), North Carolina and Maryland have been provided to assist in locating pre-war residences of the freedmen.

GENERAL SERVICES ADMINISTRATION:
National Archives and Records Service
National Archives Microfilm Publications: #M1048
Roll 57, Virginia Records:
Records of the Assistant Commissioner For the State of Virginia Bureau of Refugees, Freedmen, and Abandoned Lands, 1865-1869.

➢ Records Relating to Destitute Freedmen and Refugees.
➢ Lists of Destitute Freedmen in Districts 1-10.
➢ Narrative Reports of Local Boards of Overseers

The section entitled, **Lists of Destitute Freedmen in Districts 1-10, March through June 1866,** was used to extract the names of the freedmen in this work. These documents consisted of reports and lists found in Target 2 of Roll 57, pages 239-590. This information was a record of rations issued to destitute freedmen. The personal information included with the name of the individual varied from locality to locality. All of the information was sent as county or town reports, and stated the names of the recipient, and where that person had lived before the war.

This abstract follows the same format: name of the jurisdiction making the report (jurisdiction's name appears in upper case letters), followed by the names of recipients listed under their pre-war residence (appearing in lower-case letters). Any personal information, such as age, description, former owner, or dependents is listed after the person's name. Age ranges are noted by the following symbols:

x - under age 14   *no symbol* - between 15 and 30
+ - between 31 and 50   * -   over age 50

An index has been provided of freedmen surnames, free blacks, and former owner's names. Those freedmen who were listed with no surname, are indexed under suname *Unknown*, followed by their first name.

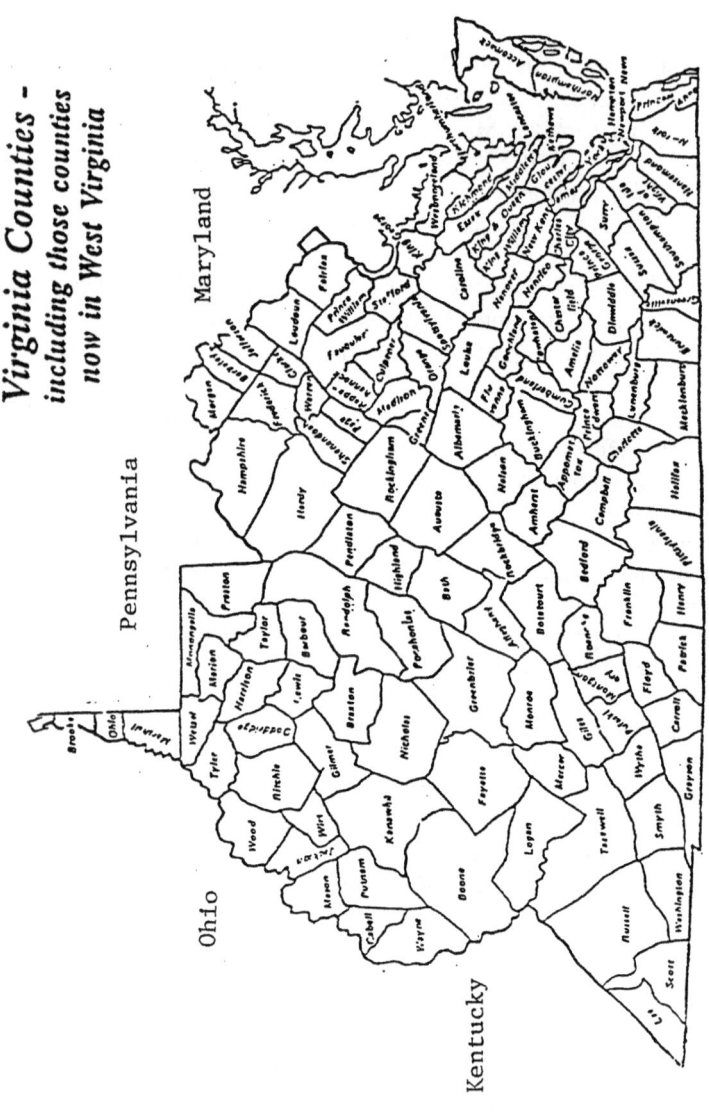

North Carolina Counties

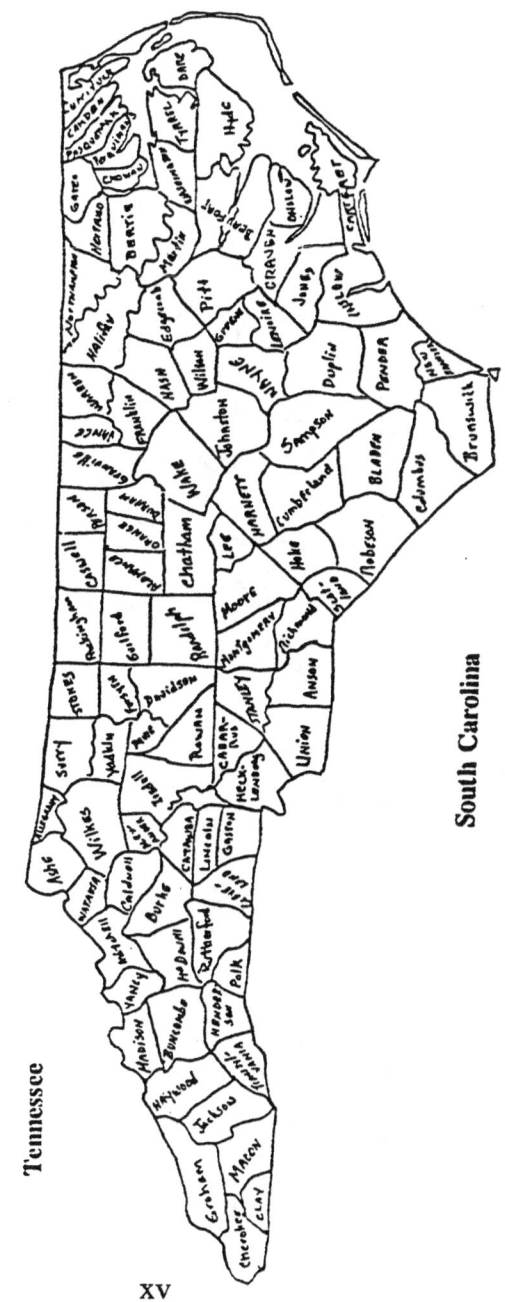

Maryland Counties

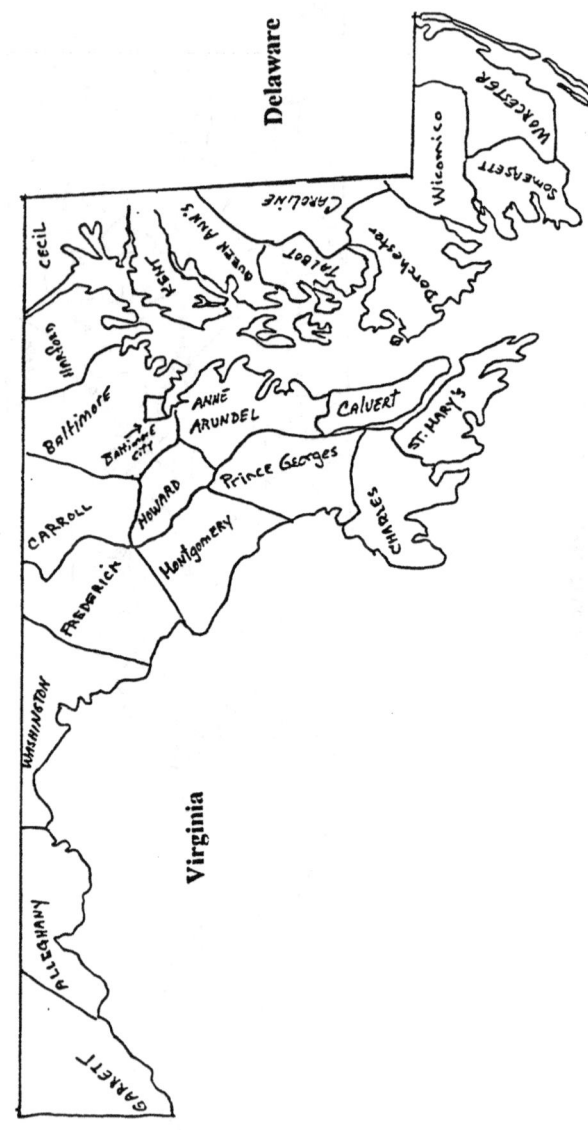

DESTITUTE FREEDMEN RECEIVING CHARITY FROM THE GOVERNMENT BUREAU OF REFUGEES AND FREEDMEN: [57.245]

DESTITUTE FREEDMEN IN FAUQUIER CO. VA

[57.247]
Fauquier Co. VA
Butler, Israel
Butler, Nancy
Combs, Agnes
Combs, Lewis
Gladdox, Elvira
Gladdox, Thomas

Jennings, Ned
Mother, Robin
Payne, George
Ransdell, Norah
Smith, Elias

From Roanoke VA
Taylor, Polly: *

Norfolk Co. VA
Baker, Paris: *
Foreman, John H: x
Foreman, Mary E: x
Shiff, Tempest: *
Walke, Milley: *

DESTITUTE FREEDMEN PRINCE WILLIAM CO. VA

Davis, Emma B: 4 small children, from Fairfax Co. VA

DESTITUTE FREEDMEN IN STAFFORD CO. VA

[57.248]
Fairfax Co. VA
Bell, David: & wife
Grey, Lewis

Grey, Richard
Jones, Winny
Meyor, Nancy
Monday, Barney

Nelson, Emilie
Warnder, Edmund
Washington, George

DESTITUTE FREEDMEN IN KING GEORGE CO. VA

King George Co. VA
Bland, Ann
Dunlop, Mary
Fitzhugh, Sophia
Green, Hannah
Key, Walker
Lucas, Winny
Lumick, Harriet
Miller, Mrs: & 2 sisters
Page, Adam
Taylor, Lucy

Unknown, Eda
Unknown, Elibeck
Unknown, Evan
Unknown, Kitty
Unknown Lewis
Unknown, Miller
Unknown, Patty
Unknown, Ralph
Unknown, Thomas
Unknown, William
West, Milley

Young, Barber
[57.249]
Bradshaw, George
Branagan, Mary
Branagan, Richard
Burl, Ettie
Burl, Jinney
Burl, John
Crigwell, Manuel
Dickens, John
Frazer, Garrett

Galvin, Thomas
Green, Hannah
Grymes, Winny
Hoe, Abraham
Jackson, Thomas
Jackson, William
Lucas, Elizabeth
Marshall, Hannah
Mirsells, Ann
Moxley, Emma

Samuel, Mrs.
Shanklins, Ann
Smith, Catherine
Starke, Virginia
Unknown, Agr?
Unknown, Beny
Unknown, Hager
Unknown, Hellon
Unknown, Jenny

Unknown, Wessley
Unknown, Winea Ann

[57.250]
Westmoreland Co.
Johnson, Eliza
Johnson, Robert
Johnson, Lindon

DESTITUTE FREEDMEN IN NORFOLK CO. VA

[57.254]
Norfolk Co. VA
Ives, Jenny
Lovis, Hannah
Lovis, Mary A.
Minkens, Charlotte
Minkens, John
Minkens, Venus
Minkins, Caroline
Person, Mary
Scott, George W.
Scott, Mary
Smith, Esther
Smith, Francis
Smith, Henry
Smith, Martha A.
Smith, Mary
Smith, Nelly
Whitehurst, Milly
Williams, Pleasant
Wilson, George T.
Wilson, Mary
Wilson, Virginia
[57.255]
Brown, Aaron
Brown, Amy
Brown, Benny

Brown, Cyrenous
Brown, Elizabeth
Brown, Frank
Brown, Georgiana
Brown, Isaac
Brown, John
Brown, Liddia
Brown, Lucy
Brown, Maggie
Brown, Mary
Brown, Matilda
Brown, Milly
Brown, Rhoda
Butt, Jack
Butt, Mary
Butt, Rachel
Butt, Ruben
Butt, Sarah
Carr, Josephus
Carr, Mary J.
Carr, Robert J.
Cherry, Ellen
Cherry, Emily
Cherry, Henry
Colden, Allen: x
Colden, Mary: x
Colden, Willie: x

Copeland, Julia
Copeland, Lizzie
Copeland, Margaret
Cuffey, Anna
Cuffey, John F: x
Cuffey, Nathaniel: x
Cuffey, William: x
Elliott, Charity: *
Elliott, Hulda
Elliott, James H: x
Elliott, Mary: x
Elliott, Solomon
Ely, Hetty
Ely, Margaret: x
Ely, Mary: x
Ely, Peter: x
Foreman, Caroline
Foreman, Mary: x
Foreman, Tyler
[57.256]
Brown, Aaron: x
Brown, Lovey: x
Brown, Lydia: x
Brown, Milly: *
Carr, Josephus: x
Carr, Mary J.
Carr, Robert J: x

Cheny, Emily
Cheny, Ellen: x
Cheny, Henry: x
Collin, Allen: x
Collin, Mary
Collin, Willis: x
Copeland, Julia
Copeland, Lizzie: x
Copeland, Margaret: x
Copper, John: x
Copper, Mollie
Copper, Penny
Copper, Samuel: x
Corprew, James E: x
Corprew, Jenny: x
Corprew, Laura
Cross, George T: x
Cross, Harriet: x
Cross, Mary
Cross, Walter: x
Cuffey, Calvin: *
Cuffey, Mahala
Cuffey, Matilda: *
Cuffey, Sarah E.
Dean, M.A.: x
Dean, Nancy A: x
Dean, Sarah
DeFord, Hannah: x
DeFord, Hilary: x
DeFord, Jacomin
Elliott, Betsey
Elliott, Charlotte: x
Elliott, Elizabeth: x
Elliott, Nancy
Fobs, Amelia
Fobs, George F.
Fobs, Sarah A.
Fogg, Alexander: x
Fogg, General Jackson: x
Fogg, Lithia
Forbes, Clarissa

Forbes, Edmond: x
Forbes, Mary: x
Foreman, Caroline
Foreman, Harrison: x
Foreman, Mary: x
Foreman, Sylvia
Fulford, Mary
Fulford, Mathew: x
Fulford, Oscar J: x
Fuller, Abbie
Fuller, Mary E. F: x
Fuller, Moses: x
Goodman, Martha
Goodman, Miles: x
Hall, Alexander: x
Hall, David W: x
Hall, Jane
Hall, Lovey
Hall, Rachel
Hodges, Indiana
Hodges, Johnson: x
Hodges, Kneeland: x
Hodges, William: x
Hoffman, Fanny: x
Hoffman, Laura: x
Hoffman, Martha
Hoffman, William: x
Hollman, Bob: x
Hollman, John: x
Hollman, Louisa
Hopkins, Frances: x
Hopkins, Jerry: x
Hopkins, Maria: x
Hopkins, Rosetha
Hopkins, Sylvia: x
Jackson, Alexander: x
Jackson, Amanda
Jackson, Henry: x
Jackson, Mary: x
Jackson, Sarah: x
Knight, Emma: x

Knight, George: x
Knight, Jane
Knight, Milly: x
Knight, Sarah: x
Land, Jack: x
Land, Joshua: x
Land, Mary: x
Land, Phillis
Land, Priscilla: x
Lovis, Hannah
Lovis, Jennie: *
Lovis, Margrett: x
Magruder, Anna: x
Magruder, Filly
Miller, Lavinia: *
Mingo, Acrious: x
Mingo, Margaret: x
Mingo, Maria
Mingo, Rondus: x
Miniver, Armetta
Miniver, Maria
Moseby, Emily: x
Moseby, Joseph: x
Moseby, Lovey
Nicholson, Essex : x
Nicholson, Frances
Nicholson, Robert: x
Peirce, Harriett: x
Peirce, Joshua
Peirce, Martha
Peldia, Penny: +
Person, Betty
Person, Mary: x
Phillips, Alvin: x
Phillips, Cally
Phillips, Charlotte
Phillips, George: x
Phillips, John: x
Phillips, Martha A: x
Pitt, John H: x
Pitt, Lenna

Pitt, Lily A.
Pitt, Mary: x
Pitt, Mary E: x
Pitt, Robert H: x
Pitt, William F: x
Pool, Cilla
Pool, Jenny: x
Posen, Alice: x
Posen, Martha
Posen, Moses: x
Reed, Amy: x
Reed, Maria: x
Reed, Rachel
Riddick, Alice: x
Riddick, Granby: x
Riddick, Jeff: x
Riddick, Linda: x
Riddick, Lucy
Riddick, Marcella
Riddick, Margaret
Riddick, Martha
Riddick, Milly
Riddick, Phillis: x
Riddick, Samuel: x
Riddick, Sarah: x
Riddick, Wanida: x
Riddick, Wise: x
Roberts, Catherine
Roberts, Lovey: x
Roberts, Samuel: x
Schuckons, John: x
Schuckons, Lovey: x
Schuckons, Mathilda
Schuckons, Washington: x
Scott, George W: x
Scott, Mary
Shephard, Jane
Sheppard, Hannah
Sheppard, John: x
Sheppard, Mary: x
Smith, Eliza

Smith, Esther
Smith, Frances: x
Smith, Henry: x
Smith, Martha A.
Smith, Nelly: x
Smith, Walter: x
Sparrow, Edmund: x
Sparrow, Isaiah: x
Sparrow, Jane: *
Sparrow, Joshua: x
Sparrow, Milly: x
Sparrow, Rosetta
Spence, Alice: x
Spence, Miria
Taylor, Joe: x
Taylor, Mary: x
Taylor, Rebecca
Taylor, William: x
Thomas, Adamanta
Thomas, Celia: x
White, George: x
White, Lidia
White, Mary: x
White, Washington: x
Wiggins, Barbara A: x
Wiggins, Eliza
Wiggins, Sarah F: x
Wilkins, Caroline: x
Wilkins, Charlotte
Wilkins, Harnett
Wilkins, Jane: x
Wilkins, John: x
Wilkins, Venus: x
Wilson, Agnes: x
Wilson, Ellen
Wilson, George T: x
Wilson, Harriett
Wilson, James: x
Wilson, Jane
Wilson, John: x
Wilson, Josephine: x

Wilson, Leah: x
Wilson, Mary E: x
Wilson, Mary E: x
Wilson, Mary
Wilson, Stephen: x
Wilson, Virginia: x
Wilson, Willis: x
[57.257]
Aikens, Eliza
Aikens, George
Aikens, Andrew
Aikens, Bailey
Aikens, Pleasant
Aikins, George L: x
Aikins, Alexander: x
Aikins, Dennis E: x
Aikins, Lucinda: *
Akins, Matilda
Akins, John: x
Akins, Jesse: x
Akins, Betty: x
Akins, Ella: x
Allen, Biddy A: x
Allen, Abbie
Armstead, Polly: *
Armstead, Harry: x
Armstrong, Fanny
Armstrong, Lewis
Armstrong, Emma
Armstrong, Milly: +
Ash, Rachel
Ash, Alfred: x
Ash, Abram: x
Baines, Phoebe
Baines, David J: x
Baker, Willis: x
Baker, Richard
Baker, Lilly
Bell, Barbara
Bell, Diana: *
Bell, Sylvia: *

Benedict, Mary: +
Bensen, Fanny: *
Berry, Charles A: x
Berry, Annie
Blanchester, Mary*
Blunt, Rachel: *
Borne, Mills
Borne, Faby
Borne, Martha J.
Bracy, Rosetta: +
Bright, James S.
Bright, Catherine
Bright, Louisa
Bright, Harriett
Bright, Jack: *
Brown, William: x
Brown, Phillis
Brown, Lucinda
Brown, Mary: x
Brown, Amanda
Brown, Louisa M: x
Burrel, Frank
Burrell, Esther: *
Capps, Nancy: *
Carter, Sarah
Carter, Caroline
Carter, Alexander
Carter, Dulaney: +
Chimes, Julia A.
Civil, James
Civil, Fanny
Civils, Virginia
Civils, Virginius: x
Civils, Charles L: x
Civils, Adolphus: x
Clark, Liny A: x
Clark, Martha
Clark, Ann E: x
Clark, Susannah
Collins, Child: x
Collins, Maria: x

Cooper, Melissa: *
Cooper, Melissa
Cooper, Pleasant
Cormick, David O.
Cormick, Sylvia
Cormick, Sylvia *
Corprew, James E.
Corprew, Laura
Corprew, Jenny
Cotten, Charlotte: +
Cross, Mary
Cross, George T.
Cross, Harriott
Cross, Walter
Cuffey, Nathaniel: x
Cuffey, Calvin
Cuffey, Louisa
Cuffey, Mahala
Cuffey, Sarah E.
Cuffey, Matilda
Cuffey, Hannah
Cuffey, Ethindger: x
Cuffey, William: x
Cuffey, Joshua: x
Cuffey, Cornelius: x
Cuffey, Thursday
Cuffey, Chloe: x
Davis, Corson: *
Deans, Tarply
Derdan, Rachel: x
Derdan, Mary
Derdan, Betsey: x
Derdan, Albert: x
Doherty, Lucy: +
Edmunds, Sarah
Edmunds, Martha: x
Edmunds, Washington: x
Edwards, James
Edwards, Thomas
Elliott, Amanda
Elliott, Jamie: x

Elliott, Elizabeth
Elliott, Bitsey
Elliott, Charles: x
Elliott, Sylvia: x
Elliott, Celia: x
Elliott, Rachel
Everedge, Robert J: x
Everedge, Barbara
Foreman, Sarah
Foreman, Edith: *
Foreman, George E: x
Fortune, Adeline: +
Foster, Maria: x
Green, Esther: +
Green, Rose: x
Green, Eliiza A: x
Harrison, Sarah: x
Harrison, Frances: x
Harrison, Mary: x
Herbert, Ellorick: x
Herbert, Charlotte
Herbert, William: x
Higgins, Sarah F.
Higgins, Eliza
Higgins, Barbara
Hodges, Daniel: +
Holmes, Lucinda: +
Hopkins, Maria: x
Hopkins, Henrietta: x
Hopkins, Ann: x
Hopkins, Jerry: x
Hopkins, Rosetta
Hopper, Lucinda: x
Hopper, Ellen
Hopper, Margrett: x
Hunter, Ann: x
Hunter, William T: x
Hunter, Fanny
Hunter, Africa
Hunter, Lydia: *
Hunter, Mary F.

James, Fanny: *
Johnson, Wilson: *
Jolly, Robert: *
Jones, Eliza
Jones, Joseph: x
Jones, Sidney: x
Joney, Tamar: *
Judkins, Louisa: *
Lafayette, Lu Johnson:x
Lafayette, Mary E: x
Lafayette, Edgar: x
Lafayette, Sarah
Langley, Julia L: x
Langley, Gawford
Langley, Jacob: x
Lawford, George: x
Lawford, Louisa
Lunford, George: x
Manning, Ann
Marshall, Mathew: x
Marshall, Frances
McKennsy, Susan
Mercer, Isaac: +
Miller, Larina
Morris, Christiania: x
Morris, Jockey
Morris, George J: x
Morris, Rose: *
Nash, Robby: x
Nash, William: x
Nash, Chloe
Olds, Peter: x
Olds, Nancy: x
Olds, Mary
Olds, Lyman: x
Parker, Cherry: +
Parker, Adna
Parker, Catherin: x
Parsens, John: +
Pegram, Marinda: *
Randolph, Bracy: +

Rawles, Joe: x
Rawles, Ben: x
Rawles, Phoebe
Rawles, Ann: x
Rawls, Sally: +
Reed, Owen
Riddick, Lucy: x
Riddick, Rosetta: x
Riddick, Georgeanna: x
Riddick, Nancy
Riddick, Margaret: x
Riddick, Anthony: +
Riddick, Martha: x
Riddick, Charles: x
Riddick, Charlotta: +
Riddick, Margaret: +
Rogers, Sallie
Rogers, Joshua
Rogers, Sallie: *
Rogers, Cintha: x
Rud, Nancy
Scott, Emma: x
Scott, Lucy: x
Shafford, Edward: x
Shafford, Chloe: *
Shafford, Lucy: x
Shafford, Esther: *
Shafford, Mary E: x
Shins?, Dennis: x
Shins?, Sarah J: x
Shins?, Silvester: x
Shins?, Sophia
Simmons, Catherine: x
Simmons, Nathaniel: x
Simmons, Prisilla
Smallwood, Nancy: *
Smith, George: +
Smith, Alice: *
Smith, Minerva: x
Smith, Thomas: x
Smith, Maria: x

Smith, Jesse: x
Smith, Nester: *
Smith, Fanny
Smith, Julia: x
Smith, James F: x
Smith, Josephine: x
Smith, Louisa
Smith, Stephen, x
Smith, Marsha
Smith, Jimmie: x
Snead, Caroline
Southall, Wiley: x
Stearns, Ann
Stone, Caroline: x
Stone, Kate: *
Tatum, Carey: *
Tatum, Ann
Tatum, Louisa: x
Tatum, John F: *
Temples, Grace: *
Thompson, Warner: *
Walke, Jeffrey: x
Walke, Susannah: x
Walke, Caroline
Walke, Maria: +
Walke, Amy: +
Walker, Mary: *
Watson, Avery: +
Watts, Amy: *
Webb, Mary
Webb, Emma: x
Webb, Max
Webb, Jerry: x
Webb, Ada: +
White, Violet
White, Phillis: x
White, Henrietta: x
White, Margaret
White, Julius B: x
Whitehurst, Jane
Whitehurst, Mary: x

Whitehurst, William: x
Whitehurst, Anna E: x
Whitehurst, David: x
Whitehurst, Fanny
Whitehurst, Charlotte:+
Whitehurst, Peter: +
Wilkins, Jane
Wilkins, Jane T: x
Wilkins, Henrietta: x
Willey, Jessee: x
Willey, Rosetta
Williams, William H: x
Williams, Chaney: x
Williams, Jane S: x
Williams, Chlorinda
Williams, Eda: *
Williams, Walter B: x
Williams, Margaret: x
Williams, Agnes: x
Williams, Angeline: x
Williams, Benjamin: x
Williams, Ellen
Williams, Lydia
Williams, Hannah
Williams, Jack: x
Williams, Fletcher: x
Wills, Child: x
Wills, Mary: +
Wilson, Sylvia: x
Wilson, Mary E: x
Wilson, Nelly: *
Wilson, L. H.: x
Wilson, Lucy
Wilson, Nancy: +
Wilson, Sallie: +
Wilson, Margrett: x
Wilson, Emeline
Wilson, George W. L: x
Wilson, William: x
Wood, Caroline
Wood, Julia A: x

Wood, Land E: x
Wood, Louisa: x
Wood, Annie
Wood, Mary: x
Wood, James: x
Wright, Isham: +
Wright, Priscilla: +
Young, Laura
Young, Hammett: x
Young, Ann: x

[57.256]
Accomac Co. VA
Williams, Emily
Williams, Laura: x

[57.257]
Brunswick Co. VA
Southold, Eliza
Southold, Julia: x
Southold, Franklin: x
Southold, Charles: x

[57.253]
Camden Co. NC
Civils, Hannah
Civils, Betty: x
Forbes, Clara
Forbes, Mary: x
Forbes, Edward: x
[57.256]
Morgan, Ann
Morgan, Charles: x
Morgan, Alice: x
Morgan, Alexander: x

Chowan Co. NC
Davenport, Sarah
Davenport, Sarah: x
Davenport, Ellen: x
Davenport, Mary

Williams, Pleasant: *

[57.252]
Currituck Co. NC
Bell, Winnie: *

[57.256]
Gates Co. NC
Rawls, Adeline
Rawls, Joseph: x
Rawls, Edmund: x
Willey, Rosetta
Willey, Kate: x
Willey, Ann: x
Willey, Davey: x
Willey, Killy: x
[57.257]
Casey, Nancy: +
Hunter, Amica: x
Hunter, Frank: x
Laster, Leah?: x
Laster, Augustus: x
Matthews, Judy: +
Matthews, Mary E: x
Morgan, Barbara
Morgan, Elinore: x
Morgan, Ann E: x
Morgan, Isaiah: x
Oflin, Silvia: x
Oflin, Caleb: x

[57.256]
Henrico Co. VA
Furtress, Sarah J.
Furtress, Mary F: x
Furtress, Emma J: x
Furtress, Miles A: x
Furtress, Emma: x
Furtress, Thomas: x
Schuchins, Louise
Schuchins, Daniel: x

Schuchins, Louisiana: x
Schuchins, Priscilla: x

[57.255]
Isle of Wight Co. VA
Sheppard, Jane
Sheppard, John
[57.256]
Shephard, Julia: x
Shephard, Anna: x

Hertford Co. NC
Kane, Doxamia
Kane, Albert
Kane, Kane
Kane, Arthur
Kane, Rose
Kain, Albert
Kain, Arthur: x
Kain, Rose: x
Goodman, Louisa
Goodman, Erastus: x
Goodman, Eva: x
[57.257]
World, Rosetta: *

[57.253]
Mathews Co. VA
Moore, Caroline: *
Moore, Frances: x
Moore, W.A.: x

[57.252]
Middlesex Co. VA
Pamels?, Catherin
Pamels?, Columbus: x
Pamels?, John R: x

[57.253]
Nansemond Co. VA
Brothers, Milly: x

Brothers, Samuel: x
Brothers, Margaret: x
Brothers, Harriet: x
[57.255]
Brinkley, Mary
Brinkley, Joe
Brinkley, Fannie
Brinkley, Rhoda
Brinkley, Harriett
Brinkly, Emily
Brinkly, Cary
Brinkly, Randall
Brinkly, Willis
Cotefield, Jane
Dean, Sarah
Dean, John
Dean, Margaret
Dean, Martha
Dean, Nelson
Elliott, Arabella
Elliott, Cornelius
Elliott, James
Missonin, Elliott
Wilson, Eliza
Wilson, Richard B.
[57.256]
Colefield, Jane
Cormick, David O: x
Cormick, Jesse: *
Cormick, Sylvia: *
Edwards, David: *
Edwards, Henrietta: x
Edwards, Henry: x
Edwards, Penny
Edwards, Rosaline: x
Elliott, Arabella
Elliott, Cornelius
Elliott, Egypt: x
Elliott, James
Elliott, Josephine: x
Elliott, Missinin?: x

Johnson, Emma: x
Johnson, Harriett
Johnson, Thomas
Liggins, Diana
Liggins, Joseph: x
Liggins, Missonn: x
Madray, Jane: x
Marshal, Hanah
Marshal, Martha: x
Marshal, Mary: x
Marshal, Robert: x
Nathan, Chloe
Nathan, Isaiah: x
Nathan, Samuel: x
Raby, Charity
Reed, Alex: x
Reed, Ame
Reed, George: x
Reed, Mills E: x
White, Ada
White, Burrel: x
White, Sarah: x
[57.257]
Calhoun, Harrison: +
Colding, Edna
Cooper, Julia: +
Copland, Mary +
Copland, Joe: x
Copland, Martha: x
Copland, William: x
Council, Patience: +
Curtis, Hester
Curtis, Henry: x
Curtis, Celia: x
Curtis, Agnes: x
McCoy, Lydia W: +
Newby, Delia
Newby, Rhoda: +
Norflet, Esther: +
Riddick, Sally: +
Riddick, Harriet: x

Riddick, Ginger: x
Riddick, Marshall: +
Riddick, Annice: x
Riddick, Maria

Pasquotank Co. NC
Williams, Hannah

[57.253]
Perquimons Co. NC
Heinger, John: x
Heinger, Henry: x

[57.252]
Princess Anne Co. VA
Bright, Cormien, *
McClennan, Rose Ellen: x
McClennan, Roseman: x
McClennan, Mary
McClennan, Cary W: x
Monday, Amy: *
Moore, Andy: x
Moore, Charles: x
Moore, Ellary *
Romey, Isaac: x
Romey, Georgeanne: x
Romey, Jane: *
Willey, Mary E: x
Willey, Phillis
Willey, Millis: x

Wondow, Martha: x
Wondow, Mary A.

[57.253]
Coleman, Mary
Coleman, Jane: x
Coleman, Eliza: x
Land, Margaret: *
Ray, Hannah
Reed, Phillis

[57.256]
Smith, Alice: x
Smith, Moses: x
Thomas, Fanny
Thomas, Richard: x
Thomas, July: x
Thomas, Martha
Thomas, Winnie: x
Thomas, Martha: x
West, Adeline
West, William H: x
West, Sarah J: x
Whitehurst, Milley
Wilson, Hannah
Wilson, Walter: x
Wilson, George: x

[57.257]
McCoy, Charlotte: +
Monday, Mary
Monday, Mary F: x

Monday, Daniel: x
Reed, Robert: x

[57.256]
From Smith Mills, NC
Proctor, Eliza
Proctor, Martha: x
Proctor, John: x

[57.254]
From St. Charles, MD
Holly, Nancy
Holly, Frank
Holly, Adelia
Holly, Sarah F.

[57.256]
From St. Mary's, MD
Dickenson, Sue
Dickenson, James: x
Dickenson, Jerome
Dickenson, Ann
Singleton, Sallie
Singleton, Frances: x
Singleton, Peter: x
Smith, Martha

[57.257]
From Summerton, NC
Williams, Chancy: +

DESTITUTE FREEDMEN IN NANSEMOND & SOUTHAMPTON COUNTIES, VA

[57.258]
Norfolk Co. VA
Elliott, Richard: x
Elliott, Jane E: x

Southampton or Nansemond Cos. VA
Bates, Isaac: *
Bates, Jane: *
Couley, Thomas

Donan, Levica
Donan, Lucinda: x
Donan, Moses: x
Masin, Eliza
Masin, George
Perry, Mathilda: *
Perry, Peter: x
Perry, Samuel: *
Perry, Samuel: x
Perry, Thomas: x

Riddick, George
Smith, Bob: *
Spratley, Benjamin: x
Spratley, George: x
Spratley, Margaret
Spratley, Sarah
Stewart, Mary
Wason, Moranda
Wright, Andres: +
Wyatt, Mahala: *
Wyatt, Phillip: *

INDIGENT FREEDMEN IN NORTHAMPTON CO. THE EASTERN SHORE OF VIRGINIA

Accommac Co. VA
Brent, Mary: x
Creppen, Margaret: x
Elliott, Anne: x
Elliott, Nancy
Goffigan, Thomas: *
Groton, Charlotta
Holland, Ned: *
Mingo, Susan: x
Parker, Allen: x
Parker, George: x
Parker, Sidney: x
Smith, Peggy: *
Snead, Bartlett:
Snead, Mary: x
Snead, Sally
Sninners?, Lucy: x
Sninners?, Matilda: x
Steley, Henry: x
Steley, Margaret: x
Steley, Martha: x
Steley, Mary
Steley, Mollie: *

Norfolk Co. VA
Beesley, John: x
Briggs, Leah: *
Bros, Sarah: x
Bros, Sophy
Brown, Eliza
Brown, Molly: x
[57.259]
Smith, Isabel: x
Turlington, Sarah: x
West, Daniel: *
Young, William

Chesapeake, VA
Bell, Lucy: x
Branch, Edward: x
Branch, Israel: x

Northampton Co. VA
Bird, Elijah
Bivins, Juliet
Bivins, Patsy
Carter, Berthie: *

Carter, Georgeanna: x
Collins, Henry
Costin, Anne: x
Costin, Daniel: *
Costin, Isaac: x
Day, Thomas
Downs, Lovilla: x
Elliott, Anna
Fisher, Ada: *
Gillet, Maria
Goffigan, Benjamin: *
Griffin, Salley
Henry, Pauline
Henry, Robert
Holden, George
Jackson, Rachel: *
Jackson, Robert: *
Joyner, Caleb
Joyner, Scipio
Kellum, Emanuel
Mapp, Isaac: *
Mason, George: x
Mason, Leah

Morris, Charles: x
Morris, Daniel: x
Morris, Henry: x
Morris, Jenny: x
Morris, Lewis: x
Morris, Margaret: x
Morris, Nannie: x
Morris, Rachel: x
Morris, William: x
Morris, Wilson: x
Nelson, Alice: x
Nelson, Avilla: x
Nelson, Rose: x
Nottingham, Ellen: x
Nottingham, George: x
Nottingham, George: x
Nottingham, Indiana
Nottingham, Leonard: x
Nottingham, Susan: x
Nottingham, Walter: x

Page, Thomas
Palmer, Sarah: *
Parker, Milborn: *
Parsons, Samuel
Powell, Tabitha
Read, James: *
Reed, Harry: *
Rivers: George: x
Rivers: Julia
Sachel, Fannie
Saunders, Laban
Saunders, Patsey: x
Savage, Henry
Savage, Jessee: x
Savage, Reuben: x
Scott, Amy: *
Shatten, Nancy: *
Small, Burrel: x
Small, Rose: *
Smaugh, Laura

Smith, Lily: x
Smith, Maria
Smith, Walker
Smith, Weller: x
Spadey, Agnes: *
Spadey, Fannie: *
Tannel, Kitty
Tazewell, Betsey
Tazewell, Martha: x
Thomas: George: x
Thomas, Louisa
Thomas, William: x
Thompson, George: x
Thurston, Phoebe: *
Titchet, Mans: x
Toavers, Leah: *
Upshur, George: *
Wescott, Isaac: x
West, Arthur
Williams, Martha

INDIGENT FREEDMEN ACCOMAC CO. VA

[57.259]
Accomac Co. VA
Allen, Joseph
Bayley, Edmond
Conquest, Bettie: *
Conquest, Clara
Coulborn, Leah
Davis, Edward
Fairford?, Kitty

Finney, Henry: *
Finney, Poliena: *
Harris, George: x
Holmes, Emma
Lewis, Winder: x
Northam, Jim: *
Parramore, Sarah
Wafe, Sarah: *
West, Rachel

Wharton, Lettie: x
Wise, Eda
Wise, Franklin
Wise, James: x
Wise, Janetta
Wise, Martha
Wise, Mary
Wright, Ani

INDIGIENT FREEDMEN IN PRINCESS ANNE CO. VA & ON GOVERNMENT FARMS

[57.261]
Camden Co. NC
Fereby, March: *
Fereby, Maria: *
Williams, Dennis: x
[57.262]
Duke, Jerry
Williams, Emily
Williams, Penny: x
Williams, Nelson: x
Williams, Alfred: x
Williams, Edmund: x

[57.261]
Charles City Co. VA
Crosby, Charles: *
Crosby, Katy: *
Hall, Fanny: *
Jackson, Fanny: x
Jackson, Louisa
Jackson, Paul: x
Jackson, Phillip: x
Jackson, Rosa: x
Jackson, Solena: x
Jones, David: x
Jones, Harriet: x
Jones, Henry: x
Jones, Thomas: x

[57.262]
Chowan Co. NC
Stafford, Elliott
Stafford, Maria
Stafford, Sawyer: x

[57.261]
Currituck Co. NC
March, Benjamin: *
March, Dorcas: *
[57.262]
Hughes, Jacob
Hughes, Milley
Lindsay, Abel
Lindsay, Jenny
Lindsay, Milley: x
McGuire, Lucy: *

Elizabeth City Co. NC
Duke, Phoebe
Duke, Harriet: x
Duke, Jerry Jr: x
Duke, Mark: x
Williams, Isaac
Williams, Betsey
Williams, Joseph
Williams, Patience
Williams, George: x
Williams, Noah: x
Williams, Charity: x
Williams, Mary: x

[57.261]
Essex Co. VA
Harrison, Millie: *
Harrison, Nancy: *
Harrison, Lucy: *

[57.265]
Young, Randall: *
Young, Anna: *
Young, Martha
Young, John H.
Young, Cornelius

[57.261]
Gates Co. NC
Brister, Eliza: *
Franklin, Margaret
Franklin, Charles: x
Franklin, Monroe: x
Franklin, Adaline: x
Franklin, Rosilla: x
Franklin, Lucy: x
Franklin, Maria: x
Moore, Rachael
Moore, Wilson: x
Moore, Mills: x
Moore, Columbus: x
Williams, Lucilla: *
Williams, Jane
[57.262]
Reddick, Wilson
Reddick, Rachel
Reddick, Valentine: x
Reddick, Sally: x
Roberts, Madeline
Roberts, Ida: x
Roberts, Frances: x
Roberts, Lee: x
Roberts, Denison

Hertford Co. NC
White, Emma
White, Anna: *
White, Celia: *

Leonards Town, MD
Hayden, Eliza
Hayden, Elen: x
Hayden, Louisa: x
Hayden, Abraham: x

[57.261]
Mathews Co. VA
White, Thomas
White, Grace
Robinson, Rosa

[57.261]
Murray, VA
Newby, Anna
Newby, Corbin: x
Newby, E: x
Newby, Elizabeth

Nansemond Co. VA
Chapman, Hester
Chapman, Lucy: x
Chapman, Mary: x
Chapman, Jacob
Chapman, Victoria: x
Chapman, William: x
Gale, Susannah: *
Gordon, Henry: *
Gordon, Eliza: *
Newfelt, Samuel: *
Newfelt, Catherine: *
Newfelt, Thomas: x
Newfelt, Rebecca
Newfelt, Georgiana: x

[57.262]
Bayner, Ellen
Bayner, Adnan: x
Bayner, Zachariah: x
Bayner, Levi: x
Sanders, Wilson
Sanders, Benny
Sanders, George
Sanders, Caroline: x
Sanders, Frank: x
[57.263)
Cross, Sally: *
Cross, Taylor
Cross, Eliza
Cross, Eli
Cross, Martha
Cross, Thomas
Cross, Lucinda
Cross, Cassandra
Cross, Taylor: x
Cross, Jane

[57.262]
Norfolk Co. VA
Walston, Malachia
Walston, Hagar
Walston, Daniel: x
Walston, Mary: x
Walston, Lemuel: x

Pennsylvania
Henley, Samuel
Henley, Johanna
Henley, Eliza: x
Henley, Thomas: x
Henley, Johanna: x

[57.261]
Prince George Co. VA
Graves, Betty: x

Princess Anne Co. VA
Bell, Fanny
Bell, Solomon: x
Bell, Mary: x
Bell, Alduston: x
Bell, John J: x
Bell, Mahala: x
Payton, Mary: x
Owens, Loveam
Owens, Charles: x
Owens, George: x
Owens, Walter: x
[57.262]
Wright, Venus

South End, NC
Gordon, Sarah
Gordon, Marietta
Gordon, Chloe
Gordon, Elizabeth

Southampton Co. VA
Tyler, Lyburn
Tyler, Penny

[57.261]
St. Mary's Co. MD
Mason, Margaret
Mason, Anna
Mason, Charles
Mason, David
Mason, Emma

DESTITUTE FREEDMEN ON THE GREGORY FARM IN PRINCESS ANNE CO. VA

[57.262]
St. Mary's Co. MD
Bros, Charity: x
Bros, Dudly: x
Bros, Mary
Love, Bruce: x
Love, Edward: x
Love, Jane
Love, Stanley
Love, Susan: x
Marshall, Malinda: *
Marshall: Margaret
McElroy, Henson: x
McElroy, Lucind
Mitchell, Amanda: x
Mitchell, John W: x
Mitchell, Matthew: x
Mitchell, Nancy: x
Mitchell, Sarah
Waters, Amelia: *
Waters, Frank: *
Waters, Mary E.
Waters, Phillis
Waters, Rebecca

Princess Anne Co. VA
Banks, Joshua: *
Cormick, Mary E: *
Cormick, Nancy
Cormick, Phillis: *
Cornick, Alice
Cornick, Harry: x
Cornick, Isabella: x
Cornick, Jenny: x
Cornick, Peter: x
Loud, Lucinda: *
Scott, Dinah: *
Simmons, Hannah: *

Simmons, William: *
Whithurst, Eliza
Whithurst, Frank
Whithurst, Jacob
Whithurst, Lucinda: x
Whithurst, Pleasant
[57.263]
Cason, Amy: x
Cason, Andover: x
Cason, Chany: x
Cason, Hannah
Cason, Mahala: x
Cason, Nancy: x
Cason, Owen: x
Cormick, Anthony:
  (on Dozier Farm)
Cormick, Fulton
Cormick, Henry
Cormick, Joseph: x
Cormick, Martha
Cormick, Mary
Cormick, Mary: x
Couch, Charles W: x
Couch, Harriett
Couch, Samuel: x
Hunter, Alexander: x
Hunter, Frank
Hunter, Jack: x
Hunter, Jordon: x
Hunter, Joseph: x
Hunter, Lizzie: x
Hunter, Lucinda:
Hunter, Maria
Hunter, Martha: x
Hunter, Mary
Hunter, Sarah
Hunter, Thomas: x
Lincoln, George: x

Valentine, Rachel: *
Weldon, Adeline
Weldon, Anthony: x
Weldon, Francis
Weldon, Lovel
Weldon, Peter
Woodhouse, Fanny: x
Woodhouse, Henry: x
Woodhouse, James: x
Woodhouse, Lucy
Dozier, Joseph: *
Dozier, Margaret: x
Dozier, Samuel: *
Dozier, Mollie: *
Dozier, Georgeanne: x
Dozier, Henry: x
Fereby, Mary
[57.264]
Canter, Mary:
  (at Bradford Farm)
Cornick, James: *
Cornick, Sally
Cornick, William
Cornick, James P.
Cornick, Amy: x
Cornick, Anthony: x
Cornick, John: x
Humphrey, Louisa: x
Humphrey, Jeffrey: x
McCoy, Henry: x
McCoy, Harriet: x
Olds, Sallie: x
Olds, Carrie: x
Palmer, Margaret: x
Parsons, Thomas: x
Parsons, James: x
Parsons, Joseph: x
Patten, Pallis: x

Steers, Alice
Snowden, George: x
Snowden, Alice: x
Whitehouse, Judy
Butt, Susan: x
Gaines, William: x
McPherson, John: x
McPherson, Chloe: x
McPherson, Alice: x
Munden, Mary
Munden, Delia: x
Munden, Sallie W: x
Munden, Obed.: x
Munden, George: x
Robinson, Fanny
Robinson, Mary: x
Robinson, Lucy P: x
Wise, Charlotte: *
[57.265]
Brock, Anthony: *
Brock, Edith
Overstreet, Clara: *

[57.263]
Isle of Wight Co. VA
Duck, Maria
Stock, Esther A.
Goodin, William H: x
Mason, Barrett: *
 (on Baxter Farm #2)
Pope, Clarissy: x
Taylor, Ann E.
Taylor, George: x
[57.264]
Watkins, Jacob: *
Watkins, Nancy: *

[57.262]
St. Mary's Co. MD
Garner, Mary
Garner, Celia: x

Garner, John: x
[57.264]
Games, Celia: x
Games, John

Charles City Co. VA
Armistead, Burrel: *
Armistead, Maria: *
Carter, Jane
Carter, Nelson: *
Partis, Eva: *

[57.262]
Middlesex Co. VA
Fleet, Archy: *
Fleet, Hannah: *
Jefferson, Ellen
Jefferson, Mary E: x
Jefferson, Charles: x
Jefferson, Alice: x
[57.263]
Robinson, Robert: *
Robinson, Lucy: *

[57.262]
Mathews Co. VA
White, Henry: *
White, Polly: *
White, Mary

Gates Co. NC
Powell, Lucinda
Powell, Israel
[57.263]
Spotman, Benjamin: x
Taylor, Louisa: (on
 Murray Farm, from
 Gates Co. NC)
Taylor, John: x
Taylor, Bragg: x
[57.264]

Hinton, Samuel: *
Hinton, Martha: *
Hinton, Sarah J: *
Hinton, Marietta: x
Hinton, Georgianna: x
Hinton, Charles W: x
Hinton, Susan: x
Hinton, Cherry S: x
Walton, Joseph: *
Walton, Patience: *
Walton, Harriett
Walton, Moses
Scutching, Joe
Bond, David: *
Bond, Esther: *
Bond, Hardy: *
Bond, Joseph: x
Harold, Jeremiah: *
Harold, Emma: *
Harold, Eddie
Harold, Delia: x
Harold, John: x
Harold, Abra: x
Walton, Granville: *
Walton, Eliza: *
Walton, Elsey
Walton, Dinah: *

[57.263]
Currituck Co. NC
Gregory, Hannah: x
Bray, George: *
Bray, Margaret: x
Bray, Thomas
Bray, Dorcas
Bray, Owen
Bray, Eliza: x
Bray, John: x
Bray, Edmund: x
Bray, Martha: x
Barrett, Charlotte

Barrett, Henry: x
Barrett, Abel: x
Barrett, Emily: x
Barrett, Nora
Dozier, Solana
Dozier, Emeline: x
Dozier, Mary: x
Dozier, Pleasant: x
Dozier, Aaron: x

Camden Co. NC
Sanlin, Phoebe
Sanlin, George
Sanlin, Charles
Sanlin, Harriett: x
Sanlin, Willis: x
Sanlin, Cherry: x
Sanlin, Elijah: x
Sanlin, Edwin W: x
Sanlin, Margaret: x
Sanlin, Emma: x

Murray, VA
Hopkins, Robin: x
Hopkins, Phillis
Hopkins, John J: x
Hopkins, David: x
Hopkins, William H: x
Hopkins, Sarah: x

Hertford Co. NC
Durden, William: x

Elizabeth City, NC
Cassen, Fanny
Cassen, Henry: x
Johnson, Harriett: *
Hannah, Crazy

Norfolk, VA
Pritchett, Atty: *

Pritchett, Clara: *

Chowan Co. NC
Riddin, Sarah
Riddin, Mary
Fereby, Lydia: x
Fereby, Jinny
Fereby, Lucinda

South End, NC
Gordon, Tony: *
Gordon, Debby
Gordon, Willey

[57.264]
Suffolk, VA
Goodsend, Aldolphus
Goodsend, Solon: x
Goodsend, Angenett: x
Goodsend, Joseph: x
Goodsend, G. Washington: x
Goodsend, Harriett: x
[57.265]
Goodsend, Harriet
Goodsend, Everett: *

[57.264]
Southampton Co. VA
Reed, Granville: *
[57.265]
Amon, Thomas: *
Gurley, Frank: *
Drew, Elenora
Drew, Hannah
Drew, Thomas
Drew, Fletcher: x
Drew, Ruberta: x
Drew, Ann: x
Drew, Abraham L: x

[57.264]
Elizabeth City Co. VA
Colins, Agnes

New Kent Co. VA
Washington, Sarah: *

Norfolk VA
Armstrong, America: x
Armstrong, Frank: x
Brown, Dennis: x
Brown, John: x
Brown, Joseph: x
Brown, Lewis: x
But, Charles
Corporal, James: x
Corporal, Nancy: x
Corporal, Washington: x
Dozier, George: x
Dozier, Harriett: x
 (on Etheridge Farm)
Wash, Alsena
Wash, Ann
Wash, Nelson
Berry, Elliza
Berry, Charles: x
Berry, Jane: x
Warden, Eliza
Warden, Georgeanna: x
Warden, Jeremiah: x
Warden, Amy: x
Warden, Maria: x
[57.265]
Douglass, George: *
Douglass, Mary
Wilson, Charlotte
Wilson, Sarah: x
Wilson, Mary: x
Wilson, Sargent: x
Wilson, Joseph: x
Wilson, Annie: x

Smith, Ann
Smith, Mary
Smith, John: x
Smith, Charlotte: x
Willey, Samuel: x
Willey, Lucy
Wise, Alfred: *
Wise, Kate: *

[57.264]
Nansemond Co. VA
Askey, Thomas: x
Baker, Ida: x
Baker, Margaret
Johnson, Edward: *
Johnson, Emily: *
Johnson, Hannah
Johnson, Kindall: *
Johnson, Phillips: *
Scutching, Paris: *
Smith, Elsa
Smith, Mary
[57.265]
Godwin, Aaron: *
Godwin, Louisa: *
Godwin, Stevens
Godwin, James
Godwin, Horace: x
Godwin, Charles
Perry, Commodore: *
Perry, Serena
Perry, Arthur: x
Perry, Isaac: x
Perry, Rebecca: x
Perry, James: x
Small, Jerry: *

[57.264]
Camden Co. NC
Fereby, Eliza: Wise Farm
Fereby, Mary E: x
Fereby, Ambrose: x
Fereby, Ely: x
Gregory, Ellen
[57.265]
Sawyer, Amy
Sawyer, Chloe
Sawyer, George: x
Sawyer, Frank: x
Sawyer, Rebecca: x
Sawyer, Thomas: x

[57.264]
Gates Co. NC
Riddick, Samuel: *
Saxe, Charles: *

Maryland:
Sewell, Mary: *

Chowan Co. NC
Warner, James: *
Warner, Susan: *
[57.265]
Bowser, Lovey: *
Bowser, Rachel: *
Elliott, Emma: J: *
Elliott, Meriam: *
Elliott, Noneh: *
 (on Hardy Farm)
Harner, Lavinia
Harner, Mary
Harner, Michael
Harner, Nathaniel: *
Warren, Nancy: *
Warren, Theresa

Gates Co. NC
Gadline, James: *
Hinton, Esther: *
James, Frances: x
Riddick, Isabella: x
Riddick, Sally
Riddick, Sam: *
Riddick, Sansbury: x
Riddick, Virginia: x
Sanders, Betty: x
Sanders, Joseph: *
Sanders, Milley
Trotman, Drucilla: *
Trotman, Sol: *
Trotman, Stephen: x
Trotman, Tamar: x
Trotman, Wright: x
Wright, Benjamin
Wright, Ellen: x
Wright, Hannah
Wright, Harriet
Wright, Isaac: x
Wright, James: *
Wright, Maria: x
Wright, Nancy: *
Wright, Rosetta: x
Wright, Sabra: x

Murfreesboro, NC
Deane, Dennis: *
Deane, Mary: *
Wise, Charlotte: *
Wise, Adelaide: x
Wells, Peggy: *
Southall, Mary
Southall, Margaret: x
Southall, Amanda: x
Southall, Osgood: x
Southall, Baby: x

Somerton, NC
Brinkley, Phillis
Brinkley, Briton: x

Warner, Melinda
Warner, Tamar: x
Warner, Mary: x

Noel, Edmund: x
Noel, Lewis: x
Noel, Katie: x

Edenton, NC
Warner, D.
Warner, Joseph: *
Warner, Merander
Warner, Ann

Charles City Co. VA
Noel, Phillips: *
(at Baker Farm)
Noel, Mary: *
Noel, Esther

[57.265]
Isle of Wight Co. VA
Norfelt, Harriet
Norfelt, Margaret
Norfelt, Guy: x
Norfelt, Thomas: x

INDIGENT FREEDMEN AT HOPKINS FARM IN PRINCESS ANNE CO., VA

[57.266]
Norfolk, VA
Crickman, Carey E: x
Crickman, Edward: x
Crickman, George: x
Crickman, Indiana F: x
Crickman, Isabella: x
Crickman, John W: x
Crickman, Josiah
Crickman, Jules: x
Crickman, Mary E: x

Crickman, Matilda A: x
Crickman, Susan W: x
Crickman, Virginia:
Foreman, Edward: x
Foreman, Elizabeth
Foreman, Jane
Foreman, Joe: x
Foreman, Sarah
Frost, Fanny: x
Frost, John D: x
Frost, Susan: x

Frost, Voilet
Frost, William T: x
Jacobs, Lydia: x
Jacobs, Mirandy: *
Jacobs, Moses: x
Johnston, Julia: x
King, Willis: *
Sanford, Isaac: *
Sinton, Maria: *
Whi e, James: *

INDIGENT FREEDMEN ON SYLVESTER FARM IN PRINCESS ANNE CO. VA

[57.266]
Norfolk, VA
Bell, Adeline: x
Bell, Daniel: x
Bell, Dina: *
Bell, Isaiah: x
Bell, Lewis: x
Bell, Mary A.
Bell, Nelson: *
Bell, Randall: x

Bolt, Emma
Bolt, James H: x
Bolt, Lydia A: x
Bolt, William E: x
Butt, Comfort: *
Cuffee, Georgiana
Cuffee, John T: x
Cuffee, Lofan: x
Cuffee, Sarah Y. ?:
Cuffee, William E: x

[57.266]
Henrico Co. VA
Reed, Jenny: x
Reed, Rosetta: x
Reed, Washington: x
Wilson, Chancy: *
Wilson, Keziah: *
Christian, Esther
Christian, Elizabeth: x
Christian, Lucy Jane: x

Christian, Anna M: x
Christian, Richard x
Johnson, Abram: *
Johnson, Ann
Johnson, Adeline: x
Lee, Adam: *

Princess Anne Co. VA
Machin, Clarissa: *
Pegram, Nancy

Pegram, Amy
Pegram, Eliza
Pegram, Beverly
Pegram, Cornelius: x
Pegram, Tasco: x

Isle of Wight Co. VA
Britcher, Osborne: *

Hertford Co. NC
Lester, Thompson: *
Lester, Minnie

Gates Co. NC
Ramsay, Margaret
Ramsay, Jim E: x
Ramsay, William H: x
Ramsay, Eli: x
Ramsay, Baby: x

INDIGENT FREEDMEN ON BILISOLY FARM
IN PRINCESS ANNE CO. VA

[57.266]
Princess Anne Co. VA
Harris, Jeff: *
Harris, Eliza
Harris, Robert: x
Harris, Agness: x
Mondon, Joseph: *
Mondon, Sarah
Mondon, Mary E.
Mondon, Martha A.
Mondon, Ellen
Mondon, Mandley

Mondon, Willie: x
Mondon, Joseph: x
Mondon, John: x
Mondon, Victoria: x

Gates Co. NC
Goodman, Willis: *
Goodman, Amy
Goodman, Henry
Goodman, Norman
Goodman, Riddick
Goodman, Casenda

Goodman, Lizzie
Goodman, Ann: x

Currituck Co. NC
Walker, Sukie: *
Walker, Charles: x *
Walker, John: x

Nansemond Co. VA
King, Eliza
King, Edley
King, Indiana

INDIGENT FREEDMEN ON LINDSAY FARM
IN PRINCESS ANNE CO. VA

Princess Anne Co. VA
Chaplin, Ann Maria
Chaplin, Eli: x
Chaplin, Martha: x
Chaplin, Salina: x
Haines, Columbus: x
Haines, Dinah

Haines, Mac: x
Haines, Walton: x
James, Mary: x
James, Nancy
James, Napoleon: x
James, Peter: *
Simmons, Fanny: *
Simmons, Robert: *

Isle of Wight Co. VA
Orcutt, Chancy
Orcutt, Benjamin: x
Orcutt, Mac: x
Orcutt, Junius: x
Orcutt, Amy: x

INDIGENT FREEDMEN ON TAYLOR FARM
IN PRINCESS ANNE CO. VA

[57.266]
Prince George Co. VA
Hatch, Thomas: *
Hatch, Eliza *
Hatch, Susanna
Hatch, Cornelius: x
[57.267]
Banister, Chloe: x
Banister, Eliza: x
Banister, Lydia W: x
Banister, Mary
Banister, Susan: x
Bonner, Eliza: x
Bonner, Hall: x
Bradley, Judith: *
Harris, Amica: *
White, Harriet: x
White, Sabra: *
Williams, Hannah: x
Williams, Jannetta: *
Williams, Louisa: *
Williams, Ned: *
Williams, Sally

[57.266]
Essex Co. VA
Garney, Cyrus: *
Garney, Cyrus Jr: x
Jones, Charles: x
[57.267]
Kidd, Mary
Kidd, Johns: x
Kidd, George W: x
Kidd, James: x
Williams, Lucy: *

Chesterfield Co. VA
Fenley, Millie
Fenley, George: x

Sussex Co. VA
Harrison, Alvenia
Harrison, Nathan: x

Charles City Co. VA
Shields, Walker: *
Shields, Malvina: *
Jones, Patsy
Jones, Cyrus: x
Cole, Nelson: *

[57.266]
St. Mary's Co. MD
Carber, Caroline
Carber, Robert C: x
Cole, Ann: x
Cole, Caroline
Cole, Cornelius
Cole, Elizabeth: x
Cole, James B: x
Cole, John M.
Dock, Alexander
Dock, Fanny: x
Dock, Rebecca: x
Fenwick, Anivesus: x
Fenwick, John: x
Fenwick, Martha
Garner, Lottie
Garner, Robert: x
Garney, Agnis
Garney, Ann M: x

Garney, Eliza A: x
Garney, George W: x
Garney, Ida C: x
Garney, James R.
Garney, Jane S.
Garney, John S: x
Garney, Louisa E: x
Garney, Mary F: x
Garney, Robert B: x
Garney, Romanis
Gunnell, Elilza: x
Gunnell, James H: x
Gunnell, John: x
Gunnell, Sarah E.
Hudgins, Henrietta
Hudgins, Virginia: *
Jones, Sol: *
Mindeth, Ann E.
Mindeth, Appalona
Mindeth, Richard H.
Phylo, Charles: x
Phylo, James: x
Phylo, Jane
Phylo, Marie: x
Phylo, Susan: x
Phylo, William: x
Taylor, John
Taylor, Nellie: x
Taylor, Peter: x
Woodhouse, Jacob: *
Woodhouse, Margaret:*
[57.268]
Brown, Lucretia
Brown, Richard: x
Buchanan, Rachael: *

Cacine, Amanda
Cacine, G[?]: x
Cacine, Jehulotto: x
Cacine, William H: x
Daly, George W: x
Daly, Henrietta: x
Daly, Hope
Daly, Lizzie: x
Daly, Robert A: x
Fenwick, Grace: *
Green, Aggis E: x
Green, Caroline: x
Green, James O: x
Green, Jerry
Green, Mary L: x
Green, William S: x
Hill, Charles H: x
Hill, Charles: *
Hill, Eliza A: x
Hill, Elizabeth: *
Hill, Jane E.
Statesman, Harriet
Statesman, Henry
Statesman, Jane R.
Statesman, Madison: x

Stone, Eliza: x
Stone, Francis: x
Stone, Martha
Swan, Joseph: x
Thomas, John L: x
Thomas, William H: x
Washington, Baby: *
Woodland, Betsy: x
Woodland, Lucy W.
Woodland, Mary C: x

[57.266]
Mathews Co. VA
Blake, Annie: x
Blake, Caroline
Blake, Georgiana
Blake, Hester: x
Blake, James: x
Blake, Lucy: x
Blake, Spencer
Lewis, Alexander: *
Phillips, Caroline
Phillips, John: *
Phillips, Mary: *

Middlesex Co. VA
Bunnill, Hannah: *
Bunnill, Sarah: x
Ransom, George: x
[57.267]
Burke, Ada: x
Carr, Polly
Carr, Nancy

[57.266]
Surry Co. VA
Cargan, Angeline
Cargan, Elizabeth
Cargan, Emma: x
Cargan, Isaac: x
Cargan, Jacob R.
Cargan, Jacob: *
Cargan, Jane
Jones, Collin: x
Jones, Elvy
Seymore, Sally: *
Sprattley, Mary: *
Washington, Ellijah A:*

INDIGENT FREEDMEN ON THE HOPKINS FARM
PRINCESS ANNE CO. VA

[57.267]
Perquimans Co. NC
Garret, Lincoln: x
Garret, Humphrey: *
Perkins, Ann
Perkins, Mary: x
Perkins, Alice: x
Perkins, Haywood: x
Perkins, Susan: x
Perkins, Indiana: x
Perkins, Abraham

[57.268]
Prince George Co. VA
Bonner, Frances
Bonner, George
Brown, Nelson: *
Burton, Franklin: x
Burton, James: x
Burton, Louisa: x
Burton, Lucinda
Fountain, Alice
Fountain, John
Fountain, Patsy: x

Harris, Elvy: x
Harris, Fanny: x
Harris, Richard: x
Laydon, Dolly: x
Laydon, Nancy
Laydon, Rachael: x
Laydon, Thomas: x
Major, Effie: x
Major, Ellen: x
Major, George: x
Major, Jacob: x
Major, Lucretia: x

Major, Martha: x
Major, Robert: *
Major, Sunny
Major, William
Paton, Albert
Paton, Cetia
Paton, Cortina: x
Paton, Melinda: x
Paton, Samuel
Paton, Sylvia
Randall, Mary: *
Steward, David: *
Steward, Eda: x
Steward, Emmeline: x
Steward, Fleming: x
Steward, Matilda
Steward, Nancy: *
Steward, Nellie
Steward, Samuel: x
Stewart, Moses: x
Stewart, Susan: x
Taylor, George: *
Taylor, Mary: *

Whitefield, Susan
Wilkins, Susan: *
Williams, Catharine: x
Williams, Joseph: *
Williams, Rebecca
Wright, Francis: x
Wright, John: x

Mathews Co. VA
Diggs, Cheney
Diggs, Richard
Diggs, Senia
Hudgins, Lucy
Hudgins, Major: *
Payton, Francis: x
Payton, Moses
Williams, Mary F.
Williams, Annie E.
Williams, Emma S.

Essex Co. VA
Holmes, Margaret
Holmes, Algerine

Camden Co. NC
Dozier, Chloe
Dozier, Eliza A: x
Dozier, Isaac: x
Dozier, William: x
Herring, Andrew J: x
Herring, Charles W: x
Holmes, Jane
Holmes, Robert: x
Sanlin, Dennis: x
Sanlin, Edmund: x
Sanlin, Jane: x
Sanlin, Mary: x
Sanlin, Penny: *
Sanlin, Peter
Sanlin, Rosetta

Currituck Co. NC
Baxter, Gabrilla
Baxter, New W: x
Baxter, Thomas L: x
Baxter, Gabrilla

DESTITUTE FREEDMEN IN HALIFAX CO. VA

[57.269]
Halifax Co. VA
Bellew, Henry
Bellew, Jennie
Bellew, Phoebe
Bellew, Joseph
Bellew, Abby
Bellew, Ephia
Bellew, Martha
Bellew, John
Bellew, Peter
Moore, Henry
Moore, Mary
Moore, Sandy: male

Moore, Martha
Moore, Joseph
Moore, Henry
Moore, Mumford
Moore, Samuel
[57.270]
Younger, America female
Younger, Amanda
Younger, Peter
Younger, Emanuel
Younger, Sampson
Moore, Richard
Moore, Cecelia

Moore, Rachael
Moore, Rebecca
Moore, Joseph
Moore, Buston
Moore, Jennie
Moore, Sammie
Moore, Lucy
Moore, Lincon
Moore, Lucinda
Pleasant, Margaret
Pleasant, Emanuel
Pleasant, Winufren
Pleasant, Eddie Jane
Pleasant, Henry

Pleasant, Shadrack
Pleasant, William
Pleasant, Robert
Pleasant, Mary Susan
Pleasant, Anna
Pleasant, James
Pleasant, Richard
Stoveall, Jackson
Stoveall, Polly
Stoveall, Georgiana
Stoveall, Dana
Stoveall, Moses
Stoveall, Parker
[57.271]
Bailey, Lizzie
Bailey, Patrick
Bailey, Pleasant
Bailey, Richard
Bailey, Walter
Cosby, Nellie
Cosby, Nelson
Cosby, Nelson Jr.
Doss, James
Edmonds, Charlotte
Edmonds, Granville
Edmonds, Jackson
Edmonds, Jennie
Edmonds, Maria
Edmonds, Millie
Edmonds, Rhoda
Edmonds, Sarah
Edmonds, Seymour
Edmonds, Stephen
Tucker, John
Tucker, Maria
Tucker, Martha Ann
Tucker, Peter

Spotsylvania Co. VA
Tucker, Stephen
Tucker, Wesley

Tucker, William
Wilson, James
Wilson, James Jr.
Wilson, Julia
Wilson, Polly
Wilson, Robert
[57.272]
Collins, Fanny
Collins, Sarah
Edmunds, Isaac
Edmunds, Isaiah
Edmunds, Nathan
Edmunds, Rachael
Edmunds, Sallie
Guthrie, Gazaline: Male
Guthrie, Jackson
Guthrie, Jetty: Female
Guthrie, John
Guthrie, Martha
Guthrie, Mary Jane
Hedgely, Washington
Kirby, Joe
Logan, Mary
Logan, Peter
Logan, Wilkins
Nunley, Emelia
Nunley, Emelia Jr.
Nunley, Richard
Stevens, James E.
Womack, Eddie
Womack, Harriet
Womack, Jemmie
Womack, Maria
Womack, Mary
Womack, Nettie
Wood, Andrew J.
Wood, Charles
Wood, Frances
Wood, Harriet
Wood, Martha
Wood, Paul E.

Wood, Robert
Wood, Stephen
[57.273]
Bennett, Rachel
Candy, Elsie
Candy, Fanny
Candy, Mary
Cratlock, David
Cratlock, Ebenezer
Cratlock, Harriet
Cratlock, Julia Ann
Cratlock, Nelson
Cratlock, Sallie
Edmunds, Elsie
Edmunds, Joseph
Edmunds, Lucinda
Edmunds, Sylvia
Este, Charles
Foster, Charles
Foster, Elsie
Foster, Maria
Foster, Peter
Foster, Phillip
Howard, Clara Lee
Howard, George
Howard, Ruth
Miles, Margaret
Pennock, Maria
Pennock, Paul
West, Enoch
West, Hannah
West, Julia
West, Katy
West, Lavinia
West, Lena
West, Melinda
[57.274]
Anderson, Elvira
Anderson, Frances
Anderson, Jane
Anderson, Mary

Anderson, Richard
Anderson, Sophia
Anderson, Thomas
Anderson, Willie
Gratcher, Elizabeth
Gratcher, Isham
Gratcher, Mary
Gratcher, Nannie
Gratcher, Rachael
Gratcher, Sarah
Hunt, Anna Maria
Hunt, Cicily
Hunt, Jack
Hunt, Martha
Jackson, Coley
Jackson, Dudley
Jackson, Jacob
Jackson, Melinda
Jackson, Michael
Jackson, Robert
Jackson, Sarah
Pennock, Ann
Pennock, Jane
Pennock, Wilhelmina
Quarles, Beverly
Quarles, Cora
Quarles, Enoch
Quarles, George W.
Quarles, Lena
Quarles, Lucy
[57.275]
Bailey, Amanda
Bailey, Carey
Bailey, Harriet
Bailey, John
Bailey, Luther
Bailey, Mary
Bailey, Simon
Bailey, Sylvia
Barnes, Henry
Farmer, Charlotte

Farmer, Enoch T.
Farmer, Henry
Farmer, Josephus
Farmer, Katy
Farmer, Maria
Farmer, Martha
Farmer, Martha
Farmer, Rodman
Farmer, Sarah
Farmer, Thomas
Hampton, Clara
Hampton, Logan
Hampton, Mary
Hughes, Andrew
Hughes, Daniel
Hughes, Lucy
Hughes, Rhody: Female
Hughes, Susan
West, Adaline
West, Malinda
West, Nat
West, Nettie
West, Polly
West, Rile: Male
West, Willis
Wood, Robert
[57.276]
Bennett, Daniel
Bennett, Eli
Bennett, James
Bennett, Sallie
Bennett, Sophia
Bennett, Susan
Easley, Dorithy
Easley, Fanny
Easley, Jamie
Easley, Luther
Easley, Mary
Easley, Obediah
Easley, Samuel
Evans, Martha

Farmer, Jesse
Farmer, Marcus
Farmer, Rebecca
Farmer, Sallie
Gerst?, Emanuel
Gerst?, Hannah
Gerst?, Isaac
Gerst?, Lena
Gerst?, Polly
Gerst?, Rose
Gerst?, William
Gerst?, Winnefred
Goodman, Aaron
Goodman, John
Goodman, Lucinda
Goodman, Millie
Ragland, Harriet
Ragland, Margaret
Ragland, Peter
Ragland, Philip
Wood, Jane
[57.277]
Easley, Amelia
Easley, Conney
Easley, Lettie
Easley, Linsa: Female
Easley, Nannie
Easley, Robert
Easley, Roger
Easley, Sallie
Edwards, Adaline
Edwards, Ann
Edwards, Handy
Edwards, Isaac
Edwards, Josephine
Edwards, Mark
Edwards, Mark Jr.
Edwards, Rachel
Edwards, Sandy
Evans, Eliza Jane
Evans, Jackson

Evans, Milton
Evans, Rhody
Evans, Susannah
Evans, Zachariah
Fourqurean, Amanda
Fourqurean, Arthur
Fourqurean, Charles
Fourqurean, Dicey
Fourqurean, Edgar
Fourqurean, Emeline
Fourqurean, John
Fourqurean, Katy
Fourqurean, Peter
Fourqurean, Susan
Wade, Amelia
Wade, Henry
Wade, Sylvia
[57.278]
Farmer, Absolom
Farmer, Amanda
Farmer, George
Farmer, Harriet
Farmer, Limsa: Female
Farmer, Rolm?: Male
Foster, Ereline
Foster, Lena
Foster, Sarah
Jennings, Fanny
Jennings, Henry
Jennings, James
Jennings, Moses
Jennings, Rhody
Jennings, Sallie
Roxam?, Lucy
Roxam?, Marcus
Roxam?, Rachel
Wade, Cecley
Wade, Christopher
Wade, Fanny
Wade, Isaiah
Wade, Joseph

Wade, Logan
Wade, Lucinda
Wade, Martha
Walthall, Andrew
Walthall, Emily
Walthall, Lavinia
Walthall, Lena
Walthall, Milly
Walthall, Simon
Walthall, Thomas
[57.279]
Clark, Ellen
Clark, Hannah
Clark, James
Clark, Rebecca
Clark, Robert
Garrett, Amanda
Garrett, Dora
Garrett, Jacob
Garrett, Lewis
Garrett, Mary
Garrett, Simon
Garrett, Sylvia
Handley, Louisa
Handley, Lucinda
Handley, Polly
Handley, Robert
Hendrick, Alexander
Hendrick, Emeline
Hendrick, Henry
Hendrick, Henry
Hendrick, Mary
Hendrick, Sallie
Hendrick, Solomon
McCraw, Ebenezer
McCraw, Edmund
McCraw, Fanny
Poindexter, George
Poindexter, Susan
Poindexter, Polly
Poindexter, Jemima

Robinson, Cecily
Robinson, Charles
Robinson, Thomas
Robinson, Thomas Jr.
Roxam, Charles
Roxam, Rena
[57.280]
Blanks, Alfred
Blanks, Cary
Blanks, Edmund
Blanks, Henry
Blanks, Kate
Blanks, Silley
Farquer, Carolina
Farquer, Ceasar
Farquer, Ellie
Farquer, Evelina
Farquer, George
Farquer, John
Farquer, Thomas
Hall, Eli
Hall, Fanny
Hall, Julia
Hall, Nellie
Hall, Rose
Handley, Catherine
Handley, Clarissa
Jennings, Amelia
Jennings, Armistead
Jennings, Mary
Jennings, Orilla
Jennings, Robert L.
Owen, Charlotte
Owen, Lavinia
Owen, Maria
Owen, Nellie
Owen, Parker
Owen, William
Vonn, Betsy
Vonn, Lizzie
Wood, Jesse

Wood, Keziah
Wood, Susan
[57.281]
Baldwin, John
Holmes, Elizabeth
Holmes, Lucy
Holmes, Milly
Holmes, Patrick
Huggins, Carey
Huggins, Ceasar
Huggins, Cecily
Huggins, James
Huggins, Press: Male
Huggins, Sarah
Pennock, Aaron
Pennock, Benjamin
Pennock, Elizabeth
Pennock, Hannah
Pennock, Lucinder
Pennock, Nellie
Taylor, Amanda
Taylor, Daniel
Taylor, Emily
Taylor, Infant
Taylor, Jackson
Taylor, Margaret
Thom, Frances
Toomes, Frances
Toomes, Jacob
Toomes, Margaret
Toomes, Press: Male
Toomes, Silvey
Wood, Charlotte
Wood, Jesse Jr.
[57.282]
Bellew, Carey
Bellew, Edward
Bellew, Edwin
Bellew, Lucinda
Johnson, Ellen
Johnson, Lucy

Lacey, Betsy
Lacey, Beverley: Male
Lacey, Eliza
Lacey, Jacob
Lacey, Mecca
Lacey, Patrick
Lacey, Rachel
Lacey, Richard
Lacey, Samuel
Lewis, Abraham
Lewis, Elvira
Lewis, Susan
Wimbush, Israel
Wimbush, Mack
Wimbush, Maria
Wimbush, Nathaniel
Wimbush, Page: Male
Wimbush, Sallie
Wimbush, Washington
[57.283]
Butt, Sallie
Danson, Claiborne
Danson, Clara
Danson, Eliza
Danson, Peter
Danson, Samuel
Danson, Simon
Danson, Susan
Gales, Fanny
Gales, Garelena: Male
Gales, George W.
Gales, Jackson
Gales, Lena
Gales, Obediah
Lewis, Amanda
Lewis, Hattie
Lewis, Nelson
Phillips, Amelia
Phillips, Rhody
Thomas, Eben: Male
Thomas, Evelina

Thomas, Maria
Thomas, Nina
Thomas, Rebecca
Thomas, Sallie
Thomas, Solomon
Thomas, Sophia
Thompson, Clement
Thompson, Maggie
Thompson, Phoebe
Thompson, Polly
Thompson, Rudolph
Thompson, Thomas
Thompson, Zackary
[57.284]
Kimbro, Alexander, Jr.
Kimbro, Alexander
Kimbro, Harriet
Kimbro, Jane
Kimbro, Patrick
Kimbro, Sarah
Kimbro, William
McPherson, Emily
McPherson, Sallie
Palmer, Abraham
Palmer, Amanda
Palmer, Elvira
Palmer, Francis: Female
Palmer, James
Palmer, Jefferson D.
Palmer, Julia
Palmer, Lucinda
Palmer, Richard
Palmer, Sallie Ann
Phillips, Annie
Phillips, James
Phillips, Lacy: Male
Phillips, Paul
Phillips, Robert
Phillips, Rolla: Male
Phillips, Ruth
Sampson, Albert

Sampson, Carey
Sampson, Ellen
Sampson, Isabella
Sampson, Mary
Smith, Charles
Smith, Fanny
Smith, Mary
Smith, Matilda

[57.285]
Brown, Adam
Brown, Ann Eliza
Brown, Elizabeth
Brown, Frederick
Brown, Jehu
Brown, Jennie
Jones, Lena
Jones, Zachariah
Lack, Armstead
Lack, Charles
Lack, Eliza
Lack, Henry
Lack, Lucy
Lack, Oney: Male
Lack, Sophrina
Lack, Thomas
Miller, Betsey
Miller, Dicey
Miller, George
Miller, Hannah
Miller, Patrick
Miller, Thomas
Parker, Adaline
Parker, Elvira

Parker, Jerry
Parker, John
Parker, Sandy
Parker, Simon
Parker, Sylvia
Peters, Amanda
Peters, Fanny
Peters, Jennie
Peters, Lemuel
Peters, Parker
Peters, Silas
Peters, Susan

[57.286]
Bostick, Ellen
Bostick, Fanny
Bostick, John Jr.
Bostick, John
Bostick, Lewis
Bostick, Mary
Bostick, Thomas
Fleming, Archer
Fleming, Polly
Fleming, Silas
Girsh, Amanda
Girsh, Greene
Girsh, Jane
Girsh, Milton
Girsh, Richard
Howard, Jackson
Howard, Sallie
Lacy, Betsey
Lacy, Fanny
Lacy, Peter
Owens, Alice
Owens, Amanda
Owens, Lincann: Male
Pennock, Andrew
Pennock, Betsey
Pennock, Lucy

Pleasant, Ellen
Pleasant, George
Pleasant, John
Pleasant, Rhody
Pleasant, Rolla: Male
Pleasant, William
Wodey, Henry
Wodey, Lucinda
Wodey, Martha
Wodey, Sallie

[57.287]
Lacy, Bristow
Lacy, David
Lacy, Elizabeth
Lacy, Fanny
Lacy, Henry
Lacy, Rebecca
Lacy, Sallie

[57.281]
Brunswick Co. VA
Stevenson, Ceily
Stevenson, James
Stevenson, Lucy
Stevenson, Richard
Stevenson, Robert
Stevenson, William

[57.283]
Charlotte Co. VA
James, Ephraim
James, Matilda
James, Sallie

Deep Black, Miss.
McCargo, Jacob
McCargo, Polly

DESTITUTE FREEDMEN GREENSVILLE CO. VA
[Note: Names followed by ages. No surnames given]

[57.289]
Greensville Co. VA
Unknown, Nat: 100
Unknown, Edmund: 12
Unknown, Sarah: 10
Unknown, Nancy: 8
Unknown, Jessie: 5
Unknown, Rainey: 4
Unknown, Aggie: 6
Unknown, Charles: 7
Unknown, Cherelyn: 5
Unknown, Barbara: 4
Unknown, Mollie: 3
Unknown, Caroline: 30
Unknown, Samuel: 12
Unknown, Charles: 10
Unknown, Ben: 7
Unknown, Clara: 6
Unknown, Thomas: 5
Unknown, Rosa: 23

Unknown, Turner: 4
Unknown, Martha: 24
Unknown, Samuel: 7
Unknown, Julia: 4
Unknown, Benjamin: 2
Unknown, Lucinda: 24
Unknown, Jesse: 5
Unknown, Maria: 3
Unknown, Green: 12
Unknown, Mary: 23
Unknown, Grace: 8
Unknown, Goodwin: 4
Unknown, John: 12
Unknown, Hannah: 12
Unknown, David: 8
Unknown, Joseph: 3
[57.291]
Unknown, Rainey: 26
Unknown, Evelina: 8

Unknown, Sarah: 6
Unknown, Andrew: 4
Unknown, Eliza: 2

[57.291]
Southampton Co. VA
Unknown, Maria: 23
Unknown, Kinda: 5
Unknown, Moses: 1

[57.290]
Nash Co. NC
Unknown, Winnie: 24
Unknown, Lucy: 7
Unknown, Eli: 5

Unknown, James: 3
Unknown, Clara: 2

DESTITUTE FREEDMAN IN DINWIDDIE COUNTY, VA

[57.293]
Dinwiddie Co. VA
Ampey, Patience: 22, 4 children
Barber, Delia: 25, 2 children
Branch, Betsy: 60, 2 children
Candar, Mesre?: 99, 2 children
Colier, Bob: 60, 2 children
Haze, Martha: 40
Hill, Nancy: 85, 2 children
Johnson, Jemy: 40, 2 children
Lettie, Fannie: 76
Lild, Martha: 45, 4 children
Mansfield, Henry: 70, 2 children
Pisan, Mary: 70
Ragsdale, Sam: 72, 2 children
Reems, Charlotte: 50, 2 children
Smith, Lucy: 50, 2 children

Valentine, Martha: 55
Watson, William: 60
Weaver, Harriet: 30, 2 children
Wilkinson, Duin?: 65, 2 children
[57.294]
Ampy, Lettis: 80
Boats, Susan: 50
Brander, Rob: 72
Chaycon, Ben: 80, 2 children
Field, Charlotte: 55
Gable, Hammer: 90
Gibson, Gideon: 80
Gilliam, Easter: 90
Gould, Mag: 20
Harris, Frank: 80
Lee, John: 16
Masters, Bob: 86

Mitchell, Ann: 70
Mynick, Sylran: 40, Male
Rainey, Lucy: 70
Ross, Mary: 74
Scott, Mary: 37
Valentine, Nancy: 65
White, Frank: 50
[57.295]
Boer, Davey: 40, 2 children
Brown, George: 50, 4 children
Caroline, Charlotte: 30
Epps, Lucy: 41, 2 children

Epps, Susan: 20, 2 children
Fitzgerald, George: 80, 8 children
Jackson, Winnie: 90
Lilds, Susan: 40, 2 children
Manford, Owen: 80, 2 children
Matthew, Jim: 4 children
Matthew, Tom: 53
Meus, Sallie: 40, 2 children
Roberts, Lasy?: 35, 2 children
Shore, Lany: 30, Female
Smith, Adlia: 50, 2 children
Wilkins, Sarah: 80, 2 children

DESTITUTE FREEMEN IN CUMBERLAND CO. VIRGINIA
{Note: all from Cumberland Co. VA before the war}

[57.297]
Absalom D: age 65
Archer, B: age 73
Albert, S: age 65, 1 child
Backey, G: age 55, 2 children
Boer, D: age 47
Backer, B: age 53, 4 children
Crowley, C: age 49, 3 children
Clowet, D: age 64, 4 dependents
Crudey, A: age 74
Dick, T: age 81
Davenport, A: age 18
David: age 62
Epeys, Am: age 57, 2 dependents
Eyloff: age 48, 1 dependent
Francys: age 46, 2 dependents
Grave, B: age 75
Grees, S: age 64, 5 dependents
Harris, T: age 54, 3 dependents
Hadley: age 73
[57.298]
Harrison, M: age 36, 1 dependent
Harris, E: age 48, 4 dependents

Harris, F: age 52, 4 dependents
Hatcher, T: age 88
Hatcher, S: age 71
Indiana: age 39, 4 dependents
Janey: age 47, 5 dependents
Johns, C: age 45, 3 dependents
Jones, A: age 35, 2 dependents
Jones, F. 49, 5 dependents
Johnson, N: age 42, 1 dependent
Johnson, S: age 37, 1 dependent
Keasey, D: age 61
Hughes, K: age 59
Lewis, F: age 41, 2 dependents
Lucy, C: age 29, 5 dependents
Locket, P: age 73, dependents
Lipscomb, S: age 42, 4 dependents
[57.299]
Lipscomb, K: age 52, 2 dependents
Lipscomb: age 46, 3 dependents
Murphey: age 42, 1 dependent
Patterson, S: age 45, 2 dependents
Pocahontas: age 37, 3 dependents
Strakin: age 61, 3 dependents

DESTITUTE FREEDMAN IN CHESTERFIELD CO. VA
{Note: The following resided in Chesterfield Co. before the war, unless otherwise noted.}

[57.302]
Allen, Jemmy
Anderson, Sarah: 4 children
Bridway, Moses
Brightwell, Moses
Brown, Carly: 1 female
Brown, Mary: 4 dependents
Brown, Sarah: 2 dependents
Chetham, Cary: 4 male dependents
Eggins, Bertha
Epps, Sally
Farmer, Sukey: 1 male, 6 children
Good, Nelson
Graves, Creed: 1 female
Hancock, Freddie: 2 dependents
Hancock, Judy: 2 dependents
Kaser, Joan
Lewis, Phillip: 5 dependents
McCray, Charlotte: 2 dependents
McCray, Charlotte: 2 children
Merrit, Spocten?
Moody, Jack: 1 dependent
Powell, Elisa: 6 dependents
Pridly, Catharina: 4 children
Randall, Lessie: 1 male, 7 children
Trent, Sam
Triss, Peter: 1 male, 1 child
Watkins, Crenshaw?: 3 dependents
Watkins, Esunguis
Watkins, Jane: 2 dependents
Watkins, John: 6 dependents
Watkins, Richardson
Wess, Philip: 2 dependents
West, James
West, Philips
Whigand, Esey: 1 female, 6 children
Wilson, Lewis
Wiss, John: 1 female, 6 children
Woody, Jack: 1 male child
Wuher?, Wyatt: 1 male, 1 child
[57.303]
Ackin, Betty
Branch, Caroline: 1 female
Bridley, Catherine: 2 dependents
Bridway, Moses
Claiborne, James
Ellett, Stephney: 1 male
Good, J.F
Gregory, Marsellus
Jeffs, Austin
Jermai?, Marie: 2 dependents
Nickys, Lucy: 6 dependents
Pegram, Easter
Pegram, Ned
Swan, Essie
Taylor, Joan
Taylor, Patrick
Wells, Isam: 1 female
[57.304]
Anderson, Sarah J.
Banks, Betsey: 6 dependents
Boyd, P: 3 dependents
Camel, Jack: 1 male
Clark, Jemmie
Coley, Phillip
Dotson, Harriet
Gilbert, Johannah: 1 dependent
Harris, Ann
Holmes, Hester
Isaaks, Caesar
Johnson, Mary: 4 dependents
Jones, Betsey
Luckes, Rachel
Mayo, Agnes: 3 dependents

Trent, Bessie: 1 dependent
Tress?, Peter: 1 dependent
Watkins, Gustavo: 1 male
Winfree, Martha
[57.305]
Akin, Jury: 1 male
Bingsley, Martha: 1 female
Bradley, Langston: 1 male
Cheatham, Creed
Cooley, Phillip: 1 female, 1 child
Ferris, George E.
Friend, Charles: 1 male, 1 female
Hicks, Eula
Holmes, McC.
Monday, Jack: 1 male
Persons, Judy
Powell, Melissa
Robinson, John
Rosse, Paten?
Spencer, Abbe
Turner, Jack

[57.306]
Banks, Betsey: 6 dependents
Bolling, Samuel: 2 dependents
Boyd, Ruffin: 2 dependents
Brightesley, Grace: 1 female
Brown, Emily: 2 dependents
Brown, Paulina: 4 dependents
Dilson, Henrietta: 5 dependents
Dilson, Phebe: 1 male, 1 female
Graves, Vallis
Hembrick, Joseph
Homes, Nelson: 1 male, 1 child
   (from King George Co. VA)
Isaaks, Rachel
Jones, Samuel
Lewis, Wilson
Loper, Crease: 2 dependents
Loper, Joan
Rowlett, Rosina: 3 dependents
Whels, Eisey
Wise, Lucian: 6 dependents

DESTITUTE FREEMDMEN CITY POINT, VIRGINIA
{Note: City Point is just outside of the
town of Hopewell, Prince George Co. VA}

[57.307]
Albemarle Co. VA
Colter, Martha: 40
Colter, Willie
Colter, Virginia
Waine, Rosetta: 49
Waine, Anthony: 8
Waine, Macajer: 10

Amelia Co. VA:
Jones, Frances: 30
Jones, Margaret: 8
Jones, William: 4

Brunswick Co. VA
Bishop, Henson: 50
Bishop, Mac: 9
Fields, Milley: 45
Fields, Francis: 10
Fields, Phillis: 8
Fields, Eliza: 6
Green, Mary: 38
Green, Charles: 12
Green, Mac: 9
[57.308]
Green, Becky: 7
Green, Mollie: 5
Hicks, Harriett: 40

Hicks, Davy: 9
Quarles, Elizabeth: 40
Quarles, Walter: 8
Quarles, Charles: 6
Quarles, Amanda: 5
Quarles, Elizabeth: 3
Parham, Priscilla: 43
Parham, Adeline: 11
Parham, Washington: 6
Salad, Ruther: 35
Mims, Emily: 30
Jones, Lucy: 35

Buckingham Co. VA
Jones, Ella: 25
Jones, Celia: 9
[57.309]
Harris, Letta: 50

Charlotte Co. VA
Morgan, Jane: 26
Reeves, Mary: 26

Dinwiddie Co. VA
Alfriend, Eliza: 65
Tillman, Elizabeth: 24
Tillman, Daniel: 7
Tillman, Sallie: 4
Gorden, Ann: 25
Gorden, Charles: 8
Palmer, Caroline: 41
Palmer, Ellis: 11
Palmer, Nora: 13
Reeves, Mary: 8
Reeves, Rosina: 36
Bolling, Caroline: 32
Bolling, Aurena: 10
[57.310]
Robinson, Lucretia: 45
Robinson, Randolph: 48
Reeves, Henry: 12

Greensville Co. VA
Buford, Cretia: 35
Buford, Robert: 16
Buford, James: 8
Fields, Minerva: 19
Fields, Winnie: 30
Mason, Jordan: 12
Mason, Henrietta: 10
Mason, Joshua: 3
Mason, Celia: 50
Mason, Sallie: 5
Mason, Harvey: 5

Lake Bolivar Co. Mississippi
Johnson, Letta: 50
Jones, Maria: 40
Jones, Eliza: 7
Jones, Thornton: 5
[57.311]
Johnson, Kesiah: 30
Johnson, Randolph: 8
Johnson, Moses: 10
Scott, Emily: 38
Scott, Matilda: 10

Lunenburg Co. VA
Carter, Lucinda: 27
Carter, Charlotte: 4
Davis, Ann: 35
Davis, Mary: 10
Davis, William: 8
Davis, Linnda: 7
Davis, Samuel: 6
Davis, Ema: 4
Randolph, Namut: 25
Randolph, William: 5
Randolph, Junius: 3
Thomas, Lucy: 45
Thomas, Washington: 8
[57.312]
Thomas, Sarah: 14

Nottoway Co. VA
Jones, Elizabeth: 70
Wright, Marandy: 35
Wright, Marandy: 9
Wright, Henry: 6
Olston, Ammy: 50
Olston, Ellen: 4
Olston, Laura: 15
Olston, Mary: 3
Olston, Nancy: 5
Lewis, Ellen: 15

Lewis, Arzelia: 9
Marshal, Harriet: 30
Marshal, Mary: 3
Marshal, Reuben: 5
Richardson, Maria: 28
Richardson, Lena: 8
Richardson, Anna: 5
Richardson, Westley: 6
Smith, Sarah: 35
Smith, Richard: 10
Smith, Susan: 8
Smith, John: 6
Smith, Charles: 5
Glover, Charlotte: 45
Glover, Sarah: 45

Plymouth, NC
Beemun, Julia: 35
Beemun, John: 12
Beemun, Maria: 7
Beemun, Sophia: 4

Prince George Co. VA
Baird, Perlina: 60
Frazer, Simon: 60
Frazer, Willie: 60
[57.313]
Harrison, Ben: 85
Harrison, Rachel: 86
Lewis, Minor: 6
Lewis, Eliza: 40

[57.314]
Sussex Co. VA
Bell, Cain: 90
Bell, Rose: 60
Branch, Margaret: 70
Briggs, Amy A: 45
Briggs, William: 12
Briggs, Littleton: 5
Epps, Sarah: 40

Epps, Sarah: 11
King, Ben: 90
King, Katy: 70
Mason, Pamley: 43
Mason, William: 12
Mason, Austin: 11
Mason, Robert: 9
Mason, Harry: 7
Mason, Mary: 27
Mason, Jack: 3
Mason, James: 12
Mason, Bettie: 8
[57.315]
Taliaferro, Lucy: 25
Tucker, Sarah: 30
Tucker, Charles: 8

Tucker, Joe: 2
Tucker, Katy: 7
Williams, Fannie: 25
Williams, Tom: 6
Wingfield, Agnes: 30
Wingfield, Walter: 9
Wingfield, Charles: 6
Wingfield, Julia: 4
Wingfield, Ann, 3
Harrison, Jane: 35
Harrison, Ellen: 10
[57.316]
Harrison, Ben: 8
Jones, Milley: 28
Jones, Westley: 6

Jones, Charles: 4
Surry Co. VA:
Drew, Nancy: 40
Drew, Moses: 6
Drew, Diana: 5
Green, Amanda: 50
Smith, Polly: 66
Ruffin, Deeza: 70
Ruffin, Mary: 10
Ruffin, Moses: 6
Lamb, Deana: 55
Lamb, Moses: 6
Lamb, John: 9
Lamb, Rosetta: 7

ORPHANS AT CITY POINT, VA

[57.317]
Sussex Co. VA
Banks, Tempy: 12
Banks, William: 6
Benjamin, Paul: 10
Briggs, Angie: 10
Briggs, Green: 8

Brown, Sarah: 9
Edwards, Claiborne: 12
Eoler, William: 12
Smith, Tom: 10

Lunenburg Co. VA
Guy, [?]: 12

From Chesterfield Co. VA
Robinson, Robert: 11

From Prince George Co. VA
Scott, Coleman: 1
Scott, Hannah
Scott, Martha: 7
Scott, Victoria: 6

DESTITUTE FREEDMEN IN CHARLOTTE COUNTY, VA

{NOTE: Names, ages, and miscellaneous remarks are listed under the pre-war residence. For those listed by first name only, "Unknown" has been used as a surname, for organizational purposes of this abstract.}

[57.319]
Halifax Co. VA
Unknown, Winnie: 25
Unknown, Sam: 7
Unknown, Phillip: 5
Unknown, Ned: 2½

Charlotte Co. VA
Unknown, Nannie: 25
Unknown, Lorenzo: 4
Brown, Bell: 1½
Unknown, Polly: 45
Coles, Lelia: 12
Unknown, Henrietta: 15
Unknown, Jemmie: 75
Unknown, Louisa: 35
Unknown, Alexander: 12
Unknown, Mary: 10
Unknown, Stevenson: 5
Unknown, Nelsons?: 2
Unknown, Judy: 29
Unknown, Henry: 12
[57.320]
Unknown, Amy: 5
Armstead, John: 2
Unknown, Priney: 1
Unknown, Gilmy: 38
Unknown, Jane: 6
Unknown, Clarissa: 67
Unknown, Delia: 27
Henry, Patrick: 6

Unknown, Susan: 7
Unknown, Sylvia: 22
Unknown, Clem: 1
Unknown, William: 6
Unknown, Julia Ann: 10
[57.321]
Unknown, Christiana: 40
Unknown, Isaac: 6
Unknown, Mary: 7
Unknown, Patty: 3
Unknown, Sarah: 12
Unknown, Ella: 8
Unknown, Richard: 7
Unknown, Isaac: 79
Bolling, Louis: 82
Unknown, William: 6
Unknown, Milly: 9
Unknown, Rosetta: 22
Unknown, Hannah: 30
Unknown, Martha: 5
Unknown, Daniel: 10
Unknown, Millie: 74
Unknown, Randal: 5
Unknown, Margaret: 5
Rice, Sucky: 66
Unknown, Sam: 75
Unknown, Thomas: 75
Unknown, Minnie: 29
Unknown, Tony: 9
Unknown, Celia: 4
Unknown, Matilda: 5

Jackson, Eliza: 50
Shepard, Joseph: 63
Shepard, Jane: 56
Crawford, Jane: 50
Unknown, Henry: 12
Edmonds, Lydia: 70
Howe, Judy: 50
Howe, Jerry: 12
[57.323]
How, Sam: 10
Unknown, Nero: 60
Nero, Eliza: 58
Unknown, Sallie: 90
Spencer, Elvira: 56
Unknown, Armstead: 70
Grisly, Millie: 45
Unknown, Agnes: 60
Unknown, James: 65
Unknown, Reuben: 60
Unknown, Jane: 57
Harrison, Daphne: 60
Sheperson, Joseph: 70
Rice, Patty: 58
Unknown, Pollie: 3
Unknown, Phillip: 1
Williams, Daniel: 75
[57.324]
Unknown, Lucretia: 12
Unknown, Isaac: 55
Unknown, Emma: 30, insane

[57.321]
Norfolk Co. VA
Marshall, Tony: 75

Campbell Co. VA
Smith, George: 104

Mecklenburg Co. VA
Robinson, Mary: 21
Unknown, Mollie: 70

[57.320]
East Tennessee
Unknown, Liza Ann: 35
Unknown, Wilson: 15

Unknown, Clark: 12
Unknown, Cynthia: 7
Unknown, John: 3
Unknown, Reuben: 6 mos.

DESTITUTE FREEDMEN BUCKINGHAM COUNTY, VA

[57.326]
Buckingham Co. VA
Bluford, Hannah
Brown, Patsey
Brown, Sary: 6 children
Coleman, Cicely
Garrett, Samuel
Gilliam, Hannah
Gough, Mary: 4 children
Granett, Mildred: 5 children
Harris, William
Hocker, F.
Hubbard, Harriett

Johnson, Elizabeth: 4 children
Jones, Obediah: 2 children
Jones, Sarah
Morris, Margaret: 3 children
Mosely, Maria: 1 child
Perkens, Hannah
Poole, Tom
Wooldridge, Mims: Female.
    6 children

[57.327]
Campbell Co. VA
Hubbard, Mary
Lease, Bettie: 4 children
Long, Adam

DESTITUTE FREEDMEN IN BRUNSWICK COUNTY, VA

[57.328]
Brunswick Co. VA
Boyd, James
Harrison, Jeremiah
Harrison, Minerva
Lashley, Alice
Lashley, Elsie
Lashley, Minerva
Lashley, Wiley
Mason, Isaac
Owens, Benjamin

Owens, Cornelius
Owens, Daniel
Owens, Frederick
Owens, Gracie
Owens, Neeley
Owens, Rose
Owens, Sallie
Owens, William
Owens, Winston
[57.329]
Clark, Rebecca

Crayton, Esther
Crayton, Flora
Crayton, Ida
Crayton, Robert
Crayton, Sallie
Easter, Susan
House, William
Jackson, Sallie
King, Ambrose
Lashley, Gracie
Lashley, Samuel

Lashley, Stephen
Lashley, Virginia
Seward, James
Shell, Martha
Shell, Mary
Shell, William
[57.330]
Cherer?, Rebecca
Dicks, Joseph
Gee, Candace?
Gee, Ceazar
Gee, Eliza

Gee, Octavia
Gee, Rosanna
Guilford, Richard
Hicks, Vamer? Male
James, Sarah
Jones, Julia
Lundy, Terry
Merritt, Bettie
Merritt, Violet
Nibby, Daniel
Nibby, Winnie
Wells, Mason

[57.331]
Archy, Washington
Blunt, Edward
Blunt, Fanny
Blunt, Lizzie
Blunt, Martha
Fowler, Elizabeth
Hatchett, Harriett
Hatchett, Robert

DESTITUTE FREEDMEN LUNENBURG CO. VA

[57.341]
Lunenburg Co. VA
Unknown, Margaret
Unknown, Scott
Unknown, Frank
Unknown, Green
Unknown, Armstead
Unknown, Samuel
Unknown, Charles
Unknown, America: Female
Unknown, Maria
Unknown, Susan
Unknown, Sini: Female
Unknown, Emma
Unknown, Duncan
Unknown, Anitha?
Unknown, Matilda
Unknown, Nancy
Unknown, George
Unknown, Minnie
Unknown, Matilda
[57.342]
Unknown, Eli
Unknown, Dennis

Unknown, Willis
Unknown, Jennie
Unknown, Cyrus
Unknown, Rose
Unknown, Addie
Unknown, Agnes
Unknown, Pochahontas
Unknown, Martha Ann
Unknown, Nellie
Unknown, Rachel
Unknown, Lucinder
Unknown, Armstead
Unknown, Dorcas
Unknown, Emily
Unknown, James
Unknown, Lucy
Unknown, Mollie
Unknown, Maria
[57.343]
Unknown, Robert
Unknown, James
Unknown, Lucy: 8
Unknown, Raymond
Unknown, Sarah: 8
Unknown, James

Unknown, Archer
Unknown, Agnes: 7
Unknown, Fannie
Unknown, Caroline
Unknown, Ann Maria
Unknown, Adner: Female
Unknown, Rachel
Unknown, Fannie
Unknown, John
Unknown, Monroe
Unknown, Moses
Unknown, Phillis
Unknown, Emeline
[57.344]
Unknown, Alice
Unknown, Lucy
Unknown, Rosa
Unknown, Amie
Unknown, Addie
Unknown, Catharine
Unknown, Peggie
Unknown, America
Unknown, Armstead
Unknown, Sandy: Male

Unknown, Margaret
Unknown, Jackson
Unknown, Mary

Unknown, Elizabeth
Unknown, Tampa: Female
Unknown, Nellie Ann

Unknown, Lucinda
Unknown, William
Unknown, Emma

DESTITUTE FREEDMEN IN MECKLENBURG CO. VA

[57.346]
Goochland Co. VA
Johnson, Charles: 82
Johnson, Margaret: 22
Johnson, Susan: 6
Johnson, Henry: 3

[57.355]
Hampton, VA
Shields, Fannie: 46
Shields, Nellie: 11
Shields, Alice: 9
Shields, Lizzie: 3
Shields, Infant:

[57.346]
Mecklenburg Co. VA
Baskerville, Albert: 4
Baskerville, Keziah: 25
Baskerville, Nancy: 24
Baskerville, Richard: 4
Mason, Bella: 2
Mason, Daniel: 5
Mason, David: 10
Mason, James: 3
Mason, Sarah: 19
Mason, Thomas: 1
Pollard, Adam: 7
Pollard, Frank: 5
Pollard, Lavina: 29
Pollard, William: 4
[57.347]
Pollard, Mary J: 12
Pollard, Edmund: 50
Jeffers, Grandison: 7
Jeffers, Maria: 1
Jeffers, Mary: 50

Jeffers, Anthony: 8
Hendricks, Amy: 40
Hendricks, Stephen: 10
Hendricks, Green: 9
Hendricks, Anaca: 5, Male
Temple, Ella: 37
Temple, Catharine: 7
Temple, Jerry: 5
Temple, John: 6
Temple, Robert: 3
Temple, Dawson: 2
[57.348]
Alexander, Ros: 75,
Cranshaw, Fannie: 50
Cranshaw, Frank: 5
Cranshaw, Louisa: 13
Hendricks, David: 1
Hendricks, Henrietta: 30
Hendricks, Horace: 7
Hendricks, Jinnie: 30
Hendricks, Mary: 25
Hendricks, Nellie: 75
Hendricks, Paul: 5
Hendricks, Peter: 9
Hendricks, Plumma: 12
Hendricks, Robert: 5
Hendricks, Sallie: 2
Hendricks, Sallie: 8
Hornes, Dollie: 75
Keaton, Fannie: 1
Keaton, P. Jane: 30
Keaton, Rebecca: 3
Keaton, Sarah: 5
[57.349]
Baskerville, Dicy: 65
Baskerville, Flora: 11

Burr, Mary: 25
Burr, Mary E: 2
Cole, Dollie: 21
Cole, Greenwood: 2
Cole, Katy: 60
Cole, Ned: 5
Hendricks, Indy: 3
Pettice, Bates: 40
Pettice, Caroline: 4
Pettice, Eliza: 30
Pettice, James: 6
Pettice, Ned: 11
Winbush, Bell: 3
Winbush, Eady: 36
Winbush, Joseph: 5
Winbush, Mary F: 8
Winbush, Sallie: 4
[57.350]
Davis, Albert: 1
Davis, Lewis: 5
Davis, Millie: 34
Davis, Osborn: 45
Davis, Sarah: 7
Keen, Francis: 13, Female
Keen, Harry: 2
Keen, James: 5
Keen, M. Ann: 10
Keen, Mary Agnes: 9
Keen, Minerva: 29
Keen, Richmond: 3
Lowns, Martha: 30
Lowns, Padin: 2, Female
Lowns, S. Ann: 1
Lowns, Susan: 5
Oliver, David: 82

Oliver, John: 9
Walker, Robert: 90
[57.351]
Davis, Jacob: 30
Jones, Cely: 7
Jones, Indiana: 23
Jones, Lavinia: 5
Jones, Louiza: 30
Jones, Lydia: 11
Jones, Mary: 7
Jones, Mary: 7
Jones, Rachel: 47
Keen, Ann: 26
Keen, Betsey: 53
Keen, Fannie: 8
Keen, Jane: 25
Keen, Queen Victoria: 9
Lownes, William: 77
Lowns, Julius: 30
Northington, John: 40
Seddon, Isaac: 90
[57.352]
Carrington, Henry: 4
Carrington, Lizzie: 25
Carrington, Thomas: 6
Hampton, Lucy: 90
Hendricks, Jane: 28
Hendricks, Laura: 26
Hendricks, Martha, 8:
Hendricks, Washington, 40
Jones, Annie: 5
Jones, Indy: 20
Jones, Jennie: 11
Jones, Lucy: 41
Jones, Susan: 4
Turner, Ann: 45
Turner, Betsey: 10

Turner, Dinah: 16
Turner, Indiana: 5
Turner, James: 2
Turner, Sila: 12
[57.353]
Baskerville, Greenville: 4
Baskerville, Amy: 60
Baskerville, Dick: 70
Baskerville, Hardy: 1
Baskerville, Lena: 8
Baskerville, Lucinder: 3
Baskerville, Matilda: 29
Baskerville, Michael: 10
Burr, Ephraim: 2
Burr, Lizzie: 22
Burr, Sallie: ½
Hase, Elizabeth: 28
Hase, Jenna: 6
Hase, Mahala: 9
Hase, Martha: 16
Hase, Octavia: 4
Hase, Rebecca: 50
Hase, Victoria: 5
Hase, William: 5
[57.354]
Baker, Absalom: 5
Baskerville, Armstead: 5
Baskerville, Edward: ½
Tally, Lizzy: 35
Baskerville, Kesiah: 2
Baskerville, Martha: 3
Coles, Angela: 20
Coles, Beverly: 4
Couch, Sally: 24
Hendricks, Harry: 1

Prior?, Anna: 7
Prior?, Benjamin: 9
Prior?, Caroline: 35
Prior?, Gray: 2
Prior?, Lee: 4
Prior?, Silas: 55
Tally, Jane
Tally, Mary: 3
Tally, Tildy: 30
William, Lewis: 4
[57.355]
Baker, Haskins: 12
Baker, Lucy: 35
Burchard, Ina: ¼
Burchard, Martha: 23
Davis, Nellie
Fields, Lucy Ann: 45
Fields, Rhodes Thomas: 9
Fields, Thomas: 7
Hendricks, Stephen: 50
Hendricks, William: ½
Johnson, Charles: 5
Johnson, James: 3
Johnson, Martha: 3
Johnson, Queentina: 2
Johnson, Rosetta: 35
Johnson, Sophia: 23
Johnson, Susan: 9
Louns, Easter: 6
Louns, Isabella: ½
Louns, Patience: 6
Louns, Peggie: 24
Pool, Hannah: 100
Wadkins, Henrietta: 25
Wadkins, Nellie: 6

DESTITUTE FREEDMEN IN NOTTOWAY CO. VA

[57.359]
Amelia Co. VA
Unknown, Susannah: 35

[57.361]
Appomattox Co. VA
Unknown, Bob: 80

[57.357]
Brunswick Co. VA
Unknown, Sally: 70

[57.359]
Dinwiddie Co. VA
Unknown, Peggie: 80
Davis, Louisa: 16
[57.362]
Grigg, Ritter: 80

[57.361]
Henrico Co. VA
Unknown, Martha: 22

[57.363]
Prince Edward Co. VA
Unknown, Isaac: 65

[57.358]
Lunenburg Co. VA
Unknown, Camblin: 75
Unknown, Martha: 60
[57.361]
Unknown, Jim: 40
[57.363]
Unknown, Anderson: 50
[57.357]
Unknown, Fanny: 70
Unknown, Lousia: 30
Unknown, Saluda: 50
Unknown, Julia: 35
Unknown, Winnie: 30
Unknown, Millie: 40

Unknown, Sylvia: 45
Unknown, Martha
Unknown, Ann: 35
Spooner, Eliza: 40
Unknown, Viney: 70
Unknown, Ida: 10
Unknown, Letcher: 8
Unknown, Pattie: 60
Unknown, Betty: 40
Unknown, Lizzie: 70
Unknown, Hannah: 75
Unknown, Mary: 70
Unknown, Peter: 80
[57.358]
Unknown, Goloah: 60
Unknown, Mollie: 60
Unknown, Phillis: 70
Unknown, Mingo: 60
Unknown, Sarah: 20
Unknown, Martha: 30
Unknown, Siam: 43, Male
Unknown, Matilda: 62
Unknown, Carney: 70, Female
Unknown, Pattie: 20
Unknown, Albert: 12
Unknown, Daniel: 40
Unknown, Prudence: 50
Branch, Pat: 50, Male
Unknown, Frances: 40
Unknown, Sarah: 50
Unknown, Louisa: 45
[57.359]
Unknown, Linda: 19
Unknown, Judy: 70
Unknown, John: 66
Unknown, Nancy: 45
Unknown, Martha: 14
Unknown, Polly: 70
Unknown, Ned: 68
Unknown, Caty: 65
Unknown, Prudence: 60

Unknown, Jennie: 70
Unknown, Weston: 80, Female
Unknown, Betsey: 75
Unknown, Tabbie: 65
Unknown, Winnie: 70
Unknown, Nancy: 12
[57.360]
Unknown, Lizzie: 80
Unknown, Isaac: 70
Unknown, Viney: 60
Unknown, Henry: 75
Unknown, Prudence: 65
Unknown, Fanny: 70
Unknown, Asa: 65
Unknown, Aggie: 50
Unknown, John: 45
Unknown, Pat: 50
Unknown, Frank: 48
Unknown, Polly: 52
Unknown, William: 60
Unknown, Henry: 65
Unknown, Armstead: 70
Unknown, Rebecca: 40
Unknown, Ned: 75
Unknown, Fibby: 45
Unknown, Agnes: 60
[57.361]
Unknown, Sophia: 85
Unknown, Lavinia: 8
Unknown, James: 13
Unknown, Daniel: 65
Unknown, Mary: 58
Unknown, Drucilla: 26
Unknown, Louisiana: 20
Unknown, Mahala: 60
Unknown, Mary: 12
Unknown, Lucy Ann: 46
Unknown, Sally: 90
Unknown, Fanny: 100
Unknown, Sally: 80
Unknown, Eliza: 40

Unknown, Mick: 55
Unknown, Solomon: 28
[57.362]
Unknown, Clarissa: 70
Unknown, Melissa: 35
Unknown, Peggie: 30
Unknown, Betsey: 60
Unknown, Lucy: 70
Unknown, Fanny: 75
Unknown, Martha: 47
Unknown, Marius: 44
Unknown, Nellie: 75
Unknown, Amy: 80

Unknown, David: 80
Unknown, Phil: 70
Unknown, Lydia: 60
Unknown, Amanda: 40
Unknown, Matilda: 35
Unknown, Lucy: 30
Cousins, Rhoda: 70
Unknown, Margaret:: 25
[57.363]
Unknown, Lewis: 120
Unknown, Peter: 70
Unknown, Heartwell: 75
Unknown, Weston: 12
Unknown, Sussex: 10

Unknown, Sally: 22
Unknown, Frank: 65
Unknown, Eliza: 14
Unknown, Sylvia: 65
Parker, William: 50
Parker, Patty: 100
Unknown, Phill: 73
Unknown, Candace: 70
Unknown, Louisa: 50
Unknown, Isaac: 65
Unknown, Lizzie: 57
Unknown, Patson: 80
Unknown, Betty: 70

DESTITUTE FREEDMEN IN THE CITY OF PETERSBURG, VA

[57.365]
Brunswick Co. VA
Edwards, Lucy
Edwards, Ruffin
[57.366]
House, Prisilla
House, Allice
House, Allen
House, Lewis
[57.367]
Edlar, Fannie
Edlar, Polly
Haskins, Violet
Jackson, Julia
Jackson, Lucy
Jackson, Rubin
Stitch, Lizzie
[57.368]
Edlar, Rosa
Edlar, Edward
Edlar, John
Wills, Martha
[57.370]
Ellis, Polly
Ellis, Estella

[57.371]
Brooks, China

Brooks, Joseph
Brooks, Mary
Brooks, Virginia
Robinson, Lucy
Robinson, Oliver
[57.372]
Good, Winnie
Good, Mary
Good, Joe
Good, Edwin
Good, Harriet
Good, Washington
Good, Branch: Female

[57.365]
Kingman, VA
Folley, Martha
Folley, Joseph
Folley, Henry

Washington, D.C.
Riddick, Richard

Mecklenburg Co. VA
Riddick, Clara
Riddick, Selia

Riddick, William
Riddick, Rose
[57.368]
Archer, Susan
Archer, Ned
[57.370]
Smith, Lucy
Smith, Elliza
[57.372]
Epps, Robert
Epps, Pheby

[57.365]
Prince Edward Co. VA
Kelly, Lucy
Kelly, Petan
Kelly, Abbie
[57.382]
Simons, Rachel
Simons, Fannie

[57.365]
Dinwiddie Co. VA
Henderson, Robert
Winfield, L: Male

[57.369]
Scott, Mason
Scott, Mary
Scott, Martha
Scott, Tom
[57.370]
Lewis, Lavinia
Lewis, Mary
Lewis, Ben
Lewis, Rose
[57.372]
Egleston, Harriet
Egleston, Emma
Egleston, Charles
Egleston, Amie
Wilson, Agness
[57.373]
Cox, Mariah
Templeton, Mat
[57.375]
Baker, Frank

[57.365]
Charlotte Co. VA
Pryor, Caroline
Pryor, Amanda
Pryor, Major
[57.366]
Ganes, Chath
Ganes, Ganes
Pryor, Mary
Pryor, Susan
[57.367]
Mosby, Manirva
[57.368]
Watkins, Sarah
Watkins, Josephine
Watkins, All
[57.369]
Mosby, Lizzie
Mosby, Josephine

Mosby, Celia
Mosby, Rose
Mosby, Tom
[57.371]
Jeffers, Lucy

[57.366]
Greensville Co. VA
Lousey, Caroline
Lousey, Sandy
Mason, Sarah
Wilkins, Frances
Wilkins, Susan
[57.367]
Chambers, Georgianna
James, Henrietta
[57.368]
Young, Eliza
Young, Hany
Young, George
Young, Lena
[57.369]
Brown, Addelin
Brown, Drusilla
Brown, Nelson
[57.370]
Robinson, Eliza

[57.365]
Sussex Co. VA
Keny, Caroline
[57.366]
Hill, Comitan?: Female
Hill, Victor
Hill, Jany
Hill, Ned
[57.371]
Williams, Mary
Williams, Celia
Williams, Elsy
Williams, Georgeanna

[57.366]
Halifax Co. VA
Crick, Suzan
Crick, James
[57.367]
Giles, Kate
[57.368]
Mason, Dolly
[57.369]
Marthan, Isabel
[57.370]
Ganet, Sarah

[57.367]
Petersburg, VA
Perry, Louisa
[57.368]
Bounce, Agnes
Bounce, Bob
Bounce, Esther
Bounce, Anthony?
Draper, Rebecca
[57.372]
Jones, Emma
[57.373]
Brown, Candus
Brown, Charlotte
Goldston, Ann
Goldston, Anner
Goldston, Eliza
Goldston, Jane
Goldston, John
Goldston, Tom
Harrison, Julia
Hill, Cornelia A.
Mason, Harriet
Valentine, Anna
Wight, Jane
Wilkinson, Celia
[57.374]
Good, Nancy

Henderson, Jemmer	Kimpt, Nancy	Jones, Clong?
Female	Lawson, Betsey	Jones, Dolly
Hunt, Polly	Lawson, Louisa	Jones, Dolly
Jackson, Amey	Lon, Sarah	Jones, Elenn
Jackson, Celia	Mack, Kate	Jones, George
Jackson, Dick	Martin, Giles	Jones, Isham
Jackson, John	Martin, Jane	Lee, Mary
Jackson, Mary	Modest, Betsy	Madock, Anna
Jackson, Ned	Moody, Marsha	Madock, Jane
Wasingburg, Alice	Moody, Sam	Mitchell, Jane
Wasingburg, John	Pegram, Mary	Mosby, Candis
Wasingburg, Kate	Pegram, Viney	Pegram, Nancy
Wasingburg, Lizzie	Rind, John	Pegram, Robert
Williams, Ann	Stewart, Miller	Pegram, Susan
Williams, Annie	Sykes, Abram	Pegram, William
Williams, Jane	Sykes, Charles	Reams, Betsey
Williams, John	Sykes, Polly	Reams, Charles
Williams, Susan	Theat, Phiby	Richardson, Elizabeth
[57.375]	Theat, Phiby	Simons, Bridy
Baker, John	Valentine, Catherin	White, Charles
Baker, Susan	White, Bob	White, Jane
Bonner, Jane	[57.380]	[57.378]
Brown, Phibby	Bell, Polly	Bird, Fannie
Cloyd, Mary	Brown, Tom	Bird, Fannie
Crawford, Silvia	Crawford, Ann	Bird, Sallie
Day, Elmer	Crawford, Jane	Day, Aron
Drummon, Agness	Day, Alice	Day, John
Edmonson, Eliza	Day, Betsy	Day, Tom
Graves, India	Day, Caroline	Hansen, Rachel
Harrison, Libbie	Day, Fanny	Hansen, Sallie
Hatcher, Potey: Female	Day, Faris: Female	[57.379]
Jenkins, Andrew	Day, Jim	Branch, Elizabeth
Jenkins, Eliza	Day, Martha	Cook, Mary
Jenkins, Mary	Fisher, Lucy	Grange, Agnes
Jenkins, Robert	Goodwin, Amie	Page, John
Jenkins, Susan	Grammer, Ann	Perkins, Sallie
Johnson, Mary	Harris, Maria	Pimeni, Green
Jones, Agnes	Jackson, Fannie	Roberts, Lizzie
Jones, Lily	Jeffries, Maria	Robinson, Esther
Jones, Mary	Jones, Caroline	Stewart, Peggy
Jones, Tom	Jones, Celia	Valentine, Sarah

White, Sam
Williams, Robert
[57.381]
Abbie, Alice
Abbie, Andrew
Abbie, Harriet
Abbie, John
Abbie, Mary
Abbie, Susan
Abbie, Tom
Bolling, Betsy
Brown, Minnie
Brown, Nancy
Filds, Martha
Holmes, Betty
Jones, Edney: Female.
Middleton, Charlotte
Miller, Martha
Parker, Gradi
Parker, Jeff
Robinson, Amelia
[57.382]
Bland, Billy
Brown, Archer
Brown, Betsey
Coleman, Martin
Colton, Pleasant
Harsin, Thomas
Johnson, Lucy
Jones, Robert
Knight, Anna
Knight, George
Knight, Isabel
Knight, James
Tisdell, Clara
Tisdell, Margareta
Tisdell, Martha
Williams, Dick

[57.367]
Nottoway Co. VA
Taylor, Betsey
Taylor, Grant
Taylor, Princess
Taylor, Sallie
[57.370]
Johnson, Lillie
Patterson, Fred

[57.367]
Lunenburg Co. VA
Jackson, Amy
Ragland, Lucy
[57.369]
Marshall, Elizabeth
[57.370]
Jackson, Nancy
Jackson, Dillia
Jackson, Tyler
[57.372]
Land, John
Land, Louisa
Land, Lucy
Land, Parhana: Female.

[57.368]
Isle of Wight Co. VA
Ream, Harriet
[57.369]
Cassell, Julia
Cassell, Manuel
Cassell, James
Cassell, Esther

[57.370]
Amelia Co. VA
Preston, Daniel
Preston, Alice
Preston, Hellen
Preston, Jane

[57.371]
Sampson Co. NC
Moon, Lucy

Southampton Co. VA
Kier, Lavinia
Kier, Emolene

[57.371]
Chesterfield Co. VA
Jarrett, Emma Fitch
Jarrett, Mary
Jarrett, Delia
Jarrett, Harriett
Jarrett, Polly
[57.373]
Baker, Lucy
Bates, Amy
[57.374]
Baker, M. Isabel
Clark, Nellie
[57.375]
Gates, Sam
Gates, Sarah
Williams?, Vinnie
Williams?, Ben
Williams?, John
Williams?, Fannie
Williams?, Susan

Prince George Co. VA
Stokes, Thoma
Shands, Indy

[57.373]
Surry Co. VA
Valentine, Betsy

DESTITUTE FREEDMEN IN POWHATAN CO. VA

[57.385]
Powhatan Co. VA
Allis, Ninny: Female
Archer, Sarah
Arthur, Jenny
Boulon, Emma: 4 children
Branch, Charlotte
Briggs, Josher
Burkes, Dick: 4 children
Carter, Martha: 1 female 4 children
Claybon, Selvin: 2 children
Cook, Rachel: 1 female, 1 child
Cosby, Nellie: 3 children. female
Ford, Donin: 1 female
Franklin, William: 1 male
Harris, Caroline: 1 female
Holland, Daniel: 1 male
Jackson, Simon: 1 male
Jenkins, Mary: 1 female, 3 children
Valentine, Artsed?: Male
[57.386]
Unknown, Peggie Ann: 1 female
Fin, Mary: 3 children

Firoled?, Lucan: child
Giles, Frank
Harris, Eliza: 3 children
Harris, Mary: 3 children
Harris, Mary: 1 female. 5 children
Logan, Ann
Logan, Kessy
Logan, Ned: 1 male
Lynch: Henny: 1 child, female
Mago, Nelson: 1 female, 1 male
Mill, Randon
Randol, Aaron
Randol, Eliza
Randol, Sam
Ranson, Nick: 1 male
Richtell, Martha
Taylor, Emmy: 1 child

[57.385]
Spotsylvania Co. VA
Bank, Rosetter: 2 children

DESTITUTE FREEDMEN PRINCE EDWARD CO. VA

[57.388]
Prince Edward Co. VA
James, William
Ross, Davy
Ross, Liza
Ross, Liza
Ross, Mag
Ross, Mary
Ross, Ticia
Wainack, Jinny
Wainack, Lucy
Walkens, George

Williams, Billy
[57.389]
Bruce, Robert
Good, Agness
Good, Joseph
Good, Wilson
Grimm, Clem
Ruggen, Eliza
Watson, Dinah
[57.390]
Bricks, Becky
Bricks, Betty

Bricks, Shedric
Bricks, Shedric
Grimm, Cisden: Female
Grimm, Herg: Female
Grimm, Mary
[57.391]
Easter, George
Easter, Jimmy
Easter, Liza
Easter, Trim
Green, Marther
Green, Rose

Matthew, Bruce
Matthew, Fanny
Matthew, Harg
Matthew, Jacob
Matthew, Lucy
Minister, Cathrain
Minister, Henry
Minister, Nathan
Minister, Robert
Tribb, James
Tribb, Olin
Tribb, William
[57.392]
Allen, Harriet
Anderson, Liza
Bartlett, Dan
Brown, Booker
Liggin, Adam
Liggin, Alicars: Male
Liggin, Elizabeth
Liggin, Harriet
Smith, Clem
Sticker, Reno
Sticker, William
Walker, Ada
Walker, Eliza
Walker, Eliza, Jr.
Walker, Jerry
Woden, Clara
Woden, John
[57.392]
Bell, Betsey
Bell, Ellen
Bell, James
Bell, Randolph
Bell, Robert
Bell, Wash
Bell, Wilsha: Male
Reed, Barba: Male
Reed, Isaac
Taylor, Abram

Taylor, Ann
[57.393]
Jackson, Celia
Liggin, Becky
Liggin, William
[57.394]
Carter, Roger
Carter, Ellen
Carter, Stuard
Carter, Allen
Clark, Rachel
[57.395]
Clark, Caroline
Clark, Doctor
Clark, Junior
Clark, Robert
Foster, Mollie
Herbert, Liza
Johnson, Luis
Johnson, Susan
Jones, Richard
McGee, Dilson
Miller, Lucy
Miller, Margaret
Miller, Sallie
Miller, Tim
Miller, William
Price, Joanna
Wainock, Fanny
[57.396]
Chaterfield, Amanda
Chaterfield, Clara
Chaterfield, Hal
Chaterfield, Richard
Clark, Fisher: Female.
Clark, John
Clark, Liza
Clark, Lucy
Clark, Martha
Clark, Susan
Clark, Wanda

Davis, Anna
Davis, Jordan
Davis, Kitty
Kearney, Annice
Kearney, Emma
Kearney, Mack
Kearney, Martha
Lang, Abram
Lang, Caroline
Lang, Cipio
Lang, George
Lang, Harriet
Lang, Henrietta
Lang, Jennie
Lang, Liza
Lang, William
McGee, Margaret Jane
McGee, Mary
McGee, Paddie: Male
McGee, Puss
McGee, Russilla
McGee, Sallie
Michel, Archer
Michel, Francis
Michel, Mollie
Michel, Spencer
Randolph, John
[57.397]
Lang, Frank
Lang, Mary
Lang, Mary
Lang, William
Smith, Fred
Smith, Henry
Smith, Martha
[57.398]
Carter, Laran: Female
Carter, Sallie
Davis, James
Francis, Clementine
Francis, Minerva

Langdon, Sarah
Unk, Sarah Maria
Walker, Henry
Young, Plummy: Male
[57.399]
Bartlett, Ellen
Bartlett, Frederic
Bartlett, Jinnie
Bartlett, Martha
Bartlett, Paul
Bartlett, Sarah
Bartlett, Woodson
Jinning, Ben
Mody, Jacob
Mody, Maria
Mody, Mingo
Mody, Paddie: Male
Mody, Rachel
Mody, Tom
Mody, Willis
[57.400]
Bartlett, James
Bartlett, George
Bartlett, Levi
Pollock, Henry
White, Betty
White, More: Female
White, Susan
[57.401]
Botts, Aaron
Jackson, Hercules
Pollard, Anna
Pollard, James
Pollard, Middir: Female
Pollard, Patience
Pollard, Prior
Pollard, Willie
Price, Millie
Terry, Eliza
Terry, James
Terry, Margarett

Terry, Peter
Trent, Fanny
Trent, Joseph
Trent, Pollie
Trent, Rhoda
Trent, Samson
[57.402]
Douglass, Delsey
Douglass, Phillis
Hutson, Addison
Lynn, Jinnie
Scott, Ann
Scott, Caroline
Scott, Minerva
Scott, Patrick
Scott, Roal: Female
Scott, Sallie
Scott, Sarah
Scott, Scott
Terry, Lucy
Terry, Martha
Terry, Tom
Terry, William
[57.403]
Francis, Daniel
Francis, Luran
Francis, Nira
Francis, Sarah
Hutson, Daniel
Hutson, Fanny
Miller, Addison
Miller, George
Miller, Lucinda
Miller, Lucy
Miller, Martha
Miller, Patrick
Miller, Rosetta
[57.404]
Goods, Isabella
Goods, Lucy
Goods, Pollie

Scott, Jeffrey
Scott, Lucy
Scott, Randol
Tucker, Dick
Tucker, Nathan
Tucker, Palina: Female
Tucker, Rosetta
Walker, Ned
White, Ella
White, Sydney
[57.405]
Douglass, James
Fountain, Dick
Fountain, Harriet
Fountain, Jane
Fountain, Robert
Gillan, Julia-Buck
Gillan, Maria
Gillan, Mary J
Green, Mary
Liggins, America:
   Female
Reed, Amanda
Reed, America
Reed, Andrew
Reed, Fannie
Reed, Harriett
Waimack, Pallace:
   Female
[57.408]
Booker, Joe
Booker, Joseph
Booker, Maria
Booker, Martha
Flood, Eliza
Wooden, Eliza
Wooden, Jesse
[57.409]
Flood, Edward
Flood, Elide
Nash, Cesar

Nash, Daniel
Rose, Charity
Rose, Ludisha
Rose, Margarett
Samson, Ezebell
Weslawn, Betty
Weslawn, Phil
Weslawn, Sallie
[57.410]
Ligon, Charlotte
Patterson, Claburn
Patterson, Julia
Patterson, Lewis
Patterson, Maria
Patterson, Mollie
Patterson, Steben
Rose, Margarett
Rose, Phil
Rose, Willie
Woodson, Doctor
Woodson, Lucy
Woodson, Minerva
Woodson, Walker
[57.411]
Egaton, Amanda
Egaton, Charles
Egaton, Martha
Egaton, Vila
Egaton, William H.

[57.388]
Buckingham Co. VA
Brindle, Phil
Findum, Tom
Hooper, Marther
[57.389]
Anderson, Henny: Female
Mills, Booker
Mills, Clara
Mills, John

Mills, Robert
[57.392]
Bartlett, Miller
[57.394]
Hooper, Sarah
Hooper, Henry
Hooper, Robert
Hooper, Mary
Venen, Catharine
Venen, Sallie
Venen, Wallace
Venen, Golen
[57.405]
Rose, Margaret
Rose, Albert

[57.388]
Lunenburg Co. VA
Branch, General
Clark, Jerry
Robinson, Andrew
Smith, Jerry
[57.389]
Didley, Becky
Didley, Jeff
Didley, Judy
Didley, Lawrence
Fig, Isaac
Williams, Henry
[57.393]
Unknown, Margaret
Ann Davis, Primas
[57.394]
Harden, Becky
[57.400]
Davis, Vina
Davis, John
[57.401]
Taylor, Amy
Taylor, Pateman
Female.

[57.409]
Hurtson, David
Hurtson, Lucy
Hurtson, Emaline
Hurtson, William
Hurtson, Peggie

[57.388]
Cumberland Co. VA
Deans, Ned
Marshall, William
[57.391]
Bartem, Edward
White, Judy
[57.392]
Woodford, Maggie
[57.394]
Micel, Jane
[57.398]
Jackson, Margaret
Jackson, Silvey
Jackson, Rose
[57.399]
Hobson, Betsey
Hobson, Stonewall
Hobson, Elisha
Hobson, Jane
[57.400]
Brown, Agnes
Brown, Anna
Brown, Daniel
Branch, Anthony
Branch, Becky
Branch, Anthony
Branch, Edward
Smith, Edward
Smith, Dollie
Jones, Redford
Jones, Lucy
Jones, Francis
Jones, Ella

Jones, Lucy
[57.405]
Bedford, Amy
Bedford, Beckey
Bedford, Floratin
Booker, Amy
Booker, George
Booker, Jackson
Booker, John
Booker, Lewis
Booker, Martha
Booker, Robert
Booker, Robert
Booker, Wilson
Jackson, Anna
Jackson, Margaret
Jackson, Robert
Jeran, Harriett
Jeran, Lucy
Jeran, William
Torvin, Alice
Torvin, Emma
Torvin, Harry
Torvin, Margarett
Torvin, Roberta
Torvin, Virginia
Watkins, Caroline
Watkins, Embra
Watkins, Sarah
Woodson, Margaret
Woodson, Maria
[57.406]
Lane, Harriett
Lane, Pollie

[57.407]
Watkins, Lucrecia
Watkins, Florence
[57.410]
Collins, Horner
Jones, Scetia: Female
Strong, Sarah

[57.389]
Nottoway Co. VA
Dickerson, Julia
Dickerson, James
Dickerson, Becky
Dickerson, Dinah
Dickerson, Jordan
Dickerson, Billy
Dickerson, Benjamin
Dickerson, Harry
Dickerson, Land: Female
Dickerson, Julius
[57.401]
Evin/Ervin, Charlotte
Jones, Sallie

[57.393]
Charlotte Co. VA
Spencer, William
[57.394]
Jones, Jane
Jones, William
Henry: James
Henry: George

[57.405]
Richard, Maria
Richard, Robert
Richard, Willie
Richard, Fanny
[57.408]
Spragon, Nancy
Spragon, Amanda
Spragon, Sarah
Spragon, Maria
Spragon, Andrew
Spragon, Oliver
Spragon, Nicy
Spragon, Solomon
Spragon, Daniel
Spragon, Harrison
Spragon, Fannie
Spragon, Paddy Female.
[57.409]
Trent, Sam

[57.401]
Mecklenburg Co. VA
Smith, Syvey
Smith, Caroline
Smith, Alice

[57.389]
Richmond Co. VA
Christian, Lucy

[57.412]
Mississippi
Evans, Harriet

DESTITUTE FREEDMEN IN PRINCE GEORGE CO. VA

[57.414]
Dinwiddie Co. VA
Green, Mason: 1 female 4 children
[57.417]
Jones, Traverse: 1 female, 1 male
Meade, Granwith: 1 female,
    4 children
[57.425]
Green, Mason
Green, Caroline
Green, Preston
Green, Sam
Green, Amy A.
[57.433]
Kennedy, Elizabeth

[57.414]
Prince George Co. VA
Bland, Mary: 3 children
Bonner, Duke
Ellis, Robert
Ellis, William: 1 female 5 children
Geary, Nancy
Hatch, Peter: 1 female 3 children
Holt, Lavinia
Hutchinson, George Ann: 4 children
Morrison, Eliza: 1 male. 4 children
Phillips, Peter
Scott, George
Sergeant, Charles: 1 female
    5 children
Sykes, Lewis: 1 female
Taylor, Clarinda: 4 children
Washington, George: 3 women,
    3 children
Wilkins, Emily: 2 children
Williamson, Rebecca: 4 children
[57.415]
Bishops, Henry: 1 male

Bland, Scott: 3 females
Boon, Sallie: 2 females. 2 children
Brown, Dick: 2 females. 4 children
Brown, Hamlin: 1 male. 1 female
Chappee?, N: 1 male
Ellis, Henry
Grammar, Richard: 1 female,
    4 children
Harrison, Stephen: 2 children
Hines, Mason: 1 female, 7 children
Hunt, Anna: 5 children
Jackson, Ambrose: 2 children
Johns, Angelina: 1 female,
    2 children
Johns, Harriett: 1 female. 2 children
Johns, Susan: 2 males, 1 female,
    4 children
Jones, Rhoda: 2 females, 2 children
Ridley, Jacob: 1 female, 4 children
Royal, William
Southall, Rosetta: 1 child
[57.416]
Beard, William: 1 female, 4 children
Bilyard, Hamlin: male, 1 female,
    1 child
Bullivant, N.P: 1 male, 2 children
Criar, Luvenia: 3 females,
    4 children
Edler, Dianah: 2 females
Eppes, Henry: 1 female, 4 children
Evans, Julia: 1 female, 2 males,
    2 children
Grammar, Andrew: 1 male
Hamlin, Sandy: 1 male, 1 female,
    1 child
Holloway, Millie: 1 child, 1 male,
    1 female
Kennedy, Elizabeth: 1 female
Marks, William: 3 children

Mason, William: male. 1 female, 4 children
McCann, Moses: 1 female
Orange, Annie: female. 1 male, 1 child
Ritchie, James
Smith, James: 4 males
Sykes, Bettie: female, 1 male, 1 child.
Turpin, Abraham: 1 female, 1 male, 1 child.

[57.417]
Bailey, Ambrose: 1 female
Barnett, Bettie: 1 female
Bowman, Amy: 3 females, 2 children
Bowman, Mary: 1 female, 5 children
Francis, Julia: 2 females
Johnson, James: 1 female, 6 children
Jordan, Amie: 3 females, 4 children
Kent, Mary E: 1 female, 2 children
Marks, Edwin A: 7 females, 3 males, 11 children
Rickes, Sallie: 1 female, 4 children
Rush, Hannah: 1 female, 4 children
Thomas, Peter: 1 male
Tucker, Cecilia: 2 females, 2 children
Wake, Thema: 1 female, 7 children
White, Pinder: 2 females

[57.418]
Brown, Lucy: 1 female, 3 children
Collier, Robert: 3 females, 3 children
Fisher, Sylvie: 1 female, 6 children
Gilchrist Harriet: 1 female, 4 children
Greaves, Isaac: 2 females
Jackson, Hester: 2 females, 1 male, 1 child
Johnson, Bob: 1 male
Jones, Harris: 2 males, 1 woman
Jones, Robert: 1 child
Lucas, Susan: 2 females, 4 children
Senley, John: 3 females, 4 males
Seward, Mary: 1 female
Thomas, Judy: 2 females, 3 children
Traverse, Nancy: 1 female, 1 child

[57.419]
Bland, LaVinia
Bland, Mary
Bland, Peteat: Male
Brown, Hamlin
Brown, Robert
Cox, Harriet
Cox, Lucinda
Cox, Richard
Cox, William
Johnson, Eliza
Johnson, Lewis
Johnson, Margarett
Johnson, Thomas
Kent, Catharine
Kent, Frances
Kent, Mary: 8 females
Sykes, Betty
Sykes, Jane
Sykes, Matthew
[57.420]
Bland, Betty
Hutchinson, George N.
Hutchinson, Ella
Hutchinson, Frances
Hutchinson, Jane
Hutchinson, Lucy
Bowman, Mary
Bowman, Eliza
Bowman, Amy
Bowman, Nathan
Bowman, Kelzie: Male
Bowman, Peter
Thomas, Peter
White, Pender: Male
White, Villie: Male
Johnson, Jim
Johnson, Mary
Johnson, George
[57.422]
Brown, Ann

Brown, Rebecca
Burnett, Betty
Francis, Emma
Francis, Julia
Jackson, Bettie
Jackson, Dick
Jackson, Edward
Jackson, James
Jackson, John
Jackson, Nancy
Johnson, Betty
Johnson, Daniel
Johnson, James
Johnson, Rochester
Jones, Lewis
Jordan, Annie
Robertson, Lizzie
[57.423]
Bailey, Ambrose
Boon, Eliza
Boon, Eliza
Boon, Taby: Female
Cox, Abner
Cox, Collin
Harrison, Logan
Harrison, Paul
Jordan, Missouri: Male
Minga, Lizzie
Ricks, Martha N.
Ricks, Mason
Ricks, Sally
Ricks, Susannah
Ricks, William
Siler, Amey
Tiler, Jane
Tiler, Martha
Tiler, Richard
Tiler, Sonny
[57.424]
Brown, Eleck
Brown, Elizabeth

Brown, Martha J.
Brown, Pallis: Female
Bush, Bucker
Bush, Edward
Bush, Hannah
Bush, John
Bush, William
Cox, Billie
Cox, Harry
Cox, Robert
Edler, Diana
Edler, Susan
Lucas, Randall
Perkins, Winnie
Turpin, Abraham
Turpin, Villina
[57.425]
Bonner, Duke
Brown, Florence
Crier, Ben
Crier, Bettie
Crier, Lavinia
Crier, Lavinia
Crier, Mahala
Crier, Palles
Crier, Rachel
Crier, Richard
Ellis, Bob
Scott, George
Seward, Maria
Sykes, Lewis
Sykes, Lucy
Wilson, Caroline
[57.426]
Brown, Darkes
Epps, Edward
Epps, Ellie
Epps, Henry
Epps, Phillis
Sergeant, Davy
Sergeant, Elick

Sergeant, Francis: Female
Sergeant, Frank
Sergeant, George
Sergeant, Lucy
Wilson, Catharine
Wilson, Lucy
Wilson, Nancy
[57.427]
Bilyard, Clara
Bilyard, Hamlin
Bishop, Henry
Chappel, N: Female
Elliot, Rebecca
Eppes, Frances
Eppes, Susan
Gilchrist, Mary
Gilchrist, William
Johns, Angelia
Johns, Delia
Johns, Edmonia
Johns, Harriett
Johns, John
Johns, Robertson
Johns, Roxanna
Johns, Sorra J: Female
Johns, Susan
Johns, Susan
[57.428]
Gilchrist, Darling
Gilchrist, Harriett
Gilchrist, Mollie
Gilchrist, Randall
Gilchrist, Thomas
Glover, Mary
Hatch, Anderson
Hatch, Anna
Hatch, Henry
Hatch, Susanna
Jones, Caroline
Jones, Easter
Jones, Virga

Morrison, Albert
Morrison, Eliza A.
Morrison, Johnnie
Morrison, Martha
Traverse, Martha
Traverse, Nancy
[57.429]
Blackwell, Louisa
Carter, Emma
Carter, John
Carter, Mollie
Carter, Sylvia
Holloway, Mike
Holloway, Millie
Jones, Allen
Jones, Ambrose
Jones, Andrew
Jones, Davy
Jones, Ephraim
Jones, Jane
Keney, John
Keney, Peter
Scott, Anna
Scott, Catharine
Scott, Charity
Scott, George
[57.430]
Evans, Julia
Evans, Maddison
Evans, William
Geary, Nancy
Holloway, Isabella
Orange, Amie
Taylor, C: Female
Taylor, Ephraim
Taylor, Irminty?: Male
Taylor, Rose
Taylor, Winn
Wilkins, Bettie
Wilkins, Emily
Wilkins, Fred

[57.431]
Brown, Betsey
Brown, John
Brown, Lucy
Ellis, Henry
Harrison, John
Harrison, John
Harrison, Luvinia
Harrison, Peter
Harrison, Rhoda
Harrison, Stephen
Holt, Luvinia
Jones, Jane
Jones, Rhoda
Royal, William
Southall, Lillie
Southall, Rosetta
Strong, John
Strong, Rinday E: Female
[57.432]
Bowman, Fleming
Bowman, John J.
Bowman, Mary
Crawley, Jennie
Jackson, Ambrose
Jackson, Diana
Jackson, Rosina
Jones, Frank
Jones, Maria
Jones, Robert
Smith, Robert
Wake, Eliza
[57.433]
Allen, Tim
Bowman, Pattie
Jones, Harriett
Marks, Alice
Marks, India
Marks, Lucy
Portriss, Bettie

Portriss, Nash
Ridley, George N.
Ridley, Mary J.
Ridley, Mason
Ridley, Robert M.
Ridley, William N.
Tucker, Cecilia
Tucker, Winni
Unknown, George
Wake, Charles
[57.434]
Cameron, Edmund
Ellis, Charles
Ellis, Emma
Ellis, Mary
Ellis, Mary
Ellis, Sarah
Ellis, William
Hines, Mason
Hunt, Anna
Hunt, Elick
Hunt, John
Hunt, Mary
Hunt, Stephen
Hunt, William
Jones, Cornelius
Williams, Jack
Williams, Jennie
Williams, Mary
Williams, William
[57.435]
Brown, Ambrose
Brown, Betsey
Brown, Jimmie
Brown, Mary
Grammar, Martha
Hines, Bob
Hines, Cecilia
Hines, Emma J.
Hines, Emmett
Hines, Eveline

Hines, Mather
Hines, Sallie
Mason, Bettie
Mason, Fred
Mason, Harriett
Mason, Nick
Mason, Phil
Phillips, Peter
Ritchie, James
[57.436]
Brown, Jennie
Brown, Lucy
Brown, Martha
Brown, Robert
Fisher, Henry
Fisher, Indiana
Fisher, Liddie
Fisher, Lucy
Fisher, Martha
Fisher, Rolla: Male
Fisher, Syliva
Gilley, Susannah
Grammar, Lillie
Lucas, Ben
Lucas, Braxton
Lucas, Mary
Lucas, Susan
Thomas, Caroline
Thomas, Judy
Thomas, Lucy
Thomas, Napoleon
[57.437]
Bird, Betsey
Bird, Elanore
Bird, John
Bird, Lew
Bird, Lucy
Bird, Maria
Bird, Martha
Bird, Martha
Bird, Mary

Bird, Rosetta
Bird, William
Smith, George
Smith, Jane
Smith, Martha
Smith, Parthenia
Washington, Dollie
Washington, George
Washington, Susan
Washington, William

[57.432]
Brunswick Co. VA
Clark, Moses
Clark, Mary
Clark, Rebecca
Clark, Casia
Clark, Douglass
Clark, Lucy
Clark, John

[57.430]
Surry Co. VA
Warren, Julia
Warren, Octavius
Warren, Thomas
Warren, Samuel
Warren, William
Warren, Emmett

[57.426]
Mississippi
Meade, Louise
Meade, Moses
Meade, Henry
Meade, Watt
Meade, Pattie

[57.427]
Missouri
Bilyard, Missouri

DESTITUTE FREEDMEN IN SURRY CO. VA

[57.440]
Sussex Co. VA
Ben, John: 77
Carr, Nellie: 60
Frazer, Jenny: 4
Frazer, Julia: 5
Frazer, Lydia: 3
Frazer, Martha: 2
Frazer, Priscilla: 12
Gillem, Jesse: 5
Gillem, John: 3
Gillem, Rosa: 8
Johnson, James: 75
Nichols, Hannah: 70
Silvey, Winnie: 65
Weich, Jonah: 45
Weich, Titus: 60
[57.441]
Bland, William: 1 year
Bland, Alice: 5
Bland, Melissa: 3
Harrison, Grace: 26
Giles, Crissy: 65
Alston, Charles: 92
Mason, Robert: 90
Brown, Silvey: 85
Benjamin, Junius: 6
Morgan, Dennis: 4
Parker, Dana: 10 mos.
Owen, Bob: 14
Owen, Lydia: 2

Seaborn, Emma: 2
Seaborn, Maria: 2
Seaborn, Lizzie: 7
Parham, Lizzie: 10
Stith, Robert: 6
[57.442]
Cox, Joseph: 3.
Cox, Lavinia: 34.
Cox, Rebecca: 10
Giles, Anna: 6
Giles, Ellen: 35
Good, Charles: 109
Powell, Archer: 8
Powell, Robert: 6
Stith, Albert: 7
Stith, Dabney: 70
Stith, Frankie: 35
Stith, John: 4
Stith, Judy: 1½
Stith, Mary: 24
Stith, Mary: 2
Waden, Harriet: 30
Waden, Scott: 5
[57.443]
Alston, Edy: 55
Brandit, Agnes: 1 year
Brandit, Archer: 37
Brandit, Madony: 5
Brandit, Mary: 45
Good, Ellen: 7
Good, Lizzie: 4

Good, Mary J: 9
Hall, Alexander: 80
Hall, Dolly: 90
Hall, Jethro: 95
Harrelton, Judy: 80
Height, Charles: 85
Honeycutt, Rebecca: 7
Honeycutt, Susannah: 5
Johnson, Lavinia: 8
Johnson, Lucy: 3
Johnson, Robert: 5
Lunder, Amy: 80
Lunder, Ellen: 110
Lunder, Landa: 8
Moss, Annica: 100
Pennington, James: 87

Spires, Adam: 90
Tatum, Anne: 2
Tatum, Bettie: 6
Tatum, Todd: 5
Taylor, Emma: 85

[57.440]
Southampton Co. VA
Parker, Tilda: 6
Parker, Nat: 5

[57.443]
Clark Co. VA
Cox, William: 5

[57.443]
Surry Co. VA
Simpson, Faithy: age 32, 3 children
Wilson, Ida: 96
Riggins, Cherry: 30, 3 children
Adney, A: 25. (Male)
Travis, Austin: 70
Bailey, Henrietta: 26, 1 child
Whitmore, David: 55

Charity, Sally Ann: 45
Ennis, Thomas: 70
Ennis, Sylvia: 40, 4 children
Ennis, Elizabeth: 65, 2 children
King, James: 50
Bird, Mary J: 55
Bailey, Nolan: 48
Bodyd, Ben: 58
Neely, Rebecca: 60, 2 children
Judkins, Elizabeth: 44

LIST OF DEPENDENTS ON THE GOVERNMENT AT HOWARD'S GROVE HOSPITAL, RICHMOND, VA, OCT. 29, 1865

[57.448]
Richmond, VA
Anderson, Lucy
Christian, Caby
Gordon, Nancy
Johnston, Henrietta
Johnston, Polly
Johnston, Sarah
Loney, Margaret
Marsh, Jane
Payne, Martha
Payne, Mary
Taylor, Sylve
[57.449]
Frazer, Ellen
Gallagher, Enoch
Jackson, Nancy
Jones, Susan
Payne, Mira
Payne, Sarah
Price Martha
Smith, Sarah
[57.450]
Breadlove, Nancy
Carey, Nathan
Collier, Julia

Lendsey, Bird
Morris, Nancy
Morris, Sam
Peadon, William
Ray, Oscar
Shores, Scott
Williams, Albert
Williams, Robert
[57.451]
Banks, William
Brown, Dolly
Brown, Rena
Gwinn, Nelly
Jackson, Harriott
Johnston, Charles
Johnston, Lucy
Johnston, Pat
Maune?, Singleton
Maune?, Carter: (from Hanover Co., but listed with Singleton Maune, of Richmond}
Morris, Margaret
Roots, Robert
Smith, Charles
Taylor, Daniel

Unknown, Annie
Unknown, Gussey
Volentine, Margaret
Volentine, Walter
[57.452]
Jackson, Isac
King, David
Moore, Jerry

[57.449]
Richmond Co. VA
Guss, Betsey
[57.451]
Robinson, Lucy
[57.452]
Baker, Alice
Loisa, Anne
Young, Adam
Young, James
Young, Susan

[57.448]
Westmoreland Co. VA
Gordon, Margaret

Loudon Co. VA
White, Fannie

Hampton, VA
Jones, Hannah

Hanover Co. VA
Jackson, Martha
Jackson, Betsey
[57.449]
Bland, Richard
Larden, Julia
[57.450]
Winston, George
[57.451]
Taylor, Thornton
[57.452]
Watkins, Fras

[57.448]
Charlottesville, VA
Brown, Sally
[57.449]
Carter, Jessey
[57.450]
Harper, Littleton
[57.451]
Banks, William
Brown, Betty
Brown, Sally
Richardson, Jane
Richardson, Peter
Richardson, Susan
Watson, Gemima
Watson, Susan

[57.448]
Brunswick Co. VA
Hill, Mason

[57.450]
Ebbs, Randall
Hall, William
Hicks, Antony
Smith, William

[57.448]
Goochland Co. VA
Smith, Harriott
Smith, Isaac
[57.449]
Smith, Mary
Payne, Eliza
Taylor, Godfrey
[57.450]
Martin, Jullian
Martin, Mira
[57.451]
Yancy, Eliza
[57.452]
Pollid, William

[57.448]
Henrico Co. VA
Wilkinson, Mary
[57.450]
Discon, Sam
[57.452]
Macus, Peter
Tolover, James

[57.449]
Fredericksburg, VA
Taylor, Catherine

Nottoway Co. VA
Robinson, Rola
Camel, Phill

[57.451]
Hyde, Millie
Hyde, Theophilis
[57.452]
Bows, Lucinda

[57.449]
Powhatan Co. VA
Bolew, Volentine
Harris, Mary
King, Solmon

Northumberland Co. VA
Williams, Hannah
[57.451]
Phantroy, Eda
Phantroy, George
Phantroy, George, Jr.

[57.449]
Chesterfield Co. VA
Walker, Morning
[57.452]
Godfrey, Mary

[57.449]
Manchester VA
Perkins, Mary
Perkins, Miley
Perkins, Pleasant
Perkins, Everett
Perkins, Warrick
[57.452]
Wheeler, Arthur

[57.449]
Danville VA
Lucy, Sarah
Brooks, Lucy
Jackson, Frederick
Watkins, Edward

[57.452]
Danville, Jemy

[57.448]
Lunenburg Co. VA
Haskins, Deliah
[57.449]
Gale, Lehiew
Washington, John
Mason, Sterling
Breadlove, Abraham
[57.451]
Bagley, Patience
Bagley, Ephraim
[57.552]
Davis, Frederick

[57.449]
Surry Co. VA
Key, Sally
[57.452]
Bookers, Frederick

[57.449]
Page Co. VA
Brimer, Emma

Middlesex Co. VA
Milliner, Henrietter

Lynchburg, VA
Brown, William

Louisa Co. VA
Williams, Buck
[57.451]
Williams, John

[57.449]
Prince Edward Co. VA
Smith, Pleasant
Blanch, Emanuel
Reid, Jerry

[57.451]
Jackson, James
[57.452]
Mekins, Moses
Douglas, Daniel
Douglas, Susan

[57.449]
Charlotte Co. VA
Mardell, Jeff
Bailey, John
Stansfield, Davis
Stansfield, Archer
[57.450]
Spencer, Sam
[57.451]
Hoskins, Lina
Hoskins, Jeff
Hoskins, Etlinah?
Hoskins, York

[57.449]
Frederick Co. VA
Johnston, Henry

Prince William Co. VA
Robinson, Charles

Pittsylvania Co. VA
Warden, Jack

Petersburg Co. VA
Brown, Ben
[57.452]
Acchols, William

Malone, Peter
Rynnall, Peter

[57.449]
Fluvanna Co. VA
Ross, Abby

Greensville Co. VA
Peters, John
Woodroffe, Peter

Charles City Co. VA
Williams, Albert
[57.451]
Lightfoot, Jessey

Caroline Co. VA
Louis, Lindon
Robinson, Rosetta

New Kent Co. VA
Holt, William

Sussex Co. VA
Bailey, Abraham
Jones, Henry
Rivers, Sam
Weldon, Tom

[57.449]
Roanoke, VA
Harrison, Cane

King & Queen Co. VA
Robinson, Major
Walker, Andrew

Dinwiddie Co. VA
Roper, Eliza
Walker, Grace
Walker, Jack

[57.451]
Norfolk, VA
Edwards, Sam

King William Co. VA
Hill, Betty
Hill, Clara
Hill, William

Appomattox Courthouse, VA
Moore, Jerry

Culpeper Co. VA
Jones, Nancy
Jones, Julia
Jones, Polly
[57.452]
Rock, William

Augusta Co. VA
Eldridge, Daniel

Farmville, VA
Woodson, Henry

Stafford Co. VA
Harburn, Henry

[57.449]
Beaufort Co. NC
Juleford, Bona
Judge, Ira

Burke Co. NC
Richardson, Elvira

Bertie Co. NC
Hogard, John

[57.451]
Darlington Co. NC
Charles, Abraham

Guildford Co. NC
Waddleton, Gabriel

Jefferson Co. VA
Williams, Maddison

Maine County
Sherrard, Rise
Dow, Precilla
Dow, William
[57.452]
Johnston, Fras.
Ross, David

[57.451]
Alabama
Marshall, Sam

South Carolina
Smith, Annie: (Charleston)

[57.451]
Murfreesboro NC
Parker, Margaret
Parker, George
[57.452]
Volentine, Robert

[57.448]
New Bern, NC
Love, Temp

Pitt Co. NC
Williams, Rose
[57.452]
Toler, Thomas

Warrenton, NC
Weleams, Matilda
[57.452]
Page, Julia: (Columbia)

Washington, D.C.
[57.449]
Dandridge, John
[57.451]
Carter, Antony

[57.448]
Hynds Co. **Mississippi**
Davis, Tempy

DESTITUTE FREEDMEN RICHMOND, VIRGINIA
{Note: Person's name followed by number of others in the household.}

[57.454]
Richmond, VA
Allen, John: 1 adults
Brown, Vina: 1 adults, 3 children
Davis, Mary: 2 adults, 4 children
Harris, Dick: 1 adult
Harris, Fanny: 2 adults, 3 children
Johnston, Mahala: 1 adult
    3 children
Smith, Date: 1 adults, 1 children
Washington, Isaac: 1 adult
Watkins, Edy: 1 adults, 6 children

Henrico Co. VA
Johnston, Nelson: 1 adult
Lyons, James: 2 adults, 4 children
Payne, Patsey: 1 adults, 5 children
Rauke, Henrietta: 1 adults,
    2 children
Robinson, Millie: 1 adults

Goochland Co. VA
Lewis, Elcy: 1 adults

Amelia Co. VA
Norfleet, Py: 1 adults, 6 children

Louisa Co. VA
Baker, Evlina: 1 adults,
    3 children
Taylor, Joanna: 2 adults,
    1 children

Rockbridge Co. VA
Fisher, Ellen: 1 adults

Fauquier Co. VA
Shelton, Mary: 1 adults,
    5 children

Hanover Co. VA
Lewis, Mary: 1 adults, 2 children

King William Co. VA
Taylor, Rosina: 2 adults,
    4 children

Charles City Co. VA
Parker, William: 2 adults

Wayne Co. NC
Dodge, Priscilla: 1 adults,
    1 child

DESTITUTE FREEDMEN IN HENRICO CO. VA

[57.455]
Richmond, VA
Bolin, Maria: 2 adults.
Craig, Susan: 1 adult, 5 children.
Dickinson, Hannah: 1 adult.
Evans, Westay: 2 adults, 3 children
Johnson, Minerva: 1 adults,
    2 children
Lee, Samuel: 2 adults, 1 children.
Olmsted, Charlotte: 1 adult.
Ross, Kitty: 3 adults, 3 children.
Tabb, Israel: 1 adult.
Thornton, Patsey: 1 adults,
    2 children
Toast, Mary: 1 adults, 1 child
Williams, Elizabeth: 1 adults,
    5 children
[57.456]
Branton, Betsy: 1 adult, 1 child
Davis, Vina: 1 adult, 1 children
Foster, Judy: 1 adult
Goldsmith, Eliza: 1 adult, 1 child
Grautein, Sam
Green, Lucinda
Hams, Phoebe: 1 adult
Harris, Kitty
Harris, Pat: 1 adult
Jefferson, Vina: 1 adult, 2 children
Marshall, Amy: 2 adults,
    3 children
Miller, Mary: 1 adult, 5 children.
Moreby, Lucile: 1 adult-5 children
Rone, Lavinia: 1 adults, 4 children
Travis, Lizzie: 1 adults, 4 children
Watkins, Lizzie: 1 adult.
[57.457]
Baker, Lucy: 1 adult
Brown, Henry: 1 adult
Jackson, James: 1 adult

Johnson, Sallie: 1 adult, 2 children
Jones, Ben: 1 adult.
Lewis, Nancy: 1 adult
Marshall, Maria: 1 adult
Morse, Celia: 1 adults, 5 children
Pittman, Stephen: 1 adult
Scott, Betsey: 2 adults, 2 children
Syles, Peggy: 1 adult, 2 children
[57.458]
Brown, Lucy: 1 adult, 2 children
Olmsted, Charlotte

[57.455]
Chesterfield Co. VA
Woolrich, Sarah: 1 adult, 1 child
Woolrich, Cornelius: 1 adult
[57.456]
Brown, Lucretia
Harris, Sallie: 1 adults, 3 children
[57.457]
Smith, Cynthia: 1 adult, 5 children

[57.456]
Henrico Co. VA
Finks, Edward
[57.457]
Burton, Caroline: 1 adults,
    2 children
Miner, Nancy: 1 adult
Allen, Jacob: 1 adult
Lucas, Amanda: 2 adults,
    4 children

[57.455]
Fluvanna Co. VA
Scott, Sallie: 2 adults, 2 children.

Caroline Co. VA
Reynolds, Catherine: 2 adults,
    5 children

Westmoreland Co. VA
Johnson, Susan: 1 adults,
    2 children

Powhatan Co. VA
Taylor, Jane: 2 adults

[57.456]
Northumberland Co. VA
Coles, Mary P: 1 adults,
    5 children

Fauquier Co. VA
Cooh, Eliza: 1 adults, 4 children

Amelia Co. VA
Mason, Betsy: 1 adult, 5 children
Morgan, Anna: 1 adults,
    3 children
Hooper, Abby: 2 adults,
    4 children

Lunenburg Co. VA
McAllister, Ann Elliza: 1 adult

Sussex Co. VA
Johnson, Phillis: 1 adult,
    4 children

[57.457]
Goochland Co. VA
Sullivan, Rachael: 2 adults

King William Co. VA
Butler, Warren: 2 adults

Augusta Co. VA
Anderson, George: 4 adults,
    3 children

Matthews Co. VA
Rillups, Fanny: 1 adults,
    2 children

Gloucester Co. VA
Carter, Sallie: 1 adults, 4 children
Bates, Robert: 1 adult

Fairfax Co. VA
Lewis, Ann: 1 adult, 1 children

Buckingham Co. VA
Gray, Saluda W: 1 adult

[57.458]
Onslow Co. NC
Henderson, Lucinder: 1 adult,
    1 child

Mobile, Alabama
Hardy, Silvia: 1 adult

DESTITUTE FREEDMEN IN GOOCHLAND CO. VA

[57.461]
Hanover Co. VA
Unknown, Phillis

Goochland Co. VA
Bowles, William
Brown, Rebecca
Green, Henry
Johnson, Milly
Unknown, Alsey
Unknown, Annie
Unknown, Anthony
Unknown, Billy
Unknown, Fanny

Unknown, Harrison
Unknown, Henry
Unknown, Jack
Unknown, Jennie
Unknown, Limus
Unknown, Lucy
Unknown, Maria
Unknown, Martha
Unknown, Matilda
Unknown, Milton
Unknown, Richard
Unknown, Samuel
Unknown, Spencer
Unknown, Sukey

[57.462]
Unknown, Phebia
Unknown, Dabney
Unknown, Philips
Unknown, Queen
Unknown, Charity
Unknown, Margaret
Unknown, Susan
Unknown, Clara
Unknown, Henry
Unknown, Jenny
Unknown, Julia
Unknown, Handy
Unknown, Archer
Unknown, Nancy

LIST OF ORPHANS IN GOOCHLAND COUNTY, VA

[57.463]
Bowles, Ida
Brown, Dolly
Brown, Henry
Brown, Sam
Brown, Winston
Cooper, Francis
Cooper, Inda
Cooper, Jack
Cooper, John
Cooper, Molly
Cooper, Rachael
Cooper, W.B.
Green, Irate
Green, Mary
Johnson, Henry
Lynch, B.
Morman, George
Morman, Winston
Red, Henry

Red, Lizzie
Red, Mary
Red, Moses
Red, Richard
[57.464]
Cunningham, E.M.
Unknown, Ellen
Unknown, Willie
Unknown, Lindsay
Unknown, Lawrence
Unknown, Indianna
Unknown, William
Unknown, James
Unknown, George
Unknown, Mary
Unknown, Preston
Unknown, Lindsay
Unknown, Harrison
Unknown, Dudley
Unknown, Indianna

Unknown, Margaret
Unknown, William
Unknown, Alice
Unknown, Robert
Unknown, Washington
Unknown, Caroline
Unknown, Buck
Unknown, Kitty
Unknown, Frank
Unknown, Eliza
Unknown, Charles
Unknown, Annie
Unknown, Sally
[57.465]
Unknown, Edward
Unknown, Jim
Unknown, Antonia
Unknown, Peter
Unknown, Sarah Jane
Unknown, Infant

DESTITUTE FREEDMEN IN GREENE CO. VA

{This section does not specify pre-war residence, but it appears that these freedmen lived in Greene County before the war. The names of their former master are listed in parentheses.}

[57.468]
Unknown, Gilbert: Child (N. Braud)
Unknown, Thomas: Child (N. Braud)
Unknown, Frank: Child (Louisa Deans) Unknown, Nelson: Child (W. White)
Unknown, Frank: Child (J. Graves)
Unknown, George: Child (S. Fishback) Unknown, Fleming: Child (Polly Timbro)
Unknown, Susan: Child (Ro. Sims) Former owner unable to support.
Unknown, Louisa: Child (Ro. Sims)
Unknown, Mary: Child (Ro. Sims)
Unknown, Rose: Woman (Ro. Sims)
Lewis, John: Child (Ro. Sims)
Unknown, Emily: Child (Ro. Sims)
Unknown, Martha: Child (Ro. Sims)
Unknown, Jennie: Child (Ro. Sims)
Unknown, Millie: Woman (R. Pritchet) Former owner deceased Estate insolvent.
Unknown, Nell: Woman. (R. Pritchet)
Unknown, Lua: Child (R. Pritchet)
Unknown, Emily: Child (R. Pritchet)
Unknown, Mary: Child (R. Pritchet)
Unknown, Gabriel: Child (R. Pritchet)
Unknown, Moses: Child (R. Pritchet)
Unknown, Betsy: Child (R. Pritchet)
Unknown, William: Child (R. Pritchet)
Unknown, Betsey: Child (E. Blakeley)
Unknown, Hannah: Child (E. Blakeley)
Unknown, John: Child (E. Blakeley)
Unknown, Maria: Child (E. Blakeley)
Unknown, Nelly: Woman. (P. Sims)
Unknown, Charlotte: (Ro. Simms) Former owner not able to support.
Unknown, Moses: Man. (Ro. Simms)
Unknown, Milly: Child (Ro. Simms)
Unknown, William: Child (Ro.Simms)
Unknown, Caroline: Child (Ro.Simms)
Unknown, Columbia: Child (Ro.Simms)
Unknown, Martha: Woman. (B. Price)
Unknown, Georgianna: Child (B.Price)
Unknown, Columba: Child (B. Price)
Unknown, Harriet: Woman. (J.B.Fleming)
Unknown, Rinda: Woman. (J.B.Fleming)
Unknown, James: Child (J.B. Fleming)
Unknown, Eliza: Child (J.B. Fleming)
Unknown, Emma: Child (J.B. Fleming)
Unknown, Robert: Child (G.W. Price) Former owner infirm Estate not able to support.
Unknown, Fanny: Woman. (G.W. Price)
Unknown, Bettie: Child (G.W. Price)
Unknown, Netty: Woman. (G.W. Price)
Unknown, Nelly: Child (G.W. Price)
Unknown, Amanda: Child (G.W.Price)
[57.470]
Unknown, Lewis: Male. (C. Conway)
Unknown, Beauty: Woman (A.A.D. Alum)
Unknown, Benjamin: Child (A.A.D. Alum?)
Unknown, Lee: Child (A.A.D. Alum?)

Unknown, Josephine: Child (A.A.D. Alum?)
Unknown, Lewis: Child (A.A.D. Alum?)
Unknown, Thornton: Man. (R.Pritchett) Former owner deceased Estate insolvent
Unknown, Fanny: Child (R. Pritchett)
Unknown, Amy: Child (R. Pritchett)
Unknown, Benjamin: Child (R.Pritchett)
Unknown, Sarah: Child (R. Pritchett)
Shirley, Reuben: Man. (Jack Miller) Aged, not able to support himself.

Slaughter, John: Man. (W. Wright)
Slaughter, Madison: Child (JaneBlakey)
Slaughter, Betty: Woman (JaneBlakey)
Slau hter, Marcus: Child (Jane Blakey)
Slaughter, Angus: Child (Jane Blakey)
Slaughter, Charlotte: Woman. (Jane Blakey)
Boras, Ro.: Child (Jane Blakey)
Boras, John: Child (Jane Blakey)
Boras, William: (Jane Blakey)

DESTITUTE FREEDMEN IN FLUVANNA CO. VA

{NOTE: Freedmen's names followed by former owner in parentheses, followed by remarks/description of freedman.}

[57.471]
Anderson, Eliza: (James Galt) Nearly blind
Banks, Samuel: (C.J. Huckstep) Old & blind
Beaver, Dosby: (B.W. Seay) Infirm
Cousins, Evalena: (W.P. Raglin) Infirm
Fox, Mary: (James Galt) Deranged
Greasy, M: (Wm. Appleberry) Infirm
Howard, Stephen: (Wm Fountain) Old
James, Daniel: (Watson Briggs) Deranged
Long, Jefferson: (James Galt) Infirm
Long, Letty: (James Galt) Scrofula
Lucas, Fanny: (Mrs. I. Staples) Old
McCary, Maria: (B.W. Seay) Infirm
McFettis, Rebecca: (Wm. Caruthers) Blind
Morton, Jane: (Wm. Bryan) Infirm
Unknown, Jacob: (Henry Woods) Old
Unknown, Hannah: (Geo.Johnson) Old, infirm

Unknown, Willie: (Geo.Johnson) Old, infirm
Unknown, Jennie: (Geo.Johnson) Old, infirm
Unknown, Fanny: (Mrs. I. Staples) Old
Unknown, Eliza: (William Hudson) Old
Unknown, Samuel: (James Galt) Infirm
Unknown, Nannie: (James Galt) Deranged
Unknown, Jolly: (Henry Woods) Deranged
Willis, Louisa: (James Galt) Infirm
Winney, Lucy: (James Galt) Infirm
[57.472]
Abraham, Ben: (Gaines Melton) Infirm
Archer, Polly: (Dr. A. Branch) Infirm
Bates, Lindsay: (John Bates) Infirm
Bowlers, Stephen: (Isaac Perkins) Infirm
Bruce, Rachel: (Wm. C. Bruce) Infirm
Cooper, John: (Wm. Payne) Cripple
Eads, James: (George Holeman) Infirm
Gray, Clara: (John R. Bryant) Invalid

Gray, Dick: (John R. Bryant) Invalid
Johnson, Billy: (Dyer Johnson) Old
Johnson, Polly: (T.F. Bashaw) Infirm
Johnson, Rose: (Dr. A. Branch) Infirm
Jones, William: (Dr. A. Branch) Infirm
Kent, Turner: (Wm. Kent) Rheumatism
Miller, Katy: (Dr. A. Branch) Infirm
Nelson, Peter: (Dr. A.G. Willis) Old
Saugon, W. Jane: (Joseph Bruce) Rheumatism
Unknown, Betsy: (H. Wood) Old
Unknown, Grace: (John G. Hughes) Infirm
Unknown, Henry: (A.B. Duncan) Asthma
Unknown, Mason: (John W. White) Invalid
Unknown, Robin: (John C. Cock) Invalid
Unknown, Ruth: (George Holeman) Deaf
Unknown, Sophia Ann: (David White) Nearly blind
Unknown, Squire: (John W. White) Old
Unknown, Wilson: (Ben Snead) Blind
Unknown, York: (R.B. Payne) Idiot
White, Hannah: (Mrs. M. Stratton) Infirm
White, Thomas: (Mrs. M. Stratton) Infirm
[57.473]
Anderson, Ned: (Joseph P. Fox) Invalid
Baily, Caroline: (Wm. P. Melone) Old
Banks, Isabella: (Wm. Caden) Old
Bowers, Reuben: (James Taylor) Old
Brown, Juda: (John D. Johnson) Old
Burks, George: (Wm. S. Lane) Old
Ferguson, Ed: (Jos. P. Fox) Idiot
Fowler, Nelly: (R.F. George) Old
Gadding, Betty: Free born- deaf-dumb
Harris, S: (Wm. Harris) Old
Jackson, John: (Wm. Appleberry) Old
Kingston, J.B: (Geo. G. Seay) Cripple
Miller, Charles: (Wm. Miller) Old
Perkins, Henry: (J. Perkins) Old
Randall, Biddie: (R.M. Cary) Old
Sauger, Lucy: (Joseph Bruce) Old
Sauger, Samuel: (Geo. W. Salad) Old
Unknown, Daniel: (A. Bleasan) Old
Unknown, David: (R. Payne) Old
Unknown, Flora: (B.V. Kidd) Invalid
Unknown, Isabella: (Washington Snows) Old
Unknown, Martha: (A. Bleasan) Old
Unknown, Mary: (D.J. Appleberry) Old
Unknown, Nanny: (Cary C. Cocks) Blind
Unknown, Sally: (Austin Seay) Infirm
Unknown, Ziddie: (H.L. Hanson) Infirm
Ware, Henry: (T.J. Clark) Old
Ware, Peter: (T.J. Clark) Old
[57.474]
Boston, Charles: (F.C. Boston) Old
Brooks, Edmund: (Dr. Wm Gray) Old
Burch, Reuben: (Wm Flannagan) Cripple
Cary, Polly: (J. Hughes) Invalid
Flowers, Malinda: (Wm D. Shepherd) Old
Hughes, Millie: (Mrs. M.A. Hughes) Old
Jackson, Sarah: (Mrs. C.M. Parish) Infirm
James, Rachel: (Henry Bower) Old
Johnson, Franklin: (Mrs. Lucy Pace) Old
Johnson, Willis: (P. Howard) Cripple
Minor, Matilda: (E. Morris) Invalid
Mutter, George: (P.J. Winn) Infirm
Payne, Alley: (J.W. Gent) Old
Payne, Polly: (Mrs. W. Johnson) Infirm
Shelton, Charity: (William Hughes) Old
Texon, James: (John R. Bryan) Infirm
Unknown, (Hampton: (J.W. Walker) Old
Unknown, Annaca: (C. Hawkins) Old
Unknown, Dolly: (W.S. McGhee) Old

Unknown, Fanny: (Mrs. P.T. Thomas) Infirm & blind
Unknown, Hannah: (R. Baseby) Old
Unknown, Laura: (J.W. Walker) Old
Unknown, Lee: (S.B. Jones) Scrofula. age 10
Unknown, Maria: 12, (S.B.Jones) Nearly blind.
Unknown, Maria: (D.D. Bryant) Old
Unknown, Polly: (John S. Kent)
Unknown, Winchester: (John R. Bryan) Infirm
Unknown, Woman: (Ed. Strange) Old
Vest, Thomas: (Mrs. Lucy Pace) Old
[57.475]
Baker, Millie: (John W. Toucy) Infirm
Carr, Madison: (M. Thomas) Crippled
Decaton, C: (John W. Cocks) Old
Decaton, Dilsa: (Mrs. F. Woodson) Old
Friday, Clary: (Ned Strange) Blind
Friday, Richard: (Henry Baskett) Infirm
Hopkins, Joshua: (Ben Hopkins) Infirm
Jackson, Lydia: (Mrs. Snotty) Infirm
Jackson, Millie: (Rich. Lovett) Infirm
Jones, Polly: (J.A. Shepherd) Old
Key, Agnes: (John W. Clark) Old
Lyons, Nancy: (B.J. Flannagan) Old
Minor, Richard: (James H. Turner) Ruptured
Moss, Elizabeth: (Jesse Pace) Old
Parish, J: (Samuel Pettit) Infirm
Parish, Lydia: (Samuel Pettit) Infirm
Prior, Matsey: (J. Flannagan) Old
Randolph, Temphy: (John Adams) Old
Ritchie, E: (Wm. Black) Old

Strong, G: (Fanny Stowe) Blind
Unknown, Dilsey: (Mrs. F. Woodson) Old
Unknown, Eliza: (W. Kidd) Old
Unknown, Gracie: (Walter J. Kidd) Old
Unknown, Hr: (Joseph Johnson) Old
Unknown, Jacob: (James P. White) Blind
Unknown, John: (James P. Whitenearly) Blind
Unknown, Malinda: (Mrs. A. Staples) Old
Unknown, Roxy: (H. Basket) Old
Unknown, Uncle Jack: (James P. White) One leg off
[57.476]
Achrell, Eliza: (James Galt) Infirm
Burton, Julia A: (Mary F. Jennie) Cripple
Crank, Housan: (James Galt) Infirm
Howard, Cary: (B. Howard) Cripple
Mosby, Malinda: (James Galt) Infirm
Ross, Jesse: (Festus Foulas) One hand off
Scott, India: (Mrs. E. Key) Deaf-dumb
Unknown, Betsy: (Geo. Holman) Infirm
Unknown, Clayborne: (Geo. Holman) Infirm
Unknown, Harriet: (George Holman) Infirm
Unknown, Jennie: (Willis Huckstep) Infirm
Unknown, Lila: (Willis Huckstep) Infirm
Unknown, Samuel: (Willis Huckstep) Blind

DESTITUTE FREEDMEN IN FREDERICKSBURG, VA

{NOTE: The names of the freedmen are followed by that of their former owner, and remarks. They are listed under their pre-war residence.}

[57.476]
Hanover Co. VA
Williams, Silvia: (Mrs. Scott)

[57.477]
Spotsylvania Co. VA
Gray, Minny: (Andrew Gordon)
Lewis, Louisa: (Hiram Gordon.)
Unknown, Hannah: (Andrew Gordon)
Unknown, Nancy: (Andrew Gordon)
Wensworth, Henry: (Richard Wallace)
Wensworth, Lucy: (Richard Wallace)
Wensworth, Mary: (Richard Wallace)
Wensworth, Melina: (Richard Wallace)
Wensworth, Moriah: (Richard Wallace)
[57.478]
Cook, Montgomery: (Thos. Anderson)
Crump, Ann: (John C. Peters)
Crump, Edward: (John C. Peters)
Crump, Georgianna: (John C. Peters)
Crump, Harris: (John C. Peters)
Crump, Mary: (John C. Peters)
Davis, Thomas: (Charles Lewis)
Davis, Tilly: (Charles Lewis)
Gallary, India: (Rowan)
Gallary, Linnia: (Rowan)
Gallary, Margaret: (Rowan)
Gallary, Mary: (Rowan)
Gallary, Sarah: (Rowan)
Hale, Millie: (William Turner)
Henry, Catharine: (Thomas Anderson)
King, Charles: (Thomas Anderson)
Lewis, Addison: (Hiram Gordon)
Lewis, Charles: (Hiram Gordon)
Lewis, Charlon: (John Saunders)
Lewis, Edward: (Hiram Gordon)
Lewis, Edward: (John Saunders)
Lewis, Hiram: (John Sudon)
Lewis, Luie: (John Saunders)
Lewis, Thomas: (Hiram Gordon)

Lewis, Thomas: (John Sudon)
Martin, Lucy: (Thomas Anderson)
Tolman, George: (Crutchfield.)
[57.480]
Johnson, Lucyh: (Paul Bryan)
Nelson, James: (Richard Terry)
Thomas, Nancy: (Catharine Goodwin)
Thompson, John: (Benjamin Spindas?)
Williams, Sippy: (Lawrence Hamphis)
[57.481]
Carter, Agnes: (Thomas Anderson)
Carter, Martha: (Thomas Anderson)

Caroline Co. VA
Coats, Benjamin: (John Washington)
Johnson, Wenna: (Francis Cameron)
Minor, Polly: (Miss Hannah Joyce)
Shepherd, James: (John Bedford)
Stafford, Emanuel: (Dr. Boston)
Stephens, Caroline: (Dr. Boston)
Stephens, Charoltte: (Dr. Boston)
Thomas, Delia: (Dr. Boston)
[57.477]
Johnson, William: (Richard Birds)
Samuel, Abbey: (Benjamin Braid)
Samuel, Mary: (Benjamin Braid)
Slaughter, Helen: (Rowan)
Tammy, Catharine: (Benjamin Braid)
Thornton, George: (Rowan)
Thornton, Millia: (Rowan)
Thornton, Ro.: (Rowan)
[57.479]
Coleman, Alice: (George Brooks)
Johnson, Caroline: (Richard Birds)
Johnson, Emily: (John Henderson)
Johnson, Sarah: (Richard Birds)
Johnson, William: (John Henderson
Pendleton, Beverly: (Thomas Chanclor)
Pendleton, Dudley: (Thomas Chanclor)
Pendleton, Fanny: (Thomas Chanclor)

Pendleton, Harriet: (Thomas Chanclor)
Pendleton, Rose: (Thomas Chanclor)
[57.480]
Johnson, Lissy: (John Washington)
Jones, Alvena: (John Washington)
Jones, William: (John Washington)
Johnson, Harrity: (John Washington)
Jones, Georgiana: (John Washington)
Jonnie, Susan: (John Garrott)
Jonnie, Lucy: (John Garrott)
Garner, Letha: (John Garrott)
Garner, James H: (John Garrott)
Garner, Margaret: (John Garrott)
Johnson, Timmy: (James Taylor)
[57.481]
Brooks, Samuel: (Gilchrist Wren)
Ewing, Ann: (William Hooker)
Ewing, Jane: (James Cronin)
Fields, Benjamin: (Gilchrist Wren)
Fields, Margaret: (Gilchrist Wren)
Thompson, Sidney: (James Cronin)
[57.480]
Lewis, Samuel: (John Bently)

King George Co. VA
Brown, Mary: (Thomas Campbell)
Johnson, Hannah: (Michael Wallace)
Johnson, Jeremiah: (Michael Wallace)
Johnson, Mary Ann: (Michael Wallace)
Johnson, Virginia: (Michael Wallace)
Lewis, Georgianna: (Thomas Jenkins)
Taplet, Anna: (William Tulliver)
Walker, James: (Michael Wallace)

Stafford Co. VA
Robinson, Elizabeth: (Capt. Green)
Robinson, Helen: (Capt. Green)
Robinson, Padda: (Capt. Green)
Robinson, William: (Capt. Green)
Willis, (Amelia: (Lewis Bogs)

[57.481]
Adamson, John: (John Hinds)
Adamson, Mary: (John Hinds)
Adamson, Seith: (John Hinds)

[57.477]
Richmond, VA
Evans, Alice: (Richard Moore)
Evans, George: (Richard Moore)
Evans, John: (Richard Moore)
Evans, William: (Richard Moore)
Evans, Marsha: (Richard Moore)
Evans, Wallace: (Richard Moore)

Fredericksburg, VA
Buckner, Sally: (Bought her freedom)
Curtis, Charlotte: (Born free)
Jackson, Jennett: (W. Wilson)
Jones, Mary: (Thomas Talber)
Lewis, William: (Born Free)
Williams, Selina: (Thomas Talber)
[57.479]
King, Fillia: (Born Free)
King, Thomas: (Born Free)

[57.480]
Slean, Margaret: (Alexander Walker)
Thornton, Antony: (Alexander Walker)

Point End, VA
Evans, Jane: (John McGorram)
Evans, Billy: (John McGorram)
Evans, Milley: (John McGorram)
Evans, William: (John McGorram)
Evans, Catharine: (John McGorram)
Evans, P: (John McGorram)
Evans, Donny: (John McGorram)

Bowling Green, VA
Harris, Hannah: (Jane Brook)
Washington, Caroline: (Holmes)

DESTITUTE FREEDMEN IN SPOTSYLVANIA CO. VA

{Note: All of the following lived in Spotsylvania Co. VA before the war.}

[57.483]
Chandler, George: age 8
Chandler, Paul: age 6
Carter, Lucy: age 86
Carter, Ned: age 80
Carter, James: age 80
Carter, Martha: age 31
Carter, Mariah: age 48
Carter, Dolly: age 18
Carter, Louisa: age 14
Carter, Jack: age 8
Carter, Mary: age 6
Carter, Katy: age 35
Carter, Alfred: age 12
Carter, Mary: age 10
Carter, Ro.: age 8
Carter, Henry: age 6
Carter, Lucy: age 4
Carter, Georgianna: age 3
Coleman, Melvina: 26
Coleman, George: age 10
Coleman, Julian: age 8
Coleman, Alfred: age 6
Cooke, Catharine: age 40
Cooke, Ellen: age 16
Cooke, William: age 13
Cooke, James: age 11
Cooke, Mary: age 10
Cooke, John: age 8
Carter, Eliza: age 30
[57.484]
Carter, Edwarda: age 8
Carter, Emma: age 6
Coats, La Ceriah: age 65
Coats, Mary: age 40
Coats, Ellen: age 12
Coats, Melvina: age 7
Coleman, George: age 78
Carter, Caroline: age 28
Dennis, Jenny: age 45
Dennis, Lucy: age 25

Dennis, Hugh: age 6
Davis, Evaline: age 32
Davis, Esther: age 16
Davis, Fountain: age 12
Duly, Alsia: age 45
Duly, Mary: age 30
Downer, Martha: age 40
Downer, Betty: age 36
Downer, Fannie: age 30
Downer, George: age 9
Downer, Leeman: age 8
Edenton, Mary: age 27
Edenton, James: age 5
Edenton, William: age 3
Edenton, Judy: age 21
Elijah, Betsy: age 34
Ellis, Reuben: age 55
Fox, Emmie: age 50
Fox, Joe: age 14
[57.485]
Fox, Louisa: age 12
Fox, Ellen: age 11
Fox, John: age 8
Frayser, Harrison: age 60
Frayser, Eliza: age 55
Fautrod, Mariah: age 37
Fautrod, Charlotte: age 11
Fautrod, Charles: age 8
Fautrod, Edgar: age 6
Gordon, Rose: age 46
Gordon, Lulan: age 7
Gordon, Emma: age 5
Goney, Pompey: age 68
Goney, Mary: age 66
Goney, Belle: age 8
Goney, Josephine: age 6
Gray, Ellen, 30
Gray, Walter: age 13
Gray, Ella: age 10
Gordon, Lucy: age 38
Gordon, Catharine: 16

Gordon, Betty: age 13
Gordon, Walker: age 11
Gordon, Minor: age 9
Henry, James: age 24
Henry, John: age 19
Henry, Mary: age 9
Holmes, Mary: age 60
Holmes, Sidney: age 9
[57.486]
Haden, Ann: age 46
Haden, Lucy: age 14,
Haden, Claud: age 13
Haden, Alexander: age 10
Haden, Georgianna: age 7
Haden, Thornton: age 5
Holmes, Louisa: age 65
Holmes, Ro.: age 10
Hocks, John: age 75
Hocks, Dolly: age 56
Jones, Sarah: age 64
Jones, Mary: age 42
Jones, Ellen: age 12
Jones, Clara: age 45
Jones, Mary: age 18
Jones, Sam: age 8
Jones, Nad: age 4
Johnson, Lincy: age 27
Johnson, Betsy: age 5
Johnson, Ro.: age 3
Johnson, Lucy: age 2
Jones, Jennie: age 77
Jackson, Mary: age 27
Jackson, Sarah: age 9
Jackson, Emma: age 4
Jackson, Ann: age 45
Jackson, Alfred: age 12
Jackson, Emma: age 39
[57.487]
Jackson, Ella: age 10
Jackson, Tom: age 8
Jackson, Georgianna: 6

Jackson, Spencer: age 5
Johnson, Thomas: age 65
Johnson, Julia: age 25
Johnson, Annie: age 9
Johnson, Mary: age 50
Johnson, Susan: age 40
Lewis, Evaline: age 55
Lewis, Billy: age 10
Lee, Jane: age 36
Lee, Louisa: age 11
Lee, Billy: age 10
Lee, Betsy: age 9
Lee, Mary: age 6
Lee, Henry: age 4
Lewis, Cattie: age 85
Lewis, Edmond: age 8
Lewis, Rose: age 6
Lewis, James: age 9
Lewis, Mary: age 50
Lewis, Levi: age 13
Lewis, Nellie: age 11
Lewis, Mariah: age 55
Lewis, John: age 15
Lewis, Jane: age 8
Lewis, Billie: age 6
Lewis, Mary: age 30
[57.488]
Lewis, Susan: age 10
Lewis, Nellie: age 8
Lewis, Martha: age 5
Lewis, Melvill: age 46
Lewis, Lucy: age 80
Lewis, Fannie: age 12
Mercer, Mary: age 30
Mercer, William: age 10
Mercer, George: age 5
Mercer, James: age 3
Minor, John: age 6
Minor, Lucy: age 50
Nomux, Eliza: age 35
Nomux, Jane: age 6
Nomux, Ann: age 5
Pates, Simon: age 70
Pates, Jack: age 18
Pates, Lucy: age 13

Pritchet, Mary: age 90
Pearl, Polly: age 28
Pearl, Carry: age 10
Pearl, Katy: age 8
Pearl, Melvina: age 6
Revel, Winney: age 84
Smith, Mary: age 80
Smith, Matilda: age 8
Saidferro, Lena: age 22
Saidferro, Nick: age 6
Saidferro, Ned: age 4
[57.489]
Stephens, Mary: age 41
Stephens, Aaron: age 71
Stong, Charlotte: age 16
Stong, Matilda: age 12
Stong, Frances: age 8
Stong, Millie: age 6
Stanard, Frances: age 35
Stanard, Ellen: age 7
Stanard, William: age 4
Smith, Elizabeth: age 65
Smith, Elizabeth: age 70
Stewart, Henry: age 84
Stewart, Louisa: age 50
Smith, Agnes: age 7
Smith, Frank: age 6
Smith, Louisa: age 3
Stanard, Ellen: age 12
Terry, Martha: age 35
Terry, Sam: age 6
Terry, Malinda: age 5
Thorn, Jane: age 60
Thorn, Charles: age 10
Talley, Eliza: age 26
Talley, George: age 4
Tillor, Eliza: age 18
Tillor, George: age 8
Tillor, Ann: age 5
Tillor, Alfred: age 20
[57.490]
Todd, John: age 20
Todd, Richard: age 8
Torrell, Charlotte: age 35
Torrell, Martha: age 9

Washington, Phill: age 50
Washington, Hannah: 10
Washington, Ella: age 8
Washington, John: age 6
Washington, Sam: age 4
Willis, Mary: age 25
Willis, Cattie: age 8
Willis, Sally: age 6
Willis, Ann: age 5
Willis, Jackson: age 4
Washington, Betsy: 60
White, Miles: age 20
White, Tom: age 40
Wilkins, Grinton: age 32
Washington, Mary: 60
Washington, Edward: 9
Washington, Ella: age 7
Wallace, George: age 20
Williams, Lucy: age 27
Williams, Addison: 10
Williams, Benjamin: 4
Williams, William: age 3
Weather, Gersetta: 80
Weather, Mary: age 75
Wilson, Mariah: age 80
[57.491]
Wilson, Margaret: age 65
Wilson, Isaac: age 5
Wigg, Lonny: age 25
Wigg, Melvina: age 8
Wigg, Dr.: age 6
Wigg, Mary: age 21
Walkins, Janna: age 41
Walkins, Ned: age 9
Walkins, George: age 6
Walkins, Jacob: age 4
Walkins, Tom: age 21
Williams, Taylor: age 13
Young, Mary: age 66
Young, Bill: age 8
[57.492]
Beverly, Harriet: age 80
Beverly, Frances: age 25
Beverly, Eliza: age 22
Brock, Lewis: age 57

Barnard, Rachel: age 67	Butlar, Mary Polly: 14	Bird, Lucy: age 35
Barnard, Ann: age 11	Bell, Katy: age 90	Bird, Lawrence: age 10
Boots, Mariah: age 26	Bell, Patsy: age 70	Bird, Julia: age 6
Boots, David: age 12	Bogg, Isabell: age 40	Bird, Wallace: age 4
Butlar, Mary: age 70	Bogg, Moses: age 10	Bird, John: age 21
Butlar, Sarah: age 37	Bogg, Albert: age 5	Chandler, Mary: age 45
	Bogg, Stephen: age 4	Chandler, Charles: 10

DESTITUTE FREEDMEN IN FREDERICK CO. VA

[57.492]
Frederick Co. VA
Barnet, William
Gramby, Polly
Harris, Harriett
Jackson, Tollins
Martin, Netty
Neilson, Martha

Parker, Emily
Tracy, James
Unknown, Bella
Unknown, Daffny
Unknown, Peggy
Whitten, Sarah
Wilkeson, Elizabeth

Augusta Co. VA
Jones, Caroline
Stewart, Martha
Williams, Charles

Warren Co. VA
Smith, James
Richardson, Dafney
Willis, Jane

DESTITUTE FREEDMEN IN JEFFERSON CO. VA

Jefferson Co. VA
Miles, Alexander
Unknown, Jugg

Nelson Co. VA
Carter, Jonah:

State of Georgia
Keeller, George:

DESTITUTE FREEDMEN IN HOSPITAL AT LYNCHBURG, VA
{Note: Freedmen are listed under pre-war residence.
Their names are followed by their age, and former masters.}

Amherst Co. VA
Anthony, Nancy: 30. Wm Mosby
Camp, Nancy: 45. Robert Camp
Dawson, Sally: 37. Sidney Dawson
Flood, Rhoda: 90. Henry Flood
Jordan, Moll: 70. William Jordan
McCue, Margaret: 24. Jas McCue
Munday, Arohy: 54. Marie Mundy

Nelson Co. VA
Campbell, James: 80. Samuel Campbell
Screggs, Dick 60. John Screggs

Campbell Co. VA
Anderson, Lucy: 90. J.W. Aderson
Blufort, Ned: 51. Seth Halsey
Brooks, Thomas: 33. Ruben Staten

Crawford, Henry: 80. Free Born
Ervin, Daniel: 75. Daniel Irvin
Floyd, Eliza: 30. Dr. Floyd
Floyd, Martha: 34. Dr. Floyd
Franklin, William: 60. Samuel Franklin
Grant, Charlotte: 23. Peter Grant
Harvey, Lucy: 24. Richard Harvey
Haydon, Ed: 70. Emily Haydon
Hosely, Celia: 70. Seth Hosely
Jackson, Jimy: 25. J. Reid
Jefferson, Frank: 18. Thomas Graff
Jenks, Mary: 80. Wm. Jenks
Johnson, Ready: 82. Seth Hosler
Jones, Letty: 38. William Jones
Pedigore, Martha: 31. James Pedigore
Rice, Booker: 23. Patterson Rice
Rosser, Selina: 40. Pleasant Rosser
Scott, Benjamin: 80. Samuel Scott
Sheer, Frank: 40. James Spelter

Lynchburg, VA
Davis, Molinda: 75. Henry Davis
Edwards, Charles: 16. E.J. Folks
Henry, Nancy: 85. Jas A. Sherman
Matthews, Jim: 18. J.W. Stine

Appomattox Co. VA
Anderson, Mary: 18. L. Anderson
Buckey, Linsey: 25. S. Whalen
Green, Leander: 23. William Green
Marshall, Anderson: 24 Marie Marshall

Bedford Co. VA
Calebee, Queen: 42. James Calebee
Crea, Smith: 23. Stephen Crea
Francis, FAnny: 30. O.G. Clay
Hill, Amy: 80. Brown Davis
Morman, Samuel: 70. Louis Mormon
Sidney, Louisa: 35. G.W. Rust

Smith, Sarah: 23. William Harris

Pittsylvania Co. VA
Coleman, Bird: 55. Cyrus Davis
Stone, Amelia: 35. Elizabeth Stone

Greenbrier Co. VA
Moss, Emma: 20. Henry Moss

Clarke Co. VA
Washington, Sally: 23. Thomas H. Crow

Giles Co. VA
Paris, Sally: 18. George Paris
Smith, Emma: 24. George Paris
Whiting, Hannah: 40. Chas. Thil

Washington Co. TN
Byers, Jane: 21. Frank Byers

Buchanan Co. VA
Russell, Elizabeth: 55. W. Kyle

North Carolina
Fields, Ann: 21. Jedediah Jones

Botetourt Co. VA
Harndall, Margaret: 40. Harry Johnson

Christiansburg, VA
Kyle, Hannah: 30. James Kyle

Rockbridge Co. VA
Irvin, Ellen: 30. Samuel Openchain

Louden Co. VA
Williams, Mary: 25. T. McFay

Charlottesville, VA
Anderson, Mary: 23.
    Rachael Sullivan

Rockingham Co. VA
Scott, William: 23. Henry Bird

Cameron Co. VA
Payne, Tom: 23. Philip Payne

Albemarle Co. VA
Robinson, Robert: 16.
    John Robinson
Perkins, Amy: 70.
    Slaughter Fickling

Sampson Co. NC
Jackson, Thomas: 32. William Atkinson

South Carolina
Genoa, Ella: 16. Cloyd Saunders

Rappahannock Co. VA
Waldron, Aaron: 66. Capt. Waldron

Richmond, VA
Ranson, Louis, 27. B. Edmonson
Ranson, Marie: 25. B. Edmonson

AMHERST CO. VIRGINIA
IN HOSPITAL AT LYNCHBURG, VA

North Carolina
Ross, Temple: 40. Peter Ross

Amherst Co. VA
Ambler, Frances: 23. John Ambler
Davenport, John: 45. Wm. Walls
Davenport, Matilda: 37 Wm. Walls
Joiner, Marie: 60. Peter Joiner

Keese, George: 53. James Kees
Pierce, Charlotte: 24. Jacob Pierce
Pierce, Clara: 67. Jacob Pierce
Pierce, Emily: 42. Jacob Pierce
Pierce, James: 49. Jacob Pierce
Pierce, Laura: 35. Jacob Pierce
Pierce, Virginia: 29. Jacob Pierce

THE FOLLOWING PERSONS IN HOSPITAL
AT AMHERST COURT HOUSE

Amherst Co. VA
Davis, Sarah J: 66. Arthur Davis
Davis, James: 70. Arthur Davis
Davis, Jacob: 37. Arthur Davis

Davis, Laura: 25. Arthur Davis
Davis, Sarah: 33. Arthur Davis
Davis, Mary: 41. Arthur Davis
Davis, Betsy: 27. Arthur Davis

THE FOLLOWING PERSONS IN HOSPITAL AT LOVINGTON, NELSON CO. VA

Nelson Co. VA
Bartlett, Daniel: 29. Wm. Reevs
Clarkson, Elva: 39 Nelson Clarkson
Giles, Dessie J: 44 years, 1 child
    Rolls Giles
Giles, Philip: 50 yrs. Rolls Giles

Giles, Sarah: 60 yrs. (& 1 child)
Johnson, Agnes: 57. Robert Reevs
Reevs, Phebe: 60. William Reevs
Robertson, Venus: 37. Hugh
    Robertson
Sampson, Samuel: 29. William
    Robertson

IN HOSPITAL AT APPOMATTOX COURT HOUSE

Appomattox Co. VA
Benton, Henry: age 2
Benton, Jennie: age 3
Bramm, Clem: age 4
Bramm, Samuel: age 5
Flood, Ben: age 75
Flood, Caroline: age 1
Flood, Edward: age 5
Flood, Ellen: age 8
Flood, Mary: age 81
Flood, Susan: age 6

Flood, Vinnie: age 2
Landrum, Toni: age 4
Matthews, Charles: age 47
Matthews, Mary: age 37
Unknown, Charles: age 85
Unknown, Charlotte Agnes: age 5
Unknown, George Henry: age 2
Unknown, James Arthur: age 3
Unknown, Mary Ellen: age 6
Unknown, Sophia Ann: age 43
Unknown, Watson: age 4

IN HOSPITAL AT LIBERTY, BEDFORD CO. VA

Bedford Co. VA
Boardwright, Robert: 30
    Harvey Boardwright
Comer, Emeline: 30. Wm. Comer
Comer, Thomas: 1. Wm. Comer
DeOde, Nelly: 60. DeOde
Graves, Anne: 27. Wm. Graves
Graves, Bob Lee: 1. Wm. Graves
Graves, Edward: 6. Wm. Graves
Unknown, Almus: age 45.
    Dr. Sanderded

Unknown, America: age 26. H. Bolt
Unknown, Ann: age 5.
    Dr. Sanderded
Unknown, Betty: age 25.
    A.B. Nickolis
Unknown, Betty: age 60.
    Dr. Sanderded
Unknown, Betty: age 2. Dr. Martin
Unknown, Blucher: 2, Fanny Bird
Unknown, Davy: age 30

Unknown, Dorcas: age 70.
   Dr. Sanderded
Unknown, Edward: age 10.
   Dr. Sanderded
Unknown, Eliza: age 25.
   Baldy Crenshaw
Unknown, Eliza: age 13.
   Baldy Crenshaw
Unknown, Ella: 5. Dr. Martin
Unknown, Ellen: 22. N. Heston?
Unknown, Ellen: age 10.
   Dr. Sanderded
Unknown, Emma: age 1.
   Dr. Sanderded
Unknown, Esther: age 18.
   Elliott Loving
Unknown, Frazer: age 6
Unknown, Henry: age 25.
   C. Beesey
Unknown, Henry: age 16
Unknown, Israel: age 60.
   Dr. Sanderded
Unknown, James: age 45.
   Dr. Sanderded
Unknown, Jeffries: age 60.
   Dr. Sanderded
Unknown, Margaret Francis: 7.
   Dr. Sanderded
Unknown, Marie: age 65.
   Dr. Sanderded
Unknown, Mary: age 30.
   Fanny Bond
Unknown, Mary: age 21.
   Dr. Sanderded
Unknown, Mary Ann: age 10.
   Thomas Rasey?
Unknown, Milton: age 7. Dr. Martin
Unknown, Minerva: age 30.
   Dr. Sanderded
Unknown, Nanda: age 30.
   Joseph Holt
Unknown, Nanda: age 34.
   Dr. Sanderded
Unknown, Neilly: age 60.
   Thomas Powell
Unknown, Peter: age 70. J. Hatcher
Unknown, Rachal: age 4.
   Joseph Holt
Unknown, Robert: age 20
Unknown, Sam: age 70.
   Dr. Sanderded
Unknown, Sarah: age 22.
   Dr. Sanderded
Unknown, Sukey: age 60
Unknown, Texanna: age 1 year.
   H. Bolt
Unknown, Virginia: age 28.
   Dr. Sanderded
Unknown, W. Henry: age 7
Unknown, Washington: age 1.
   Joseph Holt
Unknown, William: age 3.
   Dr. Sanderded
Unknown, Willie: 21.
   Thomass Creesey

Rappahannock Co. VA
Unknown, John: age 1 year
Unknown, Susan Mary: age 5
Unknown, Louisa: age 1 year

Bristol, TN
Unknown, Mary: age 25.
   John Hamilton
Unknown, Kissy: age 6.
   John Hamilton
Unknown, Davy: age 5.
   John Hamilton

Jefferson Co. VA
Unknown, Mary: 26. Louis Owen
Unknown, Jim: age 16. Louis Owen

NAMES OF PERSONS DEPENDENT ON THE GOVT. RATIONED AT FORT MONROE, VA

{NOTE: Listed under their former residence. Name of freedman is followed by the name of his former owner.}

Henrico Co. VA
Blunt, Mariah: Wm. Allen
[57.517]
Hubbard, George: Wm. Allen
Hubbard, Mary: Wm. Allen
Hubbard, George: Wm. Allen
[57.523]
Clayman, Louisa: Wm. Allen
[57.536]
Barden, Polly: Wm. Allen
[57.538]
Norris, Mary: John Tolliver
Norris, Anna: John Tolliver
Norris, Thomas: John Tolliver
Norris, Sally: John Tolliver
[57.541]
Garo, Robert: Williamson Allen
[57.546]
Ruffin, Nelly: Wm. Allen
[57.547]
Jeffers, Henry: Maj. Wm. Allen
Jeffers, Cane: Maj. Wm. Allen
[57.549]
Wm.s, Betsey: Wm. Allen
Williams, Susan: Wm. Allen
Williams, Katy: Wm. Allen
Williams, Betsy: Wm. Allen
[57.551]
Bardon, Polly: Wm. Allen
Bardon, Randall: Wm. Allen
Bardon, Edwin: Wm. Allen
Bardon, Mary: Wm. Allen
Bardon, Robert: Wm. Allen
Bardon, Marthy: Wm. Allen

Comer, Nelly: Wm. Allen
Comer, Andrew: Wm. Allen
[57.552]
Harris, Lizzie: Wm. Allen,
Harris, Laura: Wm. Allen,
Harris, Chaney: Wm. Allen,
Wm.s, Livinia: Wm. Allen
Wm.s, James: Wm. Allen
Williams, Rosetta: Wm. Allen
Williams, Elp: Wm. Allen
White: Molly: Wm. Allen
White: Jacob: Wm. Allen
[57.554]
Marshall, Franky: John Robinson
[57.556]
Freeland, Fanny: Wm. Allen
Clary, Beckey: Wm. Allen
[57.559]
Derriga, Nancy: Wm. Allen
Derriga, William: Wm. Allen
[57.563]
Jones, Sarah: Wm. Allen
Jones, Andrew: Wm. Allen
Jones, Sarah: Wm. Allen
Jones, Lavina: Wm. Allen
Jones, Miles: Wm. Allen
[57.567]
Green, Lovly: Benjamin Green
White, Susan: Wm. Allen
White, Alie: Wm. Allen
White, Pheby: Wm. Allen
White, Lawrence: Wm. Allen
[57.570]
Goodman, Hannah: Wm. Allen

Goodman, Betsy: Wm. Allen
Goodman, Minnie: Wm. Allen
[57.572]
Jones, Nancy: Wm. Allen
Smith, Nancy: Edward Cox

[57.507]
Hanover Co. VA
Keninton, Caroline: Dr. Gaines
Keninton, Roy: Dr. Gaines
Keninton, Johnson: Dr. Gaines
Keninton, Michell: Dr. Gaines
Keninton, Albert: Dr. Gaines
Henry, Caroline: Richard Huntly
Henry, Lucy: Richard Huntly
Henry, Richard: Richard Huntly
Henry, Martha: Richard Huntly
Henry, Ann: Richard Huntly
Donel, Jessie: Wm. Baker
[57.517]
Griswell, Cecilia: Wm. Brokenberry
Griswell, Mary: Wm. Brokenberry
Griswell, Armstead: Wm.Brokenberry
Grey, Clarisey: Wm. Pretty
[57.522]
James, Susan: Dr. Gaines
[57.524]
Govener, Caroline: Dr. Wm. Gaines
Govener, Roy: Dr. Wm. Gaines
Govener, Johnson: Dr. Wm. Gaines
Govener, Albert: Dr. Wm. Gaines
Govener, Bailey: Dr. Wm. Gaines
[57.536]
Johnson, Louisa: Wm. Toland
[57.540]
Quarrels, Charlett: Thomas Tyler
[57.544]
Maison, Fanny: Richard Henly
Lewis, Matilda: Phillip Winston
Lewis, Denice: Phillip Winston
[57.551]

Crane, Thomas: Wm. Winston
[57.554]
Gaines, Catharine: Dr. Gaines
Gaines, Peter: Dr. Gaines
Gaines, Aaron: Dr. Gaines
Gaines, Silvia: Dr. Gaines
Gaines, Benjamin: Dr. Gaines
Johnson, Eliza: Dr. Wm. G. Gaines
Johnson, Patsey: Dr. Wm. G. Gaines
Johnson, James: Dr. Wm. G. GainesDr. Wm. G. Gaines
Johnson, Robert: Dr. Wm. G. Gaines
Johnson, Washington: Dr. W G. Gaines
Ellis, Dilsey: Temple Elliott
[57.557]
Grain, Harriet: Dr. Wm. G. Gaines
[57.561]
Brey, Claresa: Wm. Phetty
[57.571]
Fukes, Sarah: John Tolliver
Fukes, Isader: John Tolliver
Fukes, Sephy: John Tolliver
Sails, Mary: John Tyler
Sails, Martha: John Tyler
Sails, William: John Tyler
Sails, James: John Tyler
Sails, Killis: John Tyler
[57.573]
Dudley, Alfred: Dr. Gaines
Grey, Dezzie: Dr. W.F. Gaines
[57.576]
Johnson, Peggy: Dr. Gaines
Johnson, Betsy: Dr. Gaines

[57.561]
Elmont, Hanover Co. VA
Battles, Mary: Robert Wheeler
James, Mariah: Robert Wheeler
James, Thomas: Robert Wheeler

[57.507]
Gloucester Co. VA
Brooks, Ann: Mr. Clark
Smith, Gissie: John Davis
[57.513]
Toliver, Hattie: Wm. Hobdy
Toliver, Agy: Wm. Hobdy
Toliver, Hattie: Wm. Hobdy
[57.515]
Reed, Sarah: Warren Jones
Williams, Frank: Dr. Carey
[57.520]
Bowker, Mary: Joseph Dobson
Bowker, Robert: Joseph Dobson
[57.524]
Braxton, Eliza: Robert Seldon
Braxton, Rose: Robert Seldon
[57.527]
Bundy, Hardy: {Betsy's husband} Taswell Thompson
Bundy, Betsy: {wife of Hardy} Taswell Thompson
Burrill, Polly: Thomas London
[57.528]
Brooks, Mary: Curren Taylor
Brooks, Martha: Curren Taylor
Brooks, Mary: Curren Taylor
[57.529]
Gardnor, Mary: Glotcher Clark
Gardnor, Sarah: Glotcher Clark
Gardnor, Lettie: Glotcher Clark
Gardnor, Lizzie: Glotcher Clark
[57.531]
Carey, Lucy Ann: Wm. Taylor
Carey, Emma: Wm. Taylor
Carey, John: Wm. Taylor
Bates, Annie: Warren Jones
Bates, Henry: Warren Jones
Bates, Ida: Warren Jones
Jones, Elizabeth: Free born.
[57.533]

Henry, Fanny: John Sinclair
Henry, Eliza: John Sinclair
Henry, Alice: John Sinclair
Henry, Jennie: John Sinclair
[57.537]
Smith, Mary K: John Fox
[57.540]
Taylor, Lucy: Thomas Holland
[57.547]
Young, Catharine: James Golden
Jackson, Louisa: John Tabb
Jackson, Robert: John Tabb
Jackson, Ellen: John Tabb
Hayes, Caroline: Free born.
Hayes, Rose: Free born.
Hayes, John: Free born.
Hayes, Henry: Free born.
[57.549]
Williams, Betsey: Wm. Smith
[57.556]
Tabb, Elizabeth: Benjamin Rowe
Tabb, William: Benjamin Rowe

[57.562]
Hews, Sally: Dr. Bird
Hews, Hews: Dr. Bird
Hews, John: Dr. Bird
Hews, William: Dr. Bird
Hews, Lizzie: Dr. Bird
Hews, Thomas: Dr. Bird
Carey, Lucy A: Richard Hogg
Carey, Emma: Richard Hogg
Carey, John: Richard Hogg
[57.565]
Kenny, Lucy: Wm. Dorbson
Kenny, Phil: Wm. Dorbson
[57.569]
Cook, Susan: Edward Rowe
[57.571]
Ray, Lucretia: Robert Selden
Ray, Dick: Robert Selden

Ray, Moseby: Robert Selden
Ray, Lucretia: Robert Selden
Ray, Thomas: Robert Selden

King and Queen Co. VA
[57.507]
Chapman, Ann E: Maj. Bland
Chapman, John: Maj. Bland
Green, Francis: Rodrick Bland
[57.515]
Hill, Catharine: Maj. Bland
[57.519]
Bagby, Lucy: Mortimore Smith
Dickerson, Sarah: Maj. Randall Bland
Dickerson, Eliza: Maj. Randall Bland
Dickerson, Milly: Maj. Randall Bland
Dickerson, Patsy: Maj. Randall Bland
[57.521]
Robinson, Isabella: Samuel Gadrey
Robinson, Rhoda: Samuel Gadrey
Robinson, Ellie: Samuel Gadrey
Robinson, Benjamin: Sam'l Gadrey
Robinson, Moses: Samuel Gadrey
[57.526]
Corwin, Lennie: James Mitchell
Corwin, Martha: James Mitchell
Corwin, John: James Mitchell
Corwin, Mary: James Mitchell
Corwin, Nelson: James Mitchell
Corwin, Isabella: James Mitchell
[57.528]
Cary, Rachael: Rodward Bland
Cary, John: Rodward Bland
Cary, Peter: Rodward Bland
[57.539]
Bundley, Fanny: James Thurston
Bundley, Ranson: James Thurston
Bundley, William: James Thurston
Bundley, Minnie: James Thurston
Bundley, Jennie: James Thurston
[57.546]

Roy, Rachael: Barnes Lawson
Roy, Simon: Barnes Lawson
[57.550]
Robinson, Pheby: Reddick Bland
Robinson, Francis Ann: Reddick Bland
Robinson, Taura: Reddick Bland
Toliver, Catharine: Robert Bland
Toliver, Sarah: Robert Bland
Toliver, Lucy: Robert Bland
Washington, Milly: Thomas Coe
Washington, Randall: Thomas Coe
Washington, Hellena: Thomas Coe
[57.557]rimes, Nerry: Peater Grey
Grimes, Ellen: Peater Grey
Grimes, Emma: Peater Grey
Grimes, Benjamin: Robert Hunter
[57.559]
Upture, Isabella: Wm. Haskins
Upture, James: Wm. Haskins
Upture, Eliza: Wm. Haskins
Upture, Emma: Wm. Haskins
Upture, Andrew: Wm. Haskins
[57.565]
Bagby, Sarah: Dr. Samuel Ganroy
Graves, Mary: Robert Bland

[57.507]
Surry Co. VA
Baker, Charlotte: Wm. Custis
Baker, Thomas: Wm. Custis
Baker, Mary: Wm. Custis
Baker, Louisa: Wm. Custis
Spradley, Ann: Henry H. Hart
Spradley, John: Henry H. Hart
Branch, Susan: Sarah Jones
[57.510]
Harrison, Gilly: Washington Edmunds
Harrison, Margaret: Washington Edmunds

Harrison, Martha:
    Washington Edmunds
[57.511]
Harris, Peter: Roland Hennican
Harris, Millie: Roland Hennican
[57.514]
Bailey, Jane: Richard Hynes
Crump, Sally: James S. Wilson
[57.520]
Wardy?, Cherry: Thomas Wren
[57.521]
Connell, Amanda: Eldridge Madery
[57.522]
Price, Mary: John Lamb
[57.524]
Harrison, Gally: Mr. Warren
Harrison, Sarah: Mr. Warren
Harrison, Rose: Mr. Warren
Barnes, Eliza: Free.
Barnes, John: Free.
Bailey, Margaret: Thomas Spratley
Bailey, Susan: Thomas Spratley
Bailey, Patsey: Thomas Spratley
Bailey, Miles: Thomas Spratley
[57.525]
Thomas, Martha: Wm. Cole
Thomas, James: Wm. Cole
Thomas, Anderson: Wm. Cole
Shepard, Rebecca: Free Born.
Shepard, Lucy: Free Born.
Shepard, George: Free Born.
Moore, Betsey: Jasper Clayton
Wilson, Joseph: John H. Hawkins
[57.526]
Carey, Ann: Wm. Jones
Carey, Manerva: Wm. Jones
Carey, Edith: Wm. Jones
[57.529]
Harrison, Martha: Wm. Dillard
Harrison, Claresa: Wm. Dillard
Harrison, Henrietta: Wm. Dillard

Harrison, Jack: Wm. Dillard
[57.530]
Parker, Ned: {husband of Patsey}
    Nancy Barrow
Parker, Patsey: {wife of Ned}
    Nancy Barrow
Bailey, Caroline: Richard Haynes
Bailey, Mary: Richard Haynes
[57.531]
Jones, Nancy: Wm. Ruffin
Jones, Alice: Wm. Ruffin
Jones, Edward: Wm. Ruffin
Jones, Charles: Wm. Ruffin
[57.537]
Hill, Nelly: Free born.
[57.539]
Branch, Susan: Henry Jones
Branch, Mary: Henry Jones
Branch, Thomas: Henry Jones
[57.548]
Jefferson, Mary: Cleyborn Jones
[57.550]
Nozery, Dinah: Richard Spradly
Nozery, William: Richard Spradly
Nozery, Catharine: Richard
    Spradly

[57.555]
Grey, Wm.: Cleyborn Jones
Vaughn, Jane: Richard Thornton
Vaughn, Emily: Richard Thornton
[57.557]
Morris, Agness: Wm. Ruffin
[57.559]
Turner, Dolly: Mary J. Johnson
Turner, Ambelice: Mary J. Johnson
Turner, Frank: Mary J. Johnson
Turner, Cornelia: Mary J. Johnson
Turner, Sylvester: Mary J. Johnson
[57.560]
Barker, Mary E: Thomas Ruffin

Barker, William: Thomas Ruffin
[57.561]
Barnes, Mary: Free Born.
[57.563]
Pierce, Adaline: Thomas Spradley
Pierce, Polly: Thomas Spradley
Pierce, Agness: Thomas Spradley
Spradley, Charlott: Punch Spradley
Spradley, Emma: Punch Spradley
Spradley, Cherry: Punch Spradley
Spradley, Gilbert: Punch Spradley
Spradley, Tirgers: Punch Spradley
[57.564]
Boykin, Millie: Edwin White
Boykin, Nancie: Edwin White
Boykin, Arther: Edwin White
Boykin, Louisa: Edwin White
Cox, Ellis: Wm. Ruffin
[57.565]
Williams, Sarah A: Phero Clemonts
Williams, Bergy: Phero Clemonts
Tolver, Lucy: Phero Clemonts
Tolver, George: Phero Clemonts
Tolver, Caroline: Phero Clemonts
Daniel, Robert: Geo. W. Andrews
Hasket, Ellick: Free Born.
Hasket, Lavinia: Free Born.
Harrison, Indiana: Free Born.
Harrison, Adeline: Free Born.
[57.568]
Page, Jennie: James Wilson
[57.571]
Epps, Rosa: Edward Epps
Epps, Temple: Edward Epps
Epps, Alice: Edward Epps
Epps, Henry: Edward Epps
[57.572]
Randall, Hannah: Thos Spradley
Randall, Lewis: Thomas Spradley
Randall, David: Thomas Spradley

Randall, Lucy: Thomas Spradley
Randall, Archie: Thomas Spradley
[57.573]
George, Eliza: Free Born
George, Woodland: Free Born
Jones, Fanny: Wm. Allen
Jones, James: Wm. Allen
Jones, Benjamin: Wm. Allen

[57.507]
Nottoway Co. VA
Ball, Betsey: Mr. Webb
Ball, Ella: Mr. Webb
Ball, Charlott: Mr. Webb
Ball, Lewis: Mr. Webb

Princess Anne Co. VA
Simons, Matilda: John Jerdan
[57.552]
Delano, Lucy: Sherno Hoget
Delano, Robert: Sherno Hoget
Delano, Daniel: Sherno Hoget
[57.555]
Oulds, Dinah: Wm. Oulds
[57.564]
Brown, Ann: James Jerdan
Brown, Elizabeth: James Jerdan
Brown, Margarett: James Jerdan

[57.507]
Northampton Co. VA
Colwell, Annie: John Addison
Andrews, Eda: Wm. Gidjet
Andrews, Mary: Wm. Gidjet
Andrews, Eda: Wm. Gidjet
Andrews, John: Wm. Gidjet
Andrews, Julia: Wm. Gidjet
Barber, John: Thomas Hogg
[57.513]
Trower, Mary A: John Trower
Trower, Butler: John Trower

Trower, Jerry: John Trower
Trower, Wadora: John Trower
Trower, Sarah: John Trower
[57.516]
Gibbs, Susan: Andrew Jackson
Gibbs, Joseph: Andrew Jackson
[57.529]
Andrews, Millie: Anams (?)
[57.534]
White, Ann: Wm. Upshure
White, John: Wm. Upshure
White, Mary: Wm. Upshure
White, Leren: Wm. Upshure
[57.541]
Beach, Margaret: John Fox
[57.542]
Risby, Jennie: Wm. Wescott
Risby, Frances: Wm. Wescott
[57.543]
Burras, Grace: Susan Gothican
Burras, Joshua: Susan Gothican
[57.544]
Savage, Peggy: Edward Gofican
Rose, Dilem: Edward Gofican
Scott, Lucinda: Edward Gofican
Scott, Clarence: Edward Gofican
[57.545]
Parker, Lucretia: James Crustine
Parker, Walker: James Crustine
Parker, James: James Crustine
Winder, Eddie: Victor Knappe
Winder, Nelson: Victor Knappe
Winder, Jack: Victor Knappe
Gidget, Rachael: William Wilkins
[57.555]
Fitchett, Carey: J.H. Fitchett
Fitchett, Nelson: J.H. Fitchett
[57.558]
Weston, Sarah: Fitts Hew
{Fitzhugh ?}

Roberts, Lydia: Leonard Nodingham
Mosby, Elizabeth: J.H. Fitchett
[57.562]
Upture, Julia: Robert Jacobs
Upture, Joseph: Robert Jacobs
[57.565]
Jacob, Sarah: Wm. Jacob
Jacob, Fanny: Wm. Jacob
Jacob, Polly: Wm. Jacob
Jacob, Horace: Wm. Jacob
Jacob, Martha: Wm. Jacob
Jacob, Lucy: Wm. Jacob
Johnson, Ferby: Susan Gougin
Johnson, Joseph: Susan Gougin
Johnson, Millie: Susan Gougin
[57.575]
Smith, Flora: Robert Custine
Smith, Harriett: Robert Custine
Smith, Sarah: Robert Custine

[57.523]
Eastern Shore,
Northampton Co. VA
Allen, Lucy: John Parker
Allen, Mary: John Parker
[57.543]
Carpenter, Julia: Leonard Nodingham
Carter, Delia: John Parker
Carter, Windfield: John Parker
[57.562]
Winder, Ann: John Winder
Winder, Frank: John Winder
Winder, Lehae: John Winder

[57.507]
King William Co. VA
Burkley, Millie: William Lipsker
Stock, Mahaley: William Hudsher
[57.512]
Recker, Julia: Richard Hubang

[57.513]
Wilson, Ann: Robert Munday
Holmes, Millie Ann: Judge Clemont
[57.514]
Taylor, Caroline: Wm. Hill
Taylor, Major: Wm. Hill
Taylor, Emma: Wm. Hill
Taylor, Fleming: Wm. Hill
Taylor, Kennald: Wm. Hill
[57.517]
Lambert, Nelly: George Taylor
Lambert, Hellen: George Taylor
Lambert, Susie: George Taylor
Lambert, Allice: George Taylor
Lambert, Andrew: George Taylor
Lispan, Charles: George Edwards
[57.519]
Henry, Charlotte: George Taylor
[57.522]
Lee, Margarett: Capt. Lipscomb
Lee, Elizabeth: Capt. Lipscomb
Lee, Samuel: Capt. Lipscomb
[57.523]
Bailey, Harriet: Wm. Garly
Bailey, Sarah: Wm. Garly
Bassa, Claresa: Wm. Hill
Bassa, Mariah: Wm. Hill
Bassa, Joseph: Wm. Hill
[57.527]
Henderson, Sarah: Ambrose White
Paul, Emeline: Butler Edwards
Paul, Patsy: Butler Edwards
Paul, Lucy: Butler Edwards
[57.528]
Brandis, Malinda: Wm. Pollard
[57.530]
Segor, Eli: Robert King
Segor, Eliza: Robert King
Segor, Lucinda: Robert King
[57.531]
Durgee, Elizabeth: Edward Page

[57.532]
Stired, Lettie: John Lipscae {Lipscombe?}
Stired, Emma: John Lipscae {Lipscombe?}
Stired, Jerry: John Lipscae {Lipscombe ?}
Jackson, Rebecca: Fanny Pinia
Jackson, Susan: Parlss Davis
Robinson, Patsey: Wm. Garey
Robinson, Nancy: Wm. Garey
Robinson, Wm.: Wm. Garey
Robinson, Susan: Wm. Garey
[57.534]
Stewart, Lettie: John Lipscon
Stewart, Emma: John Lipscon
Stewart, Jerry: John Lipscon
[57.535]
Coleman, Sally: Robert Gombley
[57.537]
Grimes, Ella: Boardman Percil
Reddick, Sarah: James Pollard
[57.538]
Armstead, Nancy: Thomas Pollard
[57.541]
Anderson, Rosetta: Wm. Pollard
Anderson, Susan: Wm. Pollard
Anderson, Pinkie: Wm. Pollard
Anderson, Charles: Wm. Pollard
[57.542]
Holmes, Mary: Dr. Grey
Turner, Sally: Benjamin Blake
Turner, Dira: Benjamin Blake
Turner, Nelsen: Benjamin Blake
Turner, Steward: Benjamin Blake
[57.543]
Collins, Emeline: Virginia Cox
Collins, Charles: Virginia Cox
Collins, Rody: Virginia Cox
[57.544]
Druge, Peter: Thomas Pollard

Harris, Jane: Thomas. S. Jones
Harris, Millie: Thomas. S. Jones
Williams, Polly: Mr. Clement
Williams, Margaret: Mr. Clement
Williams, Elisha: Mr. Clement
[57.545]
Tompson, Eliza: Ira Clements
Sherman, Anna: Thomas Pollard
[57.546]
Mapp, Catharine: Richard Hinebark
Mapp, Charlott: Richard Hinebark
Mapp, Thomas: Richard Hinebark
Turner, Sally: Benjamin Blake
Turner, Phil: Benjamin Blake
Turner, Dora: Benjamin Blake
Turner, Stewart: Benjamin Blake
[57.547]
Hickman, Emeline: Warner Edwards
Hickman, Charles: Warner Edwards
Hickman, Agness: Warner Edwards
Parker, Penny: George Edwards
Gowens, Sarah: Dr. Gay
[57.552]
Harris, Claben: (Mackin Winston)
[57.559]
White, Iras: George Taylor
[57.560]
Robinson, Ann: George Edwards
Thomas, Mariah: John Stephens
Thomas, Nancy: John Stephens
Clasisen, Clary: Rheuben Davis
Clasisen, James: Rheuben Davis
Clasisen, Clara: Rheuben Davis
[57.561]
Lambert, Susan: George Tayler
Lambert, Fanny: George Tayler
Lambert, Edward: George Tayler
Lambert, Charles: George Tayler
[57.563]
Nelson, Susan: Henry Colton
Nelson, Manuel: Henry Colton
Nelson, Kitty: Henry Colton
Seldon, Emily: Benjamin Pollard
Seldon, Marshall: Benjamin Pollard
Seldon, Fannie: Benjamin Pollard
[57.564]
Braxton, Harriett: James Pollard
Copeland, W.T: Free Born.
[57.565]
Grimes, Isaac: Wm. Hill
Henry, Charlott: James Johnson
Henry, Rosa: James Johnson
Henry, Lizzie: James Johnson
Reed, Judy: Wm. Dabney
[57.572]
White, Armstead: Thomas Pollard

Essex Co. VA
[57.508]
Grimes, Benjamin: Robert Hunter
[57.515]
Rice, Martha: Theodore Barn
Rice, William: Theodore Barn
Rice, George: Theodore Barn
Rice, Robert: Theodore Barn
Rice, Sarah: Theodore Barn
[57.516]
Dennis, Ellen: Richard Bailey
Dennis, Simond: Richard Bailey
Dennis, Joshua: Richard Bailey
[57.517]
Garnett, Mary J: Richard Bailey
Garnett, Tanny: Richard Bailey
[57.524]
Loyd, Kitty: Richard Crockston
[57.533]
Warren, Eliza: Thomas Huntley
Warren, Lizzie: Thomas Huntley
Warren, Elic: Thomas Huntley
Warren, Cornelia: Thomas Huntley
Warren, Magdaline: Thos Huntley

[57.537]
Thomas, Mary: Wm. Wright
[57.539]
Brooks, Mariah: Dr. Jeffers
Brooks, Florence: Dr. Jeffers
[57.555]
Haskins, Matilda: Wm. Wright
[57.556]
Grimes, Madison: Robert Hunter
[57.564]
Bush, Mariah: Richard Baylor
Bush, Pidgeon: Richard Baylor
Bush, Angella: Richard Baylor
[57.569]
Fenton, Lucy A: Austin Brokenburg
[57.570]
Wallace, Eliza: Thomas Jones
[57.575]
Braxton, Fannie: Wm. Wright
Braxton, Anderson: Wm. Wright

[57.507]
Isle of Wight Co. VA
Simpson, Mary: Free born.
Simpson, Lizzie: Free born.
Dix, Eliza: Free Born.
Dix, Sarah: Free Born.
[57.508]
Andrews, Ann: Wm. Casey
Andrews, Rachael: Wm. Casey
Andrews, Thomas: Wm. Casey
Andrews, Soloman: Wm. Casey
Andrews, Martha: Wm. Casey
Lawrence, Emily: Free born.
Lawrence, Ellen: Free born.
Lawrence, Allice: Free born.
[57.510]
Cole, Rose: Albert Wren
Cole, Annie: Albert Wren

[57.511]
Jerdan, Eliza: John Scott
Jerdan, Henrietta: John Scott
Jerdan, Ellie: John Scott
Jerdan, Emily: John Scott
[57.514]
Wilson, Nellie: Samuel White
[57.517]
Tabb, Mary: Sarah Newman
Tabb, Jake: Sarah Newman
Tabb, Lizzie: Sarah Newman
Dix, Eliza: Free Born.
Dix, Mary: Free Born.
[57.519]
Wilson, Ben: Robert Wilson
Wilson, Matilda: Robert Wilson
[57.525]
Jubilee, Sally: Dr. Boykin
Jubilee, Benjamin: Dr. Boykin
Wilson, Millie: Dr. Boykin
Young, Francis A: Dr. R. Wilson
[57.529]
Nichols, Emma: Stephen Southhould
Nichols, Jennie: Stephen Southhould
Nichols, Mary: Stephen Southhould
Nichols, Kate: Stephen Southhould
Nichols, Henry: Stephen Southhould
[57.530]
Marshall, Charlotte: John Hall
Marshall, Benjamin: John Hall
Marshall, Collins: John Hall
Bailey, Oriaden: Free Born.
Bailey, Amelia: Free Born.
[57.531]
Smith, Lizzie: Free born.
Smith, Ida: Free born.
Smith, Mariah: Free born.
Smith, Cheny: Free born.
Smith, George: Free born.
Smith, Eliza: Free born.

[57.532]
Holland, Margaret: Augustus Ballard
Syner, Ann: Daniel Badden
Syner, Lewis: Daniel Badden
Syner, Margaret: Daniel Badden
Robinson, Martha: Thomas Goodson
[57.537]
Garden, Emmie: Edmund Morrison
[57.538]
Jerdon, Caroline: Joseph Custer
Jerdon, Johana: Joseph Custer
Jerdon, Samuel: Joseph Custer
Jerdon, Emma: Joseph Custer
Wren, Eda: Thomas Wren
Folger, Jane: George Anderson
Folger, Peter: George Anderson
[57.540]
Gale, Mary L: Free born.
Gale, John: Free born.
[57.541]
Coe, Richard: Nathan Young
Chapman, Emma:
      Mrs. Fletcher Chapman
[57.545]
Edwards, Louisa: David Edwards
[57.546]
Thomas, Lucy: Richard Thomas
[57.548]
Tynes, Angeline: Free born.
Tynes, Mary: Free born.
Bailey, Polly: Free born.
Bailey, Thomas: Free born.
[57.550]
Tomlin, Almedia: Joseph M. Custer
Tomlin, Susana: Joseph M. Custer
Tomlin, Rose: Joseph M. Custer
Tomlin, Michael: Joseph M. Custer
[57.553]
Thomas, Polly: Archie Atkins
Williams, Delia: Free born.
Williams, Susie: Free born.

Robinson, Marthy: Free born.
Tynes, Lilly: Willis Wilson
Carey, Mary A: H. Atkinson
Carey, Isaac: H. Atkinson
Carey, Lizzie: H. Atkinson
Carey, Mary: H. Atkinson
[57.555]
Jones, Ester: Frank Boynton
Jones, Byren: Frank Boynton
Jones, Jeff Davis: Frank Boynton
Jones, Walter: Frank Boynton
[57.556]
Thomas, Silvey: John E. Thomas
Thomas, John: John E. Thomas
Thomas, Mary: John E. Thomas
Wilson, Pauline: Frank Shelley
Wilson, Sam: Frank Shelley
Wilson, George: Frank Shelley
Graindier, India: John Adams
Graindier, John: John Adams
[57.559]
Pitt, Lucinda: Lewis Knox
Pitt, Wright: Lewis Knox
Pitt, Francis: Lewis Knox
Pitt, Caleb: Lewis Knox
[57.560]
Davis, Mary: Wm. Casey
Davis, Ann: Wm. Casey
[57.564]
Brown, Matilda: Dr. Howard
Brown, Francis: Dr. Howard
Brown, Jack: Dr. Howard
[57.565]
Scott, Martha: Free Born.
Scott, Margarett: Free Born.
Scott, Caroline: Free Born.
Scott, John: Free Born.
[57.570]
Wilson, Lucy: Robert Wilson
Wilson, Jordan: Robert Wilson
Wilson, William: Robert Wilson

Wilson, George: Robert Wilson
Wilson, Nellie: Robert Wilson
[57.571]
Gorden, Serinda: Burden Jones
Gorden, Martha: Burden Jones
Gorden, Lizzie: Burden Jones
Gorden, James: Burden Jones
Gorden, Sarah: Burden Jones
[57.572]
Williams, Rhoda: Free Born.
Williams, James: Free Born.
Williams, John: Free Born.
Williams, Hannah: Free Born.
Williams, George: Free Born.
[57.573]
Jones, Victoria: Free Born.
Jones, Susan: Free Born.
Jones, Julia A: Free Born.
Jones, Elizabeth: Free Born.
Jones, Margaret: Free Born.
Jones, Eliza: Free Born.
[57.574]
Parker, Ester: George Parker
Parker, James: George Parker

[57.507]
Elizabeth City Co. VA
Tabb, Amy: Sylvester Malcott
Tabb, Laura: Sylvester Malcott
Tabb, Carey: Sylvester Malcott
Tabb, Willie: Sylvester Malcott
Booker, Matilda: Wm. Smith
Washington, Fanny: Wm. Smith
Washington, Matilda: Wm. Smith
[57.510]
Buckers, Nettie: Jackson Parris
Buckers, Nancy: Jackson Parris
Buckers, Esaae (Esau?):
    Jackson Parris
[57.512]
Taylor, Judy: Thomas Twine

Taylor, Marthia: Thomas Twine
Taylor, Cornelius: Thomas Twine
Taylor, Margaret: Thomas Twine
Taylor, Mary Ann: Thomas Twine
Wm.s, Margaret: Canen Whiting
Williams, Frank: Canen Whiting
Williams, Dabney: Canen Whiting
Williams, Samuel: Virginia Booker
Foster, Margaret: Thomas Twine
Foster, Thomas: Thomas Twine
Foster, George: Thomas Twine
Jackson, Lavina: Wm. Norrill
Jackson, Martha: Wm. Norrill
[57.513]
Dunn, Lockey: Fanny Savage
Jones, Sarah: Geret Gett
Jones, Phillip: Geret Gett
Jones, Hester: Geret Gett
Jones, William: Geret Gett
Jones, Indiana: Geret Gett
Robinson, Nancy: Charles Hickman
[57.514]
Benjamin, James: George Bates
[57.515]
Bright, Eliza: Jefferson Sinclare
Bright, Phillip: Jefferson Sinclare
Adams, Mary: Henry Watkins
Adams, Edward: Henry Watkins
Adams, Diza: Henry Watkins
[57.516]
Wallace, William: Robert Hudgins
Wallace, Eliza: Robert Hudgins
Watts, Robin: Thomas Watts
Watts, Nancy: C. Thompson
Watts, Robin: C. Thompson
[57.517]
Jasper, Phillips: John Brown
Jasper, Adolphus: John Brown
[57.518]
Smith, Hannah: Jacob Vaughn
Smith, Abram: Jacob Vaughn

Smith, Rosa: Jacob Vaughn
Smith, Rachael: Jacob Vaughn
Green, Bob: Eldridge Madway
Green, Catharine: Eldridge Madway
Smith, Johnson: Owen Smith
Smith, Hannah: Owen Smith
Smith, Rosa: Owen Smith
Smith, Luck: Owen Smith
Smith, Abram: Owen Smith
Smith, Rachael: Owen Smith
[57.522]
Billups, Julia A: John Beans
[57.523]
Allen, Adeline: Thomas Herbert
Allen, Matilda: Thomas Herbert
Allen, Eli: Thomas Herbert
Allen, Cornelius: Thomas Herbert
Allen, Edwin: Thomas Herbert
Allen, Charlotte: Thomas Herbert
Allen, Nancy: Thomas Herbert
[57.524]
Butts, Jane: Capt. John Dennis
Butts, Henry I: Capt. John Dennis
[57.525]
Baker, Rachael: Jefferson Phillips
Baker, Susan: Jefferson Phillips
Baker, Indiana: Jefferson Phillips
[57.527]
Washington, Eliza: Free born
Washington, Sarah: Free born
Washington, Rose: Free born
Washington, William: Free born
Davis, Sarah: Samuel Cheesman
Davis, Jane: Samuel Cheesman
Davis, Billy: Samuel Cheesman
Williams, Jane: Richard Booker
[57.530]
Patrick, Ellen: W.S. Smith
Patrick, Sella: W.S. Smith
Patrick, Peter: W.S. Smith
[57.531]
Wallace, Julia: Parce Leonard
Smith, Patsy: Lewis Davis
Stevens, Liskie A: George Garrett
Winder, Harry: John Winder
Winder, Dolly: John Winder
[57.532]
Jones, Nancy: Carey Jones
Jones, Ella: Carey Jones
Jones, Margarett: Carey Jones
[57.533]
Allen, Patsey: Nat Gamerell
Booker, Eda: Wm. Myers
Armstead, Lockey: Weston Armstead
[57.535]
Patrick, Lucretia: Wm. Dawson
Patrick, Isaac: Wm. Dawson
Patrick, Levi: Wm. Dawson
Patrick, John: Wm. Dawson
Patrick, Andrew: Wm. Dawson
[57.536]
Henton, Noah: M. Twine
Wilson, Christian: Dr. Wilcox
Wilson, Benjamin: Dr. Wilcox
Wilson, Frederick: Dr. Wilcox
Hope, Fanny: Wm. Morral
Hope, Charles: Wm. Morral
Hope, Merritt: Wm. Morral
Hope, Lucy: Wm. Morral
Hope, Jane: Wm. Morral
Hope, Jane: Thomas Phillips
Hope, Mary: Thomas Phillips
[57.537]
King, Betsy: Free born
[57.539]
Cam, Sally: Capt. George Elliott
Cam, Ellick: Capt. George Elliott
Cam, Cornelia: Capt. George Elliott
Cam, William: Capt. George Elliott
Cam, Georgetta: Capt. George Elliott

Cam, Silvey: Capt. George Elliott
[57.540]
Thomas, Nelly: Edward Savage
[57.541]
Pitchford, Caroline: John P. Jones
[57.542]
Selden, Jack: Ned King
Selden, Eliza: Ned King
[57.543]
Billups, Fannie: Wm. Cassey
Billups, Betsy: Wm. Cassey
Billups, Ned: Wm. Cassey
[57.546]
Randall, Bridget: Gilbert Myers
Randall, Mary: Gilbert Myers
Randall, Abram: Gilbert Myers
Randall, Henry: Gilbert Myers
Randall, Solomon: Gilbert Myers
[57.548]
Collins, Mahaley: Sylvestor Kelley
Collins, Alice: Sylvestor Kelley
Collins, Amelia: Sylvestor Kelley
Collins, Sally: Sylvestor Kelley
Jackson, Harmond: John Herbert
[57.554]
Marshall, Charlotte: Wm. Wood
Marshall, Jacob: Wm. Wood
Marshall, Susan: Wm. Wood
[57.555]
Davis, Amanda: Robert Hudgins
Davis, Indiana: Robert Hudgins
Davis, Charity: Robert Hudgins
Hare, Francis: Thomas Crandall
[57.557]
Howard, Pheby: Henry Whiting
[57.558]
Shepherd, Eliza: Wm. Hickman
Blue, Betsey: John Elliott
Goodman, Mary: Sarah Twine
[57.559]
Patrick, Frank: John Carey

Johnson, Catharine: Thomas Twine
[57.560]
Edney, Penny: Richard Felton
[57.563]
Carter, Lizzie: Carey Jones
[57.565]
Morris, Kitty: Canon Whiten
Morris, Patsy: Canon Whiten
Morris, Moses: Canon Whiten
[57.568]
Webster, Mary: John Parish
[57.569]
Tucker, Slara: Wm. Ivey
Gillah, Delia: Wm. Ivey
[57.570]
Wallace, William: George Booker
[57.571]
Shune, Catharine: Wm. Lee
[57.574]
Weston, Elizabeth: Jerry Kape
Weston, John: Jerry Kape
Weston, Rachael: Jerry Kape
Weston, Lucy: Jerry Kape
Weston, Sally: Jerry Kape
[57.575]
Jones, Jennie: Dr. Vaughn

[57.564]
**Hampton,
Elizabeth City Co. VA**
Andrews, Hannah: George Hoop
Andrews, John: George Hoop
Andrews, Eliza: George Hoop
Andrews, Mary J: George Hoop

**Back Water,
Elizabeth City Co. VA**
Bell, Lucy: James Bell
Bell, John: James Bell
Bell, William: James Bell

[57.507]
Prince George Co. VA
Harrison, Angeline: Wm. B. Harrison
Harrison, Nancy: Wm. B. Harrison
[57.511]
Lansin, Jessie: Ann Brighten
Lansin, Viene: Ann Brighten
[57.513]
Davis, Rena: George E. Harrison
[57.515]
Glenfoot, Eliza: Thomas G. Fenno
Taylor, Jane: Charles H. Searber
Taylor, Adeline: Charles H. Searber
Taylor, Francis: Charles H. Searber
Taylor, Joseph: Charles H. Searber
Taylor, Jacob: Charles H. Searber
[57.516]
Rice, Hannah: Maurice Gilham
Rice, Darley: Maurice Gilham
Rice, Wm.: Maurice Gilham
Rice, Robert: Maurice Gilham
[57.518]
Washington, Patsy: John Blare
Washington, James: John Blare
Washington, Sarah: John Blare
Washington, Henry: John Blare
[57.524]
Unknown, Eliza: Dr. Epson
Unknown, Randlie: Dr. Epson
[57.525]
Prophit, Ebrie: Edmon Ruffin
Prophit, Rose: Edmon Ruffin
Prophit, Alda: Edmon Ruffin
[57.527]
Washington, Rebecca: Edmund Ruffin
Washington, Richard: Edmund Ruffin
Washington, Milly: Edmund Ruffin
Washington, Julia: Edmund Ruffin
Washington, Randall: Edmund Ruffin
Washington, Richard: Edmund Ruffin
Washington, Sarah: Edmund Ruffin

[57.528]
Wilkins, Ester
Wilkins, Patience
Wilkins, James
Wilkins, Washington
Wilkins, Henry
Crumson, Sarah: Wm. B. Harrison
Crumson, Nancy: Wm. B. Harrison
Crumson, Napoleon: Wm. B. Harrison
Harrison, Adeline: Wm. B. Harrison
Harrison, Claresa: Wm. B. Harrison
Harrison, Mariah: Wm. B. Harrison
Bailey, Margaret: Montgomery Osborn
Bailey, Virginia: Montgomery Osborn
Bailey, William: Montgomery Osborn
Bailey, Mariah: Montgomery Osborn
Bailey, Peter: Montgomery Osborn
Bailey, Lucy: Montgomery Osborn
Bailey, Sarah: Montgomery Osborn
[57.533]
Harris, Ellen: Richard Pierson
Harris, Indiana: Richard Pierson
Harris, Julia: Richard Pierson
Harris, James: Richard Pierson
Jones, Mariah: Richard Harrison
[57.534]
White, Catharine: Dr. Epps
White, Rosa: Dr. Epps
White, Louisa: Dr. Epps
White, Louisa: Dr. Epps
[57.536]
Holdon, Susan: Dr. Richard Epps
Holdon, Robert: Dr. Richard Epps
Holdon, Josaphine: Dr. Richard Epps
Palister, Lucy: Dr. Richard Epps
Palister, Simond: Dr. Richard Epps
Palister, Benjamin: Dr. Richard Epps
Palister, Harriet: Dr. Richard Epps
Green, Ann: John Wobb (?)
Green, James: John Wobb (?)
Jackson, Vinnery: Charles Friend

[57.537]
Riles, Daniel: Windfield Harrison
[57.538]
Garly, Mary: Windfield Harrison
Harrison, Ellen: Windfield Harrison
Harrison, Louisa: Windfield Harrison
Harrison, Walter: Windfield Harrison
Harrison, Richard: Windfield Harrison
Marshall, David: Jacob Wilcox
Jones, Henry: Windfield Harrison
[57.539]
Brown, Catharine: Edwin P. Warren
Brown, William Henry: Edwin P. Warren
Johnson, Ann: orphan
[57.540]
Walker, Margaret A: Richard Epps
Walker, Charlotte: Richard Epps
Walker, John: Richard Epps
Walker, Richard: Richard Epps
[57.544]
Morrison, Millie: James Cox
Morrison, Soloman: James Cox
Ruffin, Sarah: Dr. Osborne
Robinson, Mariah: Petan Stock
Robinson, Fannie: Petan Stock
Robinson, Isham: Petan Stock
[57.545]
Harnett, Charlett: William Smith
Harnett, Emma: Wm. Smith
Jones, Jane: Richard Harrison
Jones, Julia: Richard Harrison
Morrison, Caroline: James Cox
Morrison, Mariah: James Cox
Morrison, Bonton: James Cox
[57.547]
Harvey, Hannah: James Cox
Harvey, Lucinda: James Cox
Harvey, Polly: James Cox
Monk, Peggy: Harrison Cox
[57.548]

Shap, Caroline: George Harrison
Shap, Milley: George Harrison
Shap, Betsey: George Harrison
Bolin, Nancy: James Cox
Bolin, Andrew: James Cox
Reed, Peggy: Edward Ruffin
Reed, Augustes: Edward Ruffin
Reed, Henry: Edward Ruffin
Reed, Indiana: Edward Ruffin
Reed, Lewis: Edward Ruffin
Reed, Clara A: Edward Ruffin
[57.550]
Jones, Patience: Julas Mocks
Willis, Hannah: Jackson Wilcox
Willis, Aaron: Jackson Wilcox
Willis, Samuel: Jackson Wilcox
Willis, Eda: Jackson Wilcox
Willis, Marshall: Jackson Wilcox
[57.553]
Slaughter, Susan: Richard Eppes
Slaughter, Peter: Richard Eppes
Slaughter, Louisa: Richard Eppes
Slaughter, Emma: Richard Eppes
[57.555]
Sweet, Margaret: George Bland
Ruffin, Maria: Harrison Cox
[57.557]
Jones, Nelly: Peater Bearch
[57.562]
Bell, Nancy: Dr. R. Epps
Bell, Sarah: Dr. R. Epps
Johnson, Silla: Dr. R. Epps
Johnson, Philip: Dr. R. Epps
Johnson, George: Dr. R. Epps
[57.565]
John, Sally: Charles Conter
Jones, Anthony: Edward Monks
[57.568]
Moore, Mariah: James B. Cox
Moore, Boylan: James B. Cox
Moore, Soloman: James B. Cox

Moore, Miller: James B. Cox
Moore, Caroline: James B. Cox
Marks, Sarah: Harrison Cox
Moody, Lucy: Harrison Cox
Moody, Nancy: Harrison Cox
King, Fanny: Harrison Cox
King, Sarah: Harrison Cox
King, George: Harrison Cox
King, Jennie: Harrison Cox
King, Ester: Harrison Cox
Young, Molly: Harrison Cox
Young, Edith: Harrison Cox
Young, Marthia: Harrison Cox
Young, John: Harrison Cox
Young, Sarah: Harrison Cox
[57.569]
Trusty, Hannah: George Harrison
Trusty, Alfred: George Harrison
Trusty, Susan: George Harrison
Trusty, Edmond: George Harrison
Trusty, Wm.: George Harrison
Wm.s, Lucy: George E. Harrison
[57.570]
Washington, Mariah: Richard Harrison
Washington, Peter: Richard Harrison
Washington, Charles: Richard Harrison
Washington, Lottie: Richard Harrison
Washington, Millie: Richard Harrison
Walker, Sarah: Richard Harrison
Walker, Ann: Richard Harrison
Walker, Sarah: Richard Harrison
[57.572]
Locklin, Fanny: Edmund Ruffin
Tolver, Spriggs: Edmund Ruffin
Tolver, Eliza: Edmund Ruffin
[57.573]
Jackson, Betsey: Windfield Harrison
Jackson, India: Windfield Harrison
Jackson, Henry: Windfield Harrison
Toliver, Sarah: Windfield Harrison
Toliver, James: Windfield Harrison

[57.574]
Jones, Kersey: Richard Jones
Jones, Alice: Richard Jones
Jones, Ida: Richard Jones
Jones, Wm.: Richard Jones
Jones, Andrew: Richard Jones
[57.575]
Strong, Martha: James Mathews
Strong, Susan: James Mathews
Strong, James: James Mathews
Strong, John: James Mathews
Strong, Betsy: James Mathews

[57.507]
Sussex Co. VA
Harrison, Matilda: Henry Jarget
Harrison, Benjamin: Thomas Blunt
[57.510]
Taylor, Michael A: John Cotten
Taylor, Jacob: John Cotten
Taylor, Thomas: John Cotten
Taylor, John: John Cotten
Taylor, Mary: John Cotten
Taylor, Catharine: John Cotten
Angrum, Eveline: Thomas Blunt
Angrum, Rose: Thomas Blunt
Angrum, Frank: Thomas Blunt
Angrum, Henrietta: Thomas Blunt
Masonberge, Polly: Thomas Blunt
Masonberge, Eliza: Thomas Blunt
[57.556]
Gray, Ann: David Taylor
Gray, Richmond: David Taylor
Gray, George Washington: David Taylor
Gray, Susan: David Taylor
[57.561]
Milkins, Lavina: John Downman
[57.571]
Wilkins, Mariah: Wm. Bishoff
Wilkins, Sandy: Wm. Bishoff

[57.575]
Moody, Cherry: Mr. Savage

[57.507]
Mathews Co. VA
Jones, Martha: Billy Wm.s
Todd, Daniel: Martha Minster
Todd, John: Martha Minster
Washington, Kittie: Wm. White
Washington, Hunter: Wm. White
Washington, Brooks: Wm. White
Knight, Ann: Joseph Knight
[57.514]
Armstead, Caroline: Susan Billups
Armstead, Albert: Susan Billups
Armstead, John: Susan Billups
Armstead, Lucy: Susan Billups
[57.515]
Brown, Christian: Christian J. Brown
Brown, Mary: Christian J. Brown
[57.516]
Dickson, Mary: Ellie Shepard
Dickson, Sarah: Ellie Shepard
[57.521]
Hill, Nanny: Andrew Brown
Hill, William: Andrew Brown
Hill, Benjamin: Andrew Brown
Hill, Maltimor: Andrew Brown
Hill, Rolsy: Andrew Brown
Hill, Catharine: Andrew Brown
[57.522]
Tompkins, Charles: John Diggs
Tompkins, Harnett: John Diggs
Tompkins, Mary: John Diggs
Thomas, Susan: Wm. Braks
Thomas, Robert: Wm. Braks
Thomas, James: Wm. Braks
[57.524]
Billups, Leach: James Garnett
Billups, Robert: James Garnett
Billups, Harriett: James Garnett
Billups, Charlott: James Garnett
[57.530]
Chainey, Tompkins: Archer Hudgins
Chainey, Mary: Archer Hudgins
Chainey, Elizabeth: Archer Hudgins
Chainey, Fridera: Archer Hudgins
Chainey, Caroline: Archer Hudgins
Colter, Emily: Sand Smith
Colter, Joseph: Sand Smith
[57.533]
Billup, Patsey: John Armstead
[57.535]
James, Peter: Christopher Brown
Collins, Grace: Francis Armstead
Collins, Harriett: Francis Armstead
Collins, Wm.: Francis Armstead
Collins, Jessy: Francis Armstead
[57.541]
Brooks, Ann: George Brooks
Cooks, Nancy: Christopher Brown
Cooks, Mary: Christopher Brown
Cooks, Margaret: Christopher Brown
Cooks, Catharine: Christopher Brown
[57.542]
Thomas, Lizzie: James Blake
Thomas, Sarah: James Blake
Thomas, Mary: James Blake
[57.543]
Carter, Polly: Robert Billups
Carter, Sarah: Robert Billups
Carter, Rebecca: Robert Billups
Carter, Dick: Robert Billups
Carter, Lucy: Robert Billups
Carter, Ned: Robert Billups
[57.550]
Buckner, Hannah: Frank Armstead
[57.552]
Johnson, Susan: Holden Hudgins
Johnson, Rosetta: Holden Hudgins
Johnson, John: Holden Hudgins
Johnson, George: Holden Hudgins

Johnson, James: Holden Hudgins
Carlton, Laura: Holden Hudgins
Carlton, Mary: Holden Hudgins
[57.553]
Jarvis, Mariah: Locken Miller
[57.558]
Jarvis, Sally: Francis Armstead
Jarvis, Margaret: Francis Armstead
Jarvis, Lina: Francis Armstead
[57.560]
Hudgins, Harriett: Albert Dip
Hudgins, Mary: Albert Dip
Hudgins, Eliza: Albert Dip
Smith, Leha: Warren Foster
Hudgins, David: Jessie Hudgins
Brombley, Lucy: Marshall Bromley
[57.562]
Lichfield, Fanny: Wm. Bohanan
Lichfield, Washington: Wm. Bohanan
Lichfield, John: Wm. Bohanan
Lichfield, Sarah: Wm. Bohanan
Coltin, Emily: Samuel Smith
Furgain, Frances: Albert Dix
Furgain, Isaac: Albert Dix
Furgain, Jacob: Albert Dix
Furgain, Robert: Albert Dix
[57.563]
Litchfield, Armstead: John Burk
Litchfield, Polly: John Burk
[57.565]
Tabb, Robert: Elleck Hudgins
[57.572]
Johnson, Mary: Robert Hudgins
Johnson, Gussie: Robert Hudgins
Johnson, Fanny: Robert Hudgins
Johnson, Oliver: Robert Hudgins

[57.507]
Williamsburg, VA
Washington, Eliza: Wm. Armstead
[57.519]
Ellis, Everett: Moses Waren
Ellis, Lizzie: Moses Waren
[57.539]
Williams, Lina:
    Maj. John D. Clayburn
Williams, Carter:
    Maj. John D. Clayburn
Williams, John:
    Maj. John D. Clayburn
Warden, Fanny: Orphan child
Warden, Ellick: Orphan child
[57.565]
Carter, Malinda: Dr. Martin
Carter, Henry: Dr. Martin

[57.507]
Suffolk, VA
Brewer, Hannah: Henry Cooper
[57.515]
Gorden, Mary: Richyard Riddick
[57.518]
Scott, Patience: Free born
[57.537]
Pierce, Martha: John Copeland
[57.542]
Sawyer, Fanny: Free born
Sawyer, Arphenia: Free born
[57.544]
Epps, Adeline: Free born.
Murry, Matilda: Dr. Murry
Murry, John: Dr. Murry
Murry, Henry: Dr. Murry
Willis, Fanny: George Garden
Spencer, Lizzie: Free black.
Spencer, Johana: Free black.
Spencer, Gertrude: Free black
Spencer, William: Free black.
[57.560]
King, Mary J: John Copeland

[57.507]
Smithfield, VA
Jerdan, Margaret: Dr. A. Boyden
Jerdan, George: Dr. A. Boyden
Jerdan, Robert: Dr. A. Boyden
[57.526]
Andrews, Lucy: Edwin Bunkley
[57.529]
Clarey, Ester: Robinson Todd
Clarey, Sarah: Robinson Todd
Clarey, Fanny: Robinson Todd
Clarey, Edwin: Robinson Todd
Gross, Chasey: John Burkley
Hankins, Margarett: Samuel P. Jerdan
Hankins, Mary: Samuel P. Jerdan
Hankins, Edward: Samuel P. Jerdan
Hankins, Martha: Samuel P. Jerdan
Hankins, Henry: Samuel P. Jerdan
Hankins, Bobby: Samuel P. Jerdan
Smith, Robert: Sterrit Whitney
Smith, Ann: Sterrit Whitney
[57.565]
Smith, Georgean: Free Born
Smith, Josephine: Free Born
Smith, Mary Francis: Free Born

[57.507]
Charles City Co. VA
Washington, Susan: Richard Barley
[57.510]
Lewis, Margaret: Dr. Epps
Lewis, Charles: Dr. Epps
Lewis, Edmond: Dr. Epps
[57.512]
Hill, Aaron: John Hall
Hill, Patsey: John Hall
[57.515]
Pride, Anthony: Hill Carter
Pride, Sarah: Hill Carter
[57.516]
Thornton, Clara: P. Stocks
Thornton, Thomas: P. Stocks
[57.518]
Harrison, Braxton: Dr. Stock
Harrison, Edmond: Dr. Stock
[57.519]
Christian, Sarah: Hill Carter
Booker, Ann: Wm. S. Smith
[57.524]
Bailey, Sally: John Smith
Bailey, Jackson: John Smith
[57.526]
Cooper, Mary: Martha Augurn
Cooper, Martha: Martha Augurn
Cooper, Mary: Martha Augurn
Cooper, Thomas: Martha Augurn
Bailey, Diana: Martha Augurn
Braxtin, Fannie: Benj. Christian
Braxtin, Charlotte: Benjamin Christian
Braxtin, Robert: Benjamin Christian
[57.527]
Smith, Susan: Dr. Epps
Smith, Rosa: Dr. Epps
Smith, Mary: Dr. Epps
[57.532]
Jackson, Hannah: Richard Bailey
James, David: Jerome Paden
[57.533]
Scott, Jessey: Dr. John Wilson
[57.535]
Armstead, Eliza: Thomas Covington
Black, Eliza: John Tyler
Black, Thadious: John Tyler
Black, Ellen: John Tyler
Black, Mary: John Tyler
Black, Joseph: John Tyler

[57.536]
Christian, Julia A: Hill Carter
[57.537]
Johnson, Betsy: Hiram Tyler

[57.538]
Shepard, Morris: Robert Vanten
Shepard, Ella: Robert Vanten
[57.540]
Gower, Sarah: James Phillips
Gower, Ellick: James Phillips
Gower, Sarah: James Phillips
Gower, Joseph: James Phillips
Gower, Maria: James Phillips
[57.541]
Bradley, Rachael: George Major
[57.543]
Christian, Julia: Hill Carter
Christian, Joseph: Hill Carter
Christian, Annie: Hill Carter
[57.544]
Robinson, Carter: Potan Stocks
Robinson, Lucy: Potan Stocks
Robinson, Rachel: Potan Stocks
[57.545]
Washington, Jane: Hill Carter
[57.546]
Henderson, Lucy: Richard Epps
Henderson, Fanny: Richard Epps
Henderson, Hannah: Richard Epps
Henderson, Mary: Richard Epps
Henderson, Albert: Richard Epps
Henderson, Cornelius: Richard Epps
Douglass, Philis: John Selden
Douglass, Lucy: John Selden
Douglass, Agness: John Selden
Douglass, Margarett: John Selden
Childs, Betsey: Free born
Childs, Milly: Free born
Childs, Amanda: Free born
[57.547]
Jones, Margaret: John Selden
Jones, Mary: John Selden
[57.549]
Robinson, Patsy: Agness Crenshaw
Robinson, William: Agness Crenshaw
Robinson, Joseph: Agness Crenshaw
Robinson, Archie: Agness Crenshaw
Johnson, Margaret: Free born
Johnson, John: Free born
Johnson, James: Free born
[57.551]
Carter, Mary: John P. Roy
Cooper, Mary: Mrs. Carter
Cooper, Mary: Mrs. Carter
Cooper, Louisa: Mrs. Carter
Cooper, Betsey: Mrs. Carter
[57.552]
Howard, Behannob: Hill Carter
Howard, Virginia: Hill Carter
[57.553]
Marrell, Hanan: W.B. Walker
[57.554]
Jefferson, Annie: Dr. Wilcox
Jefferson, Maria: Dr. Wilcox
Jefferson, Allen: Dr. Wilcox
[57.560]
Edlay, Martha: Westmore Wilcox
Edlay, Fleming: Westmore Wilcox
[57.561]
Washington, Liddy: Hill Carter
Morris, Betsey: Hill Carter
Morris, Phillis: Hill Carter
Morris, Lillie A: Hill Carter
Morris, Elijah: Hill Carter
[57.563]
Green, Malinda: William Upture
[57.565]
Phillips, Ann: Charles Page
Phillips, Delia: Charles Page
Phillips, Richard: Charles Page
Shepard, Rena: Charles Page
[57.568]
Terrall, Elliza: Hill Carter
Terrall, William: Hill Carter

[57.569]
Wilson, Sarah: Charles Lariby
Rogister, Nancy: Wm. H. Southold
Henderson, Mary: Henry Payton
Henderson, Isaac: Henry Payton
Henderson, Moses: Henry Payton
[57.572]
Hall, Patsey: Dr. Wm. Wilcox
Hall, Hatty: Dr. Wm. Wilcox
Hall, Patsy: Dr. Wm. Wilcox
Hall, Sarah: Dr. Wm. Wilcox
[57.573]
Carter, Patience: John Selden
Julias, Francis: John P. Ronett
Harrison, Millie: Dr. Stocks
Harrison, Armstead: Dr. Stocks
[57.574]
Jackson, Mary: Hill Carter
Jackson, Almina: Hill Carter
Jackson, Jennie: Hill Carter
Jackson, Wm.: Hill Carter
Jackson, Hill: Hill Carter
Jackson, Amosan: Hill Carter

[57.510]
Accomac Co. VA
Wise, Rosetta: Wm. H. Custis
Wise, Sarah: Wm. H. Custis
[57.512]
Jerson, Laurance: George Seasber
[57.569]
Upher, Louisa: George W. Parker
Upher, Hellen: George W. Parker
Upher, Georgiania: George W. Parker
Upher, Nat: George W. Parker

[57.511]
Lancaster Co. VA
Hawkins, Mary A: James Grasham
[57.556]
Yearby, Sharlett: Baldwin Kenny

[57.511]
York Co. VA
Westen, Susan:
    Josaphene Rodringham
Westen, Martha:
    Josaphene Rodringham
Thomas, Martha: Free born.
Thomas, Mary: Free born.
Thomas, Levi: Free born.
Thomas, Soloman: Free born.
[57.520]
Gatens, Polly: Edmond Winn
Russell, Lucy: Edmond Winn
Russell, George: Edmond Winn
Russell, Hanah: Edmond Winn
Russell, Laura: Edmond Winn
Russell, Lizzie: Edmond Winn
[57.521]
Minkin, Malinda: Wm. P. Taylor
Minkin, Amy: Wm. P. Taylor
[57.522]
Williams, Phillis: Marshall Davis
Thomas, Peter: Charles Hopkins
Thomas, James: Charles Hopkins
[57.524]
Cook, Dafney: Frank Smith
[57.530]
Washington, Sally: John Taylor
Washington, Nace: John Taylor
Dickerson, Nace: Orphan child.
    John Taylor
[57.531]
Baker, Betsey: W.P. Taylor
Baker, William: W.P. Taylor
[57.532]
Bangs, Jerry: Wilet Crockett
[57.536]
Dennis, Millie: John Dennis
[57.541]
Bailey, Francis: Howard Dunn
Bailey, Matilda: Howard Dunn

Bailey, Rosa: Howard Dunn
Carey, Francis: Thomas Dunn
[57.542]
Gales, Susan: George Smith
[57.545]
Jones, Sarah: F. Holt
Jones, Lucy: F. Holt
Jones, Jane: F. Holt
Jones, Lizzie: F. Holt
[57.549]
Milborn, Lalie: Wm. Adams
Milborn, David: William Adams
Milborn, Francis: Wm. Adams
[57.558]
Willams, Hellena: J.D. Cleyborn
Willams, Carter: J.D. Cleyborn
Willams, John: J.D. Cleyborn
Willams, Fanny: J.D. Cleyborn
Willams, Elec: J.D. Cleyborn
[57.565]
Dennis, D: James Wilson
Johnson, Sarah Ann: John Tennis
Johnson, William: John Tennis
[57.569]
Jones, Paul: Hawkins Reed
[57.570]
Harmen, Richard: W. Crockett
Harmen, Jacob: W. Crockett
Harmen, George: W. Crockett
Harmen, Charles: W. Crockett
Harmen, Edward: W. Crockett

[57.527]
Yorktown, VA
Johnson, Emma: Lyons Farren
Johnson, Ella: Lyons Farren

[57.511]
New Kent Co. VA
Page, Lucy: Ballard Sherman
Megins, Louisa: Ballard Sherman

Fox, Hannah: Braxton Garlic
Fox, Fanny: Braxton Garlic
Stewart, Winnie: Braxton Garlic
[57.514]
King, Amy: Dr. Samuel Webb
King, Nelson: Dr. Samuel Webb
[57.517]
Taylor, Elizabeth: Mastin Sherman
[57.518]
Brown, Millie: Samuel Webb
[57.520]
Christian, Rosetta: Bat Christian
Christian, Rosa: Bat Christian
Christian, Jane: Bat Christian
[57.522]
More, Patsey: Braxton Gallie
{Garlick?}
More, Sh[ ]: Braxton Gallie
{Garlick?}
More, Daniel: Braxton Gallie
{Garlick?}
Mickens, Louisa: Benjamin Sherman
Christian, Lucy: Benjamin Sherman
[57.528]
Webb, Jane: Joseph Weed
Webb, Burrell: Joseph Weed
Webb, Jackson: Joseph Weed
[57.534]
Williams, Mary: Jocklin Dexter
Williams, Joseph: Jocklin Dexter
Williams, Jerdon: Jocklin Dexter
Williams, Isabella: Jocklin Dexter
Webb, Catharine: Georgeana Ward
Webb, Jane: Susan Joseph
[57.537]
Nash, Kesiah: Braxton Garlic
[57.539]
Robinson, Julia: Mr. Sherman
[57.540]

King, Caroline: Samuel Webb
King, Polly: Samuel Webb
King, Logan: Samuel Webb
King, Dinah: Samuel Webb
King, Mary: Samuel Webb
Granton, Margaret: Wm. C. Christian
Granton, Fanny: Wm. C. Christian
[57.542]
Robinson, Sally: Henry Webb
Slate, Clarisa: Henry Webb
[57.545]
Allen, Margaret: Ann Johnson
Allen, Lavinia: Ann Johnson
Allen, Malinda: Ann Johnson
Allen, Emeline: Ann Johnson
[57.553]
Quolls, Susan: Logan Elliott
Quolls, Isaac: Logan Elliott
[57.554]
Bolding, Caroline: Harrison Crump
[57.558]
Gaines, Ann: Henry Toller
Gaines, Michell: Henry Toller
[57.565]
Fisher, Mary: Braxton Garlic
Fisher, Eldridge: Braxton Garlic
[57.572]
Samuel, Lucy: Dr. Leonard Crump
[57.574]
Smith, Louisa: Henry Webb
Smith, Ellen: Henry Webb
Smith, Henry: Henry Webb
Meekes, Caroline: Headley Sherman
Meekes, Fleming: Headley Sherman
Meekes, Littleton: Headley Sherman
Meekes, Elle E: Headley Sherman
Meekes, Caroline: Headley Sherman

[57.512]
Cumberland Co. VA
Jackson, Fanny: John Slocum
Jackson, Walter: John Slocum
Jackson, Emily: John Slocum
Edmonds, Agness: John Slocum
[57.534]
Jeofers, Jenott: John Price
Jeofers, George H: John Price
Jeofers, Henry: John Price
[57.535]
Clark, Eliza: Oscar Blackman
Clark, Eli: Oscar Blackman

[57.513]
Richmond, VA
Weston, Louisa: Maj. Custis
[57.521]
Durgen, Sallie: Dr. Epps
Durgen, Mary: Dr. Epps
Durgen, Susan: Dr. Epps
Jupee, Amanda: Carter Whitney
Jupee, Alice: Carter Whitney
[57.526]
Barnes, Mary: Free Born
Barnes, Nathan: Free Born
Barnes, Ames: Free Born
Barns, Ann Eliza: Free Born
Barns, John: Free Born
[57.559]
Slaughter, Sarah: Dr. Epps
[57.575]
Moore, Nancy: Free Born
Moore, Rebecca: Free Born
Moore, Jane: Free Born

[57.514]
James City Co. VA
Dennis, Nancy: Wilmot Jones
Dennis, Lilley: Wilmot Jones
Dennis, Seldun: Wilmot Jones
[57.533]
Bryant, Fanny: Thomas Carrington

[57.538]
Douglass, Matilda: Michael Warren
Douglass, Matilda: Michael Warren
Douglass, Fanny: Michael Warren
Douglass, Lucy: Michael Warren
Douglass, Betsy: Michael Warren
[57.539]
Booker, Jane: Dr. Epps
Booker, Ida: Dr. Epps
Booker, Fanny: Dr. Epps
[57.565]
James, Caroline: Nathaniel Picket
James, Sally: Nathaniel Picket

[57.510]
Nansemond Co. VA
Parker, Ann: Jessie Barley

[57.514]
Jerdan, Nancy: Free born
Jerdan, Amy: Free born
[57.516]
Small, Margaret: Jassett Everett
[57.520]
Clay, Almedra: John Turner
Clay, Josephine: John Turner
Russell, Maria: Elisha Norlet
[57.521]
Simonds, Matilda: Abram Dukes
Dexter, Hester: Dempsy Difen
Dexter, Miles: Dempsy Difen
[57.523]
Bath, Nancy: Capt. Gaskin
Bath, Martha: Capt. Gaskin
Bath, Elizabeth: Capt. Gaskin
Bailey, Rebecca: Capt. Gaskin
Bailey, Nancy: Capt. Gaskin
Bailey, Laura: Capt. Gaskin
Bailey, Fannie: Capt. Gaskin
Brown, Claresa: Walter Livingston
Brown, Caledonia: Walter Livingston
Brown, George: Walter Livingston
Copeland, Richard: Free born
Copeland, Lindey: Free born
Copeland, Harriett: Free born
[57.532]
Fladden, Jane: Free Born
Fladden, James: Free Born
Fladden, George: Free Born
[57.535]
Camford, Clarisa: Ashfille Wilson
[57.537]
King, Louisa: Edwin King
[57.540]
Reddick, Armassa: Free born
Reddick, Wealthy: Free born
Reddick, Willis: Free born
[57.549]
Carson, Lourice: Joshua Simonds
[57.556]
Nelson, Toney: Joseph Nelson
[57.557]
Savage, Eliza: John Yates
[57.563]
Brown, Delia: Wm. Jerdon
Brown, Mary: Wm. Jerdon
[57.565]
Garrett, Nancy: Ashby Wilson
[57.570]
Richards, Precilla: Free Born
Richards, Julia: Free Born
Richards, Mary: Free Borr
[57.573]
Johnson, Elizabeth: Free Born
Johnson, Martha: Free Born
Johnson, Peter: Free Borr
[57.575]
Wilson, Martha: Henry Burr
Wilson, Abram: Henry Burr

[57.517]
Portsmouth, VA
Wilson, Mary A: Free born
Wilson, John: Free born
Wilson, Henry: Free born
[57.533]
Moore, Annie: Martha Livingston
Moore, George: Martha Livingston
[57.575]
Henderson, Millie: John Benisonk
Henderson, Matilda: JohnBenisonk
Henderson, Louisa: John Benisonk
Henderson, Willis: John Benisonk

[57.519]
Eastern Shore, VA
Johnson, Martha: Wm. Bucket
[57.564]
Custer, Susan: Edward Holland
Custer, John: Edward Holland
Custer, Wm.: Edward Holland
Custer, Mary A: Edward Holland

[57.519]
Southampton Co. VA
Simond, Reno: Madisen Ganie
Simond, James: Madisen Ganie
Simond, Buck: Madisen Ganie
Simond, Ellie: Madisen Ganie
[57.520]
Lightfoot, Agnes: Chestine Maggett
[57.551]
Jerdon, Hariett: Wm. Jones
Jerdon, Henry: Wm. Jones
Jerdon, Elizabeth: Wm. Jones
Jerdon, Lindy: Wm. Jones
Jerdon, Miles: Wm. Jones
[57.556]
Simonds, Samuel: James Acket
Simonds, Ann: James Acket

[57.519]
Chesterfield Co. VA
Hood, Ann: Wm. Gregory
Hood, Mary: Wm. Gregory
[57.520]
Henderson, Millie: Richard Epps
Henderson, Randall: Richard Epps
Henderson, Alexander: Richard Epps
Henderson, Matilda: Richard Epps
Henderson, Hesekiah: Richard Epps
[57.541]
Cogsnell, Betsey: Thomas Howler
[57.543]
Cox, Marthy: Thomas Howdy
Cox, Lucy: Thomas Howdy
Cox, John: Thomas Howdy
Cox, Martha: Thomas Howdy
Cox, Jerdan: Thomas Howdy
Cox, Mary: Thomas Howdy
[57.552]
Williams, Betsey: Edward Watkins
Williams, Lizzie: Edward Watkins
Williams, Fanny: Edward Watkins
Williams, Peter: Edward Watkins
[57.553]
Boykin, Elizabeth: Wm. Parker
Boykin, Charlett: Wm. Parker
Boykin, Agness: William Parker
Boykin, Charles: Wm. Parker
Boykin, Robert: Wm. Parker
[57.556]
Wm.s, Patsey: Edward Watkins
Williams, Fanny: Edward Watkins
Williams, Lizzie: Edward Watkins
Williams, Peache: Edward Watkins
[57.562]
Dungy, William: Free Born.
Sweet, Primus: James Howlet

[57.565]
Good, Peggy: Wm. Gregory
Good, Joseph: Wm. Gregory
Good, John: Wm. Gregory
Good, Sarah: Wm. Gregory
[57.574]
Chapman, Emma: Mr. Moody
Chapman, Sarah: Mr. Moody
Chapman, Joseph: Mr. Moody

[57.519]
Louisa Co. VA
Jones, Susan: Granville Bullock
Jones, Lucy: Granville Bullock
Jones, Martha: Granville Bullock
Jones, Overton: Granville Bullock
[57.547]
Garrett, Sarah A: Granville Bullock
Garrett, Thomas: Granville Bullock
Garrett, Eliza: Granville Bullock
[57.549]
Trace, Walker: Robert Harris
Bullock, Clara: Granville Bullock
Bullock, John: Granville Bullock
Bullock, Mary: Granville Bullock
[57.558]
Robinson, Esther: Granville Bullock
[57.575]
Overton, Alexander: R.B. Davis

[57.520]
Dinwiddie Co. VA
Epps, Ned: John Dorson
[57.525]
Murry, Ann: Christian Sulivan
Murry, Fannie: Christian Sulivan
Murry, Jennie: Christian Sulivan
[57.543]
Bland, Nancy: Dr. Epsey

[57.522]
Norfolk, VA
Sawyer, W.H: Free born
[57.551]
Brown, Benjamin: Alexander Bell
Brown, Julia: {wife of Benjamin} Alexander Bell
[57.560]
Judon, Amand: Mr. Smith
[57.569]
Malery, Lucy: Joseph Freeman

[57.522]
Petersburg, VA
Willis, Lucretia: Jacob Wilcox
[57.535]
Bundy, Elizabeth: Free born
Tyler, Lucy A: Free born
Tyler, Thomas: Free born
Tyler, William: Free born

[57.525]
Richmond Co. VA
Marshall, Robert
Jefferson, Cox: {husband of Patsey}
Jefferson Patsey: {wife of Jefferson}
Marshall, Patsey: {wife of Robert}
Marshall, Robert: {husband of Patsey}
Washington, Saderfield: Thomas Wiley
Washington, Daniel: Thomas Wiley
Washington, Jackson: Thomas Wiley
[57.572]
Sidney, Winnie: John Graham

[57.526]
Goochland Co. VA
Boyden, Rosey: Wm. Simonds
Boyden, Delia: Wm. Simonds
Boyden, Joseph: Wm. Simonds
Boyden, Manuel: Wm. Simonds
Boyden, Mariah: Wm. Simonds

[57.529]
Nelson Co. VA
Rankle, William: Wm. Randle
[57.556]
Randall, William: Wm. Randall

[57.557]
Fredericksburg, VA
Maisen, Lydia: John Allen
Maisen, James: John Allen
Maisen, Georgeana: John Allen
Maisen, Lydia: John Allen
Maisen, Mary: John Allen
Maisen, Kesiah: John Allen
Maisen, Manuel: John Allen
Gatter, Nellie: Richard Bailey
Gatter, William: Richard Bailey
Gatter, Nellie: Richard Bailey
Gatter, Anthony: Richard Bailey
Gatter, Mary: Richard Bailey

[57.532]
Amelia Co. VA
Washington, Frank: John Fenny
[57.555]
Wilson, General: Mr. Wilson

[57.558]
Albemarle Co. VA
Anderson, Lavenia: Richard Wild
Anderson, Lucy: Richard Wild
Anderson, Fanny: Richard Wild
[57.575]
Marshall, Lucy: Thomas Gallen
Marshall, Lizzie: Thomas Gallen

[57.558]
Clark Co. VA
Bright, Sallie: John Foster
[57.559]
Hunt, Francis: Wm. Hunt
Hunt, Robert: Wm. Hunt
Hunt, Henry: Wm. Hunt
Hunt, Susan: Wm. Hunt

[57.530]
Westmoreland Co. VA
Armstrong, Ann: Thomas Murphy
Armstrong, Joseph; Thomas Murphy

[57.533]
Buckingham Co. VA
Mitchell, Eliza: Mr. C. Paterson
Mitchell, Samuel: Mr. C. Paterson
Mitchell, Sophia: Mr. C. Paterson

[57.534]
Middlesex Co. VA
Washington, George: Miles Mason

Winchester Co. VA
Burrace, Lucy: Free born.

[57.514]
Virginia (place not stated)
Bailey, Semple: Lucy Hill
Bailey, William: Lucy Hill
Bailey, Virginia: Lucy Hill
Bailey, Louisa: Lucy Hill
Bailey, Tempy: Lucy Hill

[57.512]
Western Virginia
Wilson, Amy: Henry Wilson

[57.514]
Grayson Co. VA
Carrol, Rachael: Mary Organ

[57.544]
Lynchburg, VA
Tanner, Amand: Dabne Pondexter

[57.549]
Caroline Co. VA
Taylor, Benjamin: James Hill
Taylor, Paul: James Hill
Taylor, John: James Hill
Taylor, Silas: James Hill

Warwick Co. VA
Robinson, Ellen: Thomas Lee
[57.565]
Hawkins, Jane: John Hawkins
Hawkins, Anthony: John Hawkins

[57.570]
Prince Edward Co. VA
Miller, Lilley: Wm. Smith

[57.555]
Northumberland Co. VA
Strong, Sarah: Hands Lewis

[57.565]
Pamunkey Co. VA
Dandridge, Lavenia: John Crump

[57.513]
St. Mary's Co. MD
Langly, Susan: Dr. Caleb Jones
[57.515]
Gough, Ann: Thomas Looker
[57.516]
Berry, Laurice: Henry Snell
Berry, George: Henry Snell

Riley, Seleshie: Henry Carrol
Riley, James: Henry Carrol
[57.534]
Quintaine, Charles: John Crocker
[57.541]
Butler, Ann: Benedict McGill
[57.549]
Watts, Adeline: Leonard Neal
Watts, George: Leonard Neal
Watts, Mary: Leonard Neal
Watts, William: Leonard Neal
[57.550]
Davis, Ann: Waller Langly
Davis, James: Waller Langly
[57.558]
Brown, Ann: Wm. Cord
Brown, William: Wm. Cord
[57.575]
Bennett, Eliza: Walter Bisker
Bennett, Rosa: Walter Bisker
Bennett, John: Walter Bisker

[57.541]
Maryland
Brown, Alice: Ann Upcher
Brown, Robert: Ann Upcher

[57.516]
Washington, D.C.
Custer, Jasper: Maj. George Custer

[57.511]
Cherry Gutt, NC
Brown, Matilda: John Boykin
Brown, John: John Boykin
Brown, Sarah: John Boykin
Brown, Henrietta: John Boykin
Brown, Peter: John Boykin

[57.512]
Edenton, NC
Spence, Martha: Catharine Sutton
[57.521]
White, Rebecca: Jackson Glover
White, Richard: Jackson Glover
[57.553]
Blend, Harnett: John Blend
Blend, Henry: John Blend
[57.557]
Vaughn, Elsie: Thomas Vaughn
Taylor, Louisa: John Smith
Taylor, Elijah: John Smith
Taylor, Sally Ann: John Smith

[57.519]
Wilmington, NC
Quince, Peggy: Charles Craig
Quince, Lewis: Charles Craig
[57.521]
Murphy, William: James Middleton

[57.540]
Plymouth, NC
Spruell, Chloe Ann: Hesekiah Spruell

[57.516]
North Carolina
Bell, Mary: No owner listed
Bell, Marthy: No owner listed

[57.522]
Perquimmons Co. VA
Rose, Charlotte: Jasher Felter

[57.518]
Gates Co. NC
Riddick, Harriet: Wm. H. Riddick
Riddick, Edward: Wm. H. Riddick
Riddick, Alfred: Wm. H. Riddick
Riddick, Molly: Wm. H. Riddick
Riddick, Nancy: Wm. H. Riddick

[57.520]
Cross, Sallie: Wm. Cross
Cross, John: Wm. Cross
Cross, Sally: Wm. Cross
Cross, Quinton: Wm. Cross
Cross, Dolphin: Wm. Cross
[57.534]
Gatlin, Mary I: Reddick Gatlin
Gatlin, Roxanne: Reddick Gatlin
Gatlin, Richard: Reddick Gatlin
[57.537]
Anderson, Sukie: Isaac Dukes
Dukes, Mariah: Isaac Dukes
[57.540]
Harold, Agness: Sam Harold
[57.549]
Gregory, Phania: Wiley Reddick
Gregory, Rebecca: Wiley Reddick
Gatlin, Anne: Reddick Gatlin
Gatlin, Rachel: Reddick Gatlin
[57.561]
Katlin, Lucy: Redick Gatlin
Gulscom, Ann: Redick Gatlin
Gulscom, Martha: Redick Gatlin
Gulscom, Ann: Redick Gatlin
Price, Ester: Wm. Reduck
Price, John: Wm. Reduck
Price, Charles: Wm. Reduck
[57.575]
Christian, Mary: David Christian
Christian, Mack: David Christian
Christian, Francis: David Christian

[57.542]
Deep Creek, South End, NC
McCoy, Surmelia: David Pritchett
McCoy, Mariso?: David Pritchett
McCoy, Angeline: David Pritchett

McCoy, Edith: David Pritchett

[57.542]
Franklin Co. NC
Jones, Eliza: Jerry Dillard
Jones, Puss: Jerry Dillard
Jones, Cornelias: Jerry Dillard
Jones, Hannah: Jerry Dillard

[57.551]
Bertie Co. NC
Askey, Margaret: John Askey
Askey, Johanna: John Askey
Askey, Thomas: John Askey
Askey, Calvin: John Askey
Askey, Betsey: John Askey
Askey, Chancy: John Askey
Askey, Henry: John Askey
Askey, Toney: John Askey
Askey, Margaret: John Askey
Askey, Martha: John Askey
[57.558]
Newell, Patsey: John Symons
[57.570]
Askey, Adaline: John Askey
Askey, William: John Askey

[57.517]
New Bern, NC
Kinsey, Ann: Joseph Skinner

[57.560]
Bryant, Lucy: Wm. Bryant
Bryant, Martha: Wm. Bryant
Bryant, James: Wm. Bryant

[57.565]
Hurtville, NC
Washington, Jane:
    William Washington
Washington, Charles:
    William Washington
Washington, Francis:
    William Washington
Simonds, Margaret: Wm. Byron
Simonds, Henry: Wm. Byron

Whiteford, NC
Crocker, Lucy: James Crocker
Crocker, Lemin: James Crocker

[57.555]
Warren, NC
Keely, Sarah: Thomas Warren
Keely, Laura: Thomas Warren

[57.553]
East Tennessee
Allen, Nancy: Lee Jessie
Allen, Catharine: Lee Jessie

[57.547]
Georgia
Stewart, Fanny: Benjamin Syke

LIST OF INDIGENT FREEDMEN AT DOWNEY FARM, VIRGINIA

{Note: Names followed by names of former owners. Freedmen listed under name of pre-war residence.}

[57.577]
Elizabeth City Co. VA
Moore, Jerrie: John Moore
Rowe, William: R. Vaughn
Taylor, Peggy: Lewis Winder
Vaughn, Eliza: Robert Vaughn
[57.577]
Austin, Ann: J.W. Downey
Austin, Earl: J.W. Downey
Austin, Wealthy Ann: J.W. Downey
Booker, Emily: Richard Gamott
Booker, Janie: Richard Gamott
Carey, Fanny: A. Booker
Carey, Maria: A. Booker
Carey, Sally: A. Booker
Cyrus Cooper: J.W. Downey
Smith, Charlote: Richard Gamott
Smith, Miranda: J.W. Downey
Thomas, Dicy: J.W. Downey
Thomas, Margaret: J.W. Downey
Thomas, Rose: J.W. Downey
[57.578]
Grey, Lucy Ann: R. Hudgins
Reams, Georgeanna: Delia Hudgins
Reams, Minerva: Delia Hudgins
Rodgers, Charey: Lewis Winder
Rodgers, Fred: Lewis Winder
Rodgers, Jim: Lewis Winder
Shields, Polly: Dr. S. Shields
Shields, Ricard: Dr. S. Shields
Vaughn, Rosetta: Robert Vaughn

[57.580]
Gatewood, Aaron: Catherine Wattes
Gatewood, Esther: Catherine Wattes
Johnson, Alice: Catherine Wattes
Johnson, Amelia Ann:
  Catherine Wattes
Parker, Isaac: Catherine Wattes
Parker, Mary Eliza:
  Catherine Wattes
Thomas, John: Henry Cox
[57.584]
Granger, Warren: Franklin Stokeley
Granger, Mary: Franklin Stokeley
Armistead, Louisa: M.H. Kelly
Armistead, Patty: M.H. Kelly
Marshall, Pleasant: Thomas Lowry
Marshall, David: Thomas Lowry
Marshall, Louisa: Thomas Lowry
Marshall, William: Thomas Lowry

[57.577]
New Kent Co. VA
Christian, Christiana: Dr. L. Crump
Christian, Isabella: Dr. L. Crump
Christian, Edward: Dr. L. Crump
[57.581]
Johnson, Nellie: Free Born
Dandridge, Elsie: Free
Dandridge, Martha: Free
Dandridge, Charlotte: Free
[57.583]
Lewon, Winnie: Dr. S. Webb
Lewon, Mary: Dr. S. Webb

[57.577]
York Co. VA
Pressey, Tom: Henry Smith
[57.578]
Brown, Callifer: Carey Crawken
Brown, Rachell: Carey Crawken
Cheeseman, Agnes: Hopkins
Purlieu, Lucy Ann: Tom Smith
Howard, Chole: Calvin Pressey
Pressey, Mary: Widow Rowell
Pressey, William: Widow Rowell
Pressey, Maria Susan: Widow Rowell
[57.579]
Hardgrove, Francis: Mrs. William Tabb
Hardgrove, Robert Henry: Mrs. Wm. Tabb
Smith, Molly: William Nottingham
[57.580]
Thomas, Alice Adelier: Henry Cox
[57.582]
Pascoll, Susan: Thomas Hoag
[57.584]
Chatman, Susan: W. Stovel

[57.577]
Portsmouth, VA
Rowe, Violet: Goodall

Williamsburg, VA
Washington, Lewis: Robert Armistead
Jones, Mary: Moses Harold
Jones, Mary Eliza: Moses Harold

Sussex Co. VA
Buster, Eliza: Free Born.
Buster, Mary Ann: Free Born
[57.580]
Jones, Robert: James Parker

[57.583]
Daugherty, Fanny: William Parker
Jackson, Hannah: James Parker

[57.577]
Surry Co. VA
Clayton, Lucy: James Hall
Clayton, Archer: James Hall
[57.581]
Coker, Caroline: Merrit Stedgt
Brigham, Pocahontas: R. Taylor
Brigham, Jesse: R. Taylor
[57.583]
Clayborns, Mirander: J. Hall
Ellis, Betsey: Free.
Harrison, Henrietta: Keziah Lane

[57.577]
James City Co. VA
Smith, Agnes: George Jones
Smith, Rebecca: George Jones
[57.578]
Randall, Eliza: George Bacon

[57.577]
Isle of Wight Co. VA
Outland, Winnie: Augustus Outland
[57.578]
Copeland, Rhoda: Free Born.
Copeland, Isam: Free Born
Copeland, Mary: Free Born
[57.580]
Good, Elizabeth: Charles Rand
Good, Robert: Charles Rand
[57.582]
Lewis, Eliza: Free.
Lewis, Oliver Ann: Free
Brigham, Bina: Fred Cooper
Bowder, Nancy: Fred Cooper
Goodwin, Margaret Ann: Free
Norfleet, Mary: Free

[57.583]
Johnson, Priscilla: Edwin Dundan
Daugherty, Pautriome: Free.
Daugherty, Jackson: Free.
Daugherty, Betty: Free.
[57.584]
Thomas, Corey: John Thomas
Thomas, Mary: John Thomas
Holman, Dianna: Dr. J. Atkins
Holman, Charlotte: Dr. J. Atkins

[57.577]
Warwick Co. VA
Corben, Mary: Dr. Carter
[57.578]
Black, Sarah: J. Lewellyn
Steptson, Ann: J. Lewellyn
Smith, Susan: John Jones
Smith, Louisa: John Jones
Smith, Mary: John Jones
Smith, Tom: John Jones
Washington, Lucy: Wm. Burnham
Jones, William: William Burnham

Charles City Co. VA
Allen, Betsy: R. Christian
Allen, Jesse: R. Christian
Armistead, Alice: Wm M. Harrison
Armistead, Cornelia: Wm. M. Harrison
Armistead, Henry: Wm. M. Harrison
Armistead, Kitty: William M. Harrison
Brown, Alexander: Edward Going
Carter, Eliza: William M. Harrison
Carter, Eliza: William M. Harrison
Carter, Louisa: William M. Harrison
Carter, Marion: William M. Harrison
Carter, Mary: William M. Harrison
Carter, Moses: William M. Harrison
Clark, Robert: Cary Chauncy
Clark, Rosetta: Cary Chauncy
Davis, Dianna: Edward Going

Harrison, Nancy: William M. Harrison
Jackson, Caroline: Dr. John Wilson
Jackson, Christiana: Dr. John Wilson
Jackson, Cornelius: Dr. John Wilson
Jackson, Edmund: Dr. John Wilson
Jackson, Elvey: Dr. John Wilson
Jackson, Henry Moler:
   Dr. John Wilson
Lewis, Peggy: John D.W. Jones
Randall, Amy: Valentine Marshall
Randall, Frank: Valentine Marshall
Randall, Marshall: Valentine Marshall
Trent, Elizabeth: William M. Harrison
Watkins, Amy: William M. Harrison
Webb, Priscilla: Ben C. Graves
Williams, Eleanor: Wm. M. Harrison
Woodson, Lucy: William M. Harrison

[57.581]
Churchill, Elizabeth: John H. Harrison
Crosly, Clemma: John Smith
Crosly, Edward: John Smith
Crosly, Lavina: John Smith
Crosly, Sandy: John Smith
Crosly, Wilbur: John Smith
Hunt, Ben: John H. Harrison
Hunt, Judy: John H. Harrison
Hunt, Louisa: John H. Harrison
Love, Caroline: John H. Harrison
Parker, Mary: John Smith
Randall, Delia: John Smith
Randall, Ida: George Major
Randall, Judy: George Major
Randall, Julia: George Major
Randall, Katy: George Major
Randall, Lavina: George Major
Rolin, Thomas: John H. Harrison
Taylor, Martha Ann: John Smith
[57.582]
Curtis, Ann: Thomas Johnson
Curtis, Sophia: Thomas Johnson

Curtis, Thomas Franklin:
    Thomas Johnson
Jordan, Austin: Austin Ferguson
Jordan, Alexander: Austin Ferguson
Jordan, Caroline: Austin Ferguson
Jordan, Matilda: Austin Ferguson

[57.578]
Prince George Co. VA
Dillard, Lucretia: Maj. Ruffin
Robinson, Daniel: John P. Wilson
Robinson, Eliza: John P. Wilson
[57.581]
Lewis, Henry: Hudson Allen
Vaughn, Martha: Hudson Allen
[57.582]
Still, Eliza: James Temple
[57.583]
Hubbard, Lucy Ann: Mary Brountey
Scott, Albert: Mary Brountey
[57.584]
Eppes, Jim: John Eppes

[57.578]
Gloucester Co. VA
Christian, Allen: Austin Kemp
[57.580]
Rhone, Agnes: William Harbody
[57.582]
Cramp, Julia Ann: Col. Joseph Hayes
Green, Betty Ann: William White
Gates, Hester Jane: William White
Gates, Dotty: William White
Gates, Lewis: William White
Smith, Francis: William White
Thomas, James: Col. Joseph Hayes

[57.578]
King William Co. VA
Brown, Ellen: Dr. Boyd

Chesterfield Co. VA
Good, Maria: E.O. Watkins
[57.580]
Johnson, Allen: Free Born.
Johnson, Francis Ann: Free Born
Johnson, Leuender Octavia:
    Free Born
Johnson, Elizabeth Charity:
    Free Born
Johnson, Christopher: Free Born
Johnson, Martha Jane: Free Born
Johnson, Mary Eliza: Free Born
Johnson, James Austin: Free Born
Johnson, Sarah Eliza: Free Born

Nansemond Co. VA
Copeland, Andrew Jackson:
    Mills Cuder
Copeland, Hannah: Mills Cuder
Copeland, Jenny: Mills Cuder
Copeland, Joseph: Mills Cuder
Goodman, Mahala: John W. Parker
Holland, Eliza: Born Free
Holland, Elizabeth: Born Free
Holland, Peter: Born Free
Holland, Sally: Born Free
[57.581]
Franklin, Mary: J.N. Franklin
Smith, Awander: Jeptha Reddick
[57.583]
Copeland, Lewis: Jacob Dougherty
Copeland, Lucy: Jacob Dougherty
Copeland, Mary E: Free.
Copeland, Merider: Jacob
    Dougherty
Copeland, Sarah: Free
Copeland, William: Free
Copeland, Wright: Free.
Gath, Kitty: Josiah Murphy
Gath, Lucy: Josiah Murphy
Gath, Mary J: Josiah Murphy

Gunn, Cherry: A. Lancaster
Gunn, Hetty: A. Lancaster
Gunn, Jack: A. Lancaster
Savage, Mary: Jesse Savage
[57.584]
Cross, Alice: J.H. Holland
Cross, Judy: J.H. Holland
Johnson, Anne: Richard Reddick
Johnson, John T: Richard Reddick
Johnson, Joseph Henry:
    Richard Reddick
Johnson, Joseph: Richard Reddick
Johnson, Mary Catherine:
    Richard Reddick
Williams, Fanny: J.H. Holland
Williams: James: Josiah Murphy
[57.585]
Keetan, Phillis: John Keetan
King, Louisa: Sylvester Wright

[57.581]
Stafford Co. VA
Jones, Amanda: A. Wallace

Hanover Co. VA
Drew, Susan: William Wickham

[57.582]
Northampton Co. VA
Norfleet, Francis: F. Anderson
Norfleet, Alfred: F. Anderson
Norfleet, Martha: F. Anderson
Norfleet, Tom: F. Anderson
Norfleet, Matilda: F. Anderson

Nelson Co. VA
Smith, Nancy Ann: Fred Calrit

[57.583]
Louisa Co. VA
Bottey, George: Sam Talley

Bottey, Agnes: Sam Talley
Jackson, Eliza: William Ronds
Jones, Ann: Dr. B. Buckner
Jones, Anna: Dr. B. Buckner
Jones, Mary: Dr. B. Buckner
Jones, Henry: Dr. B. Buckner
Jones, Comoro: Dr. B. Buckner

[57.584]
Virginia Co. VA
Sykes, Eliza: Michael Sykes
Sykes, Laura: William Nelrum or Nelson

Middlesex Co. VA
Bauks, Polly: Lewis Jones

Goochland Co. VA
Boles, Caroline: J. Grooms

[57.585]
Henrico Co. VA
Peyton, Eliza: H. Kemp
Peyton, Ben: H. Kemp
Peyton, Walker: H. Kemp
Peyton, Clara: H. Kemp
Peyton, Mary Alice: H. Kemp
Matthews, Betsey: Simon Golding
Matthews, Dick: Simon Golding

[57.580]
Eastville, Eastern Shore, VA
Knight, Leah: Leroy Oldhern
Knight, Francis: Leroy Oldhern

[57.582]
White Stone, VA
Brigham, Charity: Major Custis
Brigham, Molly: Major Custis
Jackson, Ann: Major Custis
Young, Jane: Major Custis

[57.580]
Gates Co. NC
Ballard, Martha: Samuel Harold
Savage, Celia A: William Jones
Morris, Susan: Thomas Brady
[57.581]
Harold, Mary: William Jones
[57.584]
Lee, Manerva: Henry Lee
Lee, Tom: Henry Lee
Lee, Augustus: Henry Lee
[57.585]
Parker, Penelpe: H.D. Parker
Parker, Samuel: H.D. Parker
Lee, Malinda: Henry Lee

[57.581]
Whiteford, NC
Pinier, Priscilla: Alvin Reddick

[57.582]
Bertie Co. NC
Ercott, Elizabeth: James Ercott
Doles, Adeline: Widow Reddick

[57.585]
Currituck Co. NC
Bolt, Betsey: John Bright
Bolt, Mary Ann: John Bright

Bolt, Victoria: John Bright
Bolt, Hezekiah: John Bright

[57.584]
St. Mary's Co. MD
Sewall, Frank: T. Burrows
Cassell, Margaret: W.H. Locke
Crawley, Jane: Dr. J.I. Shaw
[57.585]
Marshall, Alice: Hezekiah Bean
Marshall, Mary Earnest:
    Hezekiah Bean
Hawkins, Eliza: Billy Thomas

Charles Co. MD
Slater, Sarah Ann: L. Webster
Slater, Lewis: L. Webster
Slater, Ann: L. Webster
Slater, Robert: L. Webster

[57.581]
Calvert Co. MD
Gladden, Sophia: John Penn
Spriggs, Eleanor: John Penn

DESTITUTE FREEDMEN AT YORKTOWN COMMISSARY, VA OCT. 16, 1865.

[57.586]
Banks, Frances
Banks, Sarah
Bright, Louisa
Bright, Mary
Bumel, Anna
Bumel, Rachel
Bumel, Susannah

Bunel, Emeline
Bunel, Joanna
Burnett, Polly
Butcher, Mary
Butcher, Nelly
Carey, Henry
Cary, Elizabeth
Churchill, Betsy

Churchill, Christopher
Cook, Kesiah
Cook, Keziah
Cook, Mary
Curtis, Betsey
Cur is, Eliza
Davis, Cherry
Diggs, Dianna

112

Gardner, Louisa	Stephens, Ann	Frazier, Catherine
Gibbs, Nancy	Stephens, Esther	Frazier, Mary Ann
Hand, Judah	Stokes, Malinda	Gardner, Clara
Harrison, Guy	Stubbs, Becca	Gardner, Lettie
Harrison, Henrietta	Stubbs, Lorenzo	Gardner, Sarah
Harrison, Jenny	Stubbs, Lucy	Gordon, Betsey
Harrison, William	Stubbs, Polly	Graham, Alice
Henry	Todd, Lavinia	Graham, John
Harrod, Catherine	Tolliver, Jane	Graham, Lucy
Hayes, Caroline	Tompkins, Hannah	Graham, Nancy
Hayes, Lucy Ann	Tompkins, Jenny	Hamad, Frank
Jackson, Rachael	Tompkins, Susan	Hamod, Amy
Jones, Susan	Totwell, Charles	Hamod, Henry
King, Becca	Totwell, Jesse	Hamod, Tappitora
King, Gabriella	Totwell, Sally	Hams, Lettie
Lewis, Mary	Totwell, Thomas	Harrad, Esther Jane
Liddleton, Kesiah	Turner, Betty	Hughs, Moses
Milsey, Oil	Turner, Samuel	Jones, Betsey
Montague: Peggy	Washington, Ellen	Jones, Margaret
Moore, Oliver	Washington, Grace	Jones, Richard
Pendleton, Dandridge	Washington, Henrietta	Lewis, Julia Ann
Penne, Mille	Washington, John	Morris, Chester
Penne, Venus	Washington, Sarah	Morris, Nancy
Pierce, Christead	Whiting, Ann	Page, Mary
Price: Lucy	Whiting, Ann	Pierce, Sarah Jane
Redman, Rebecca	Whiting, Maria	Randall, Joneta
Robinson, Dolly	Whiting, Thomas	Robertson, Rose Ann
Robinson, Edward	Williams, Betsey	Robinson, Israel
Robinson, Mahala	Wilson, Mary	Smith, Mary
Robinson, Matilda	Wormley, Mary	Smith, Moses
Roy, Pinkie	Wormley, Sally	Smith, Peggy
Scott, Ambrose	Young, Emily	Smith, Roberta
Scott, James	[57.587]	Sparks, George
Scott, Mary	Booth, Amy	Sparks, Martha
Scott, Winnie	Booth, Mary	Thurston, Joseph
Shields, Sally	Booth, Noah	Wise, General
Shields, William	Burnet, Coleman	Wital, Winnie
Singleton, Eliza	Cook, Henry	[57.588]
Singleton, Howard	Cook, Susan	Cook, Charlie
Singleton, Rachel	Diggs, Ann	Cook, Jenny
Spurlock, Charles	Fox, Martha	Gardner, Ceressy

Gardner, Mary	[57.589]	[57.589]
Henning, Rachael	Allen, James	Anderson, Lucy
Johnson, Margaret	Braxton, Jacob	Billups, Ann E
Johnson, Maria	Carter, Mary	Billups, Mary
Johnson, Polly	Cheens, Dolly	Billups, Sarah
Loomis, Abby	Field, Hannah	Callis, George
Loomis, Henrietta	Field, Mary	Callis, Kesiah
Loomis, Lucy	Field, William	Callis, Mary
Mason, Catherine	Fields, Albert	Cook, Lucy
Mason, Cyrus	Fields, Manj.	Cook, Mary E.
Mason, Peggy	Goldman, Maria	Dix, Julia Ann
Miegs, Alice	Graves, Mary Jane	Dix, Robert
Miegs, George	Graves, Nancy	Dix, Seymore
Reed, Nancy	Graves, Victoria	Hollins, Anna
Robins, Mary	Griffin, Henry	Hollins, George
Rowe, Matilda	Griffin, Maria	Hollins, Mary
Rowe, Warner	Hall, Indianna	Hollins, Richard
Scott, Eliza	Hughes, Martha	Hughes, Danny
Scott, Gregory	Jones, Jenny	Hughes, John
Scott, Jack	Montacue, Catherine	Jones, Harry
Stokes, Esther	Montacue, Zacharier	Jones, Sally
	Nealy, Hannah	Lee, Martha
New Kent Co. VA	Page, Susan	Lee, Winnie
Gaines, Dianna	Riley, Martha	Marsh, Hester
Gaines, Malinda	Robinson, Adelaide	Marsh, Vilet
Grantum, John	Scott, Robert	
Grantum, Margaret	Spencer, Betsey	**Mathews Co. VA**
Grantum, Moses	Spencer, Hannah	Miller, Jesse
Holmes, Alice	Spencer, Winnie	Miller, Octavia
Holmes, Charlotte	Thomas, Charlie	Moore, Pompey
Holmes, Hannah	Ward, Rebecca	Robinson, Betsey
Lee, Sally	Washington, James	Robinson, Catherine
Lee, Susan	Washington, Margaret	Robinson, Martha E.
Nash, Kesiah	Washington, Martha	Smith, Elsie
Nash, Nelson	Washington, Mary E.	Smith, Harry
Nash, Peggy	Whiting, James	Smith, Lucy
Spencer, Betsey	Whiting, Mary	Smith, Mary
Spencer, Dianna	Wilson, Senna	Smith, Milly
Spencer, Elizabeth	Wood, Samuel	Smith, Rebecca
Stokes, Abe L.		Smith, Terra
Washington, Eliza		Tabb, Emily

Warner, Silva
Washington, Sarah
Washington, Walter
White, Cerra
Williams, Jesse

[57.589]
King & Queen Co. VA
Brookins, James
Field, Hezekiah
Field, Nancy
Guerson, John
Guerson, Mahala
Hawkins, Mary
Johnson, Vilet
Kidd, Louisa
Kidd, William H

Muse, Louisa
Muse, Sarah Jane
Ricks, Jennie
Russell, Frances
Thornton, Peggy
Thornton, Polly
Walker, Mary Jane
Walker, Milly
Walker, Sarah
Webb, Molly
Wormley, Mary
Wormley, Mary Jane

[57.590]
Warwick Co. VA
Winn, Mat
Lee, Lucy
Winn, Peggy

King William Co. VA
Hamilton, Julia
Dabney, Caroline
Dabney, Richard
Braxton, Lucy Ann
Lightfoot, Elizabeth
Redman, Betty
West, Letty
Cook, Charles
Wormley, Peter
Lee, Silas
Lee, Cyrus Lee
Phillips, William
Phillips, Hetty
Birdewell, Pine
Monroe, Isabella
Brooker, Walter
Harris, James T.

FORMER SLAVE OWNERS LISTED
WITH THEIR FREED SLAVES

{NOTE: Part II is not part of the original microfilmed record of Reel 57. All of the slaves which appeared in the previous lists with the names of their former masters have been re-arranged in this section to enable the researcher to find individuals using the record of the former owner. The format used in this sections lists the former masters (names in bold-face) with their place of residence. The freedmen are listed under their current (post-war) residence. It is assumed that the freedmen's pre-war residence was the same as their former master.}

[57.556]
Acket, James:
Southampton Co. VA
At Fort Monroe, VA:
Simonds, Samuel
Simonds, Ann

[57.475]
Adams, John:
Fluvanna Co. VA
At Fluvanna Co. VA:
Randolph, Temphy:
Old age

[57.556]
Adams, John:
Isle of Wight Co. VA
At Fort Monroe, VA:
Graindier, India
Graindier, John

115

[57.548]
Adams, William:
York Co. VA
At Fort Monroe, VA:
Milborn, Lalie
Milborn, David
Milborn, Francis

[57.581]
Allen, Hudson:
Prince George Co. VA
At Downey Farm, VA:
Vaughn, Martha
Lewis, Henry

[57.557]
Allen, John:
Fredericksburg VA
At Fort Monroe, VA:
Maisen, Lydia
Maisen, James
Maisen, Georgeana
Maisen, Lydia
Maisen, Mary
Maisen, Kesiah
Maisen, Manuel

Allen, William: (Maj.)
Henrico Co. VA
At Fort Monroe, VA:
[57.507]
Blunt, Mariah
[57.517]
Hubbard, George
Hubbard, Mary
Hubbard, George
[57.523]
Clayman, Louisa

[57.536]
Barden, Polly
[57.546]
Ruffin, Nelly
[57.547]
Jeffers, Henry
Jeffers, Cane
[57.549]
Williams, Betsey
Williams, Susan
Williams, Katy
Williams, Betsy
[57.551]
Bardon, Polly
Bardon, Randall
Bardon, Edwin
Bardon, Mary
Bardon, Robert
Bardon, Marthy
Comer, Nelly
Comer, Andrew
[57.552]
Harris, Lizzie
Harris, Laura
Harris, Chaney
Williams, Livinia
Williams, James
Williams, Rosetta
Williams, Elp
White, Molly
White, Jacob
[57.556]
Freeland, Fanny
Clary, Beckey
[57.559]
Derriga, Nancy
Derriga, William
[57.563]
Jones, Sarah
Jones, Andrew

Jones, Sarah
Jones, Lavina
Jones, Miles
[57.567]
White, Susan
White, Alie
White, Pheby
White, Lawrence
[57.570]
Goodman, Hannah
Goodman, Betsy
Goodman, Minnie
[57.572]
Jones, Nancy

[57.573]
Allen, William:
Surry County, VA
At Fort Monroe, VA:
Jones, Fanny
Jones, James
Jones, Benjamin

[57.541]
Allen, Williamson:
Henrico Co. VA
At Fort Monroe, VA:
Garo, Robert

[57.470]
Alum?, A.A.D:
Greene Co. VA
At Fredericksburg, VA
Unknown, Beauty:
Unknown, Benjamin:
    Child
Unknown, Lee: Child
Unknown, Josephine:
    Child
Unknown, Lewis: Child

116

[57.502]
Ambler, John:
Amherst Co. VA
At Lynchburg Hospital,
Amherst Co. VA:
Ambler, Frances: 23

[57.529]
Anams?:
Northampton Co. VA
At Fort Monroe, VA:
Andrews, Millie

[57.582]
Anderson, F:
Northampton Co. VA
At Downey Farm,
Princess Anne Co. VA:
Norfleet, Francis
Norfleet, Alfred
Norfleet, Martha
Norfleet, Tom
Norfleet, Matilda

[57.538]
Anderson, George:
Isle of Wight Co. VA
At Ft. Monroe, VA
Folger, Jane
Folger, Peter

[57.500]
Anderson, J.W:
Campbell Co. VA
At Lynchburg Hospital,
Amherst Co. VA:
Anderson, Lucy: 90

[57.501]
Anderson, L:
Appomattox Co. VA
At Lynchburg Hospital,
Amherst Co. VA:
Anderson, Mary: 18

[57.476]
Anderson, Thomas:
Spotsylvania Co. VA
At Fredericksburg, VA:
Cook, Montgomery
Martin, Lucy
King, Charles
Henry, Catharine

[57.481]
Carter Agnes
Carter, Martha

[57.566]
Andrews, George W:
Surry Co. VA
At Fort Monroe, VA:
Daniel, Robert

[57.473]
Appleberry, D.J:
Fluvanna Co. VA
At Fluvanna Co. VA:
Unknown, Mary:
Old Age

[57.471]
Appleberry, William:
Fluvanna Co. VA
At Fluvanna Co. VA:
Greasy, M: Infirm
Jackson, John: Old Age

[57.577]
Armistead, Robert:
Williamsburg, VA
At Downey Farm,
Princess Anne Co. VA:
Washington, Lewis

[57.535]
Armstead, Francis:
Mathews Co. VA
At Fort Monroe, VA:
Collins, Grace
Collins, Harriett
Collins, William
Collins, Jessy

[57.550]
Armstead, Frank:
Mathews Co. VA
At Fort Monroe, VA:
Buckner, Hannah

[57.533]
Armstead, John:
Mathews Co. VA
At Fort Monroe, VA:
Billup, Patsey

[57.533]
Armstead, Weston:
Elizabeth City Co. VA
At Fort Monroe, VA:
Armstead, Lockey

[57.509]
Armstead, William:
Williamsburg, VA
At Fort Monroe, VA:
Washington, Eliza

[57.551]
Askey, John:
Bertie Co. NC
At Fort Monroe, VA:
Askey, Margaret
Askey, Johanna
Askey, Thomas
Askey, Calvin
Askey, Betsey
Askey, Chancy
Askey, Henry
Askey, Toney
Askey, Margaret
Askey, Martha
[57.570]
Askey, Adaline
Askey, William

[57.553]
Atkins, Archie:
Isle of Wight. Co. VA
At Fort Monroe, VA:
Thomas, Polly

[57.584]
Atkins, J: (Dr.):
Isle of Wight Co. VA
At Downey Farm,
Princess Anne Co. VA:
Holman, Dianna
Holman, Charlotte

[57.553]
Atkinson, H.:
Isle of Wight Co. VA
At Fort Monroe, VA:
Carey, Mary A.
Carey, Isaac
Carey, Lizzie
Carey, Mary

[57.502]
Atkinson, William:
Sampson Co. NC
At Lynchburg Hospital,
Amherst Co. VA:
Jackson, Thomas: 32

[57.526]
Augurn, Martha:
Charles City Co. VA
At Fort Monroe, VA:
Cooper, Mary
Cooper, Martha
Cooper, Mary
Cooper, Thomas
Bailey, Diana

[57.578]
Bacon, George:
James City Co. VA
At Downey Farm, VA:
Randall, Eliza

[57.532]
Badden, Daniel:
Isle of Wight Co. VA
At Fort Monroe, VA:
Syner, Ann
Syner, Lewis
Syner, Margaret

[57.532]
Bailey, Richard:
Charles City Co. VA
At Fort Monroe, VA:
Jackson, Hannah

Bailey, Richard:
Essex Co. VA
At Fort Monroe, VA:
[57.516]
Dennis, Ellen
Dennis, Simond
Dennis, Joshua
[57.517]
Garnett, Mary J.
Garnett, Tanny

[57.557]
Bailey, Richard:
Fredericksburg VA
At Fort Monroe, VA:
Gatter, Nellie
Gatter, William
Gatter, Nellie
Gatter, Anthony
Gatter, Mary

[57.509]
Baker, William:
Hanover Co. VA
At Fort Monroe, VA:
Donel, Jessie

[57.532]
Ballard, Augustus:
Isle of Wight Co. VA
At Fort Monroe, VA:
Holland, Margaret

[57.510]
Barley, Jessie:
Nansemond Co. VA
At Fort Monroe, VA:
Parker, Ann

[57.509]
Barley, Richard:
Charles City Co. VA
At Fort Monroe, VA:
Washington, Susan

[57.515]
Barn, Theodore:
Essex Co. VA
At Fort Monroe, VA:
Rice, Martha
Rice, William
Rice, George
Rice, Robert
Rice, Sarah

[57.530]
Barrow, Nancy:
Surry Co. VA
At Fort Monroe, VA:
Parker, Ned: (Patsy's husband)
Parker, Patsy:(Ned's wife)

[57.474]
Baseby, R.:
Fluvanna Co. VA
At Fluvanna Co. VA:
Unknown, Hannah: Old age

[57.472]
Bashaw, T.F:
Fluvanna Co. VA
At Fluvanna Co. VA:
Johnson, Polly: Infirm

[57.475]
Basket, H.:
Fluvanna Co. VA
Unknown, Roxy: Old age

[57.475]
Basket, Henry:
Fluvanna Co. VA
Fluvanna Co. VA
Friday, Richard: Infirm

[57.514]
Bates, George:
Elizabeth City Co. VA
At Fort Monroe, VA:
Benjamin, James

[57.472]
Bates, John:
Fluvanna Co. VA
At Fluvanna Co. VA:
Bates, Lindsay: Infirm

[57.564]
Baylor, Richard:
Essex Co. VA
At Fort Monroe, VA:
Bush, Mariah
Bush, Pidgeon
Bush, Angella

[57.585]
Bean, Hezekiah:
St. Mary's Co. MD
At Downey Farm, VA:
Marshall, Alice
Marshall, Mary Earnest

[57.522]
Beans, John:
Elizabeth City Co. VA
At Fort Monroe, VA:
Billups, Julia A.

[57.557]
Bearch, Peater:
Prince George Co. VA
At Fort Monroe, VA:
Jones, Nelly

[57.477]
Bedford, John:
Caroline Co. VA
At Fredericksburg, VA
Shepherd, James

[57.504]
Beesey, C.:
Bedford Co. VA
At Hospital At Liberty, Bedford Co. VA:
Unknown, Henry: 25

[57.551]
Bell, Alexander
Norfolk VA
At Fort Monroe, VA:
Brown, Benjamin: Husband of Julia
Brown, Julia: Wife of Benjamin

[57.564]
Bell, James:
Back Water,
Elizabeth City Co. VA
At Fort Monroe, VA:
Bell, Lucy
Bell, John
Bell, William

[57.575]
Benisonk, John:
Portsmouth, VA
At Fort Monroe, VA:
Henderson, Millie
Henderson, Matilda
Henderson, Louisa
Henderson, Willis

[57.480]
Bently, John:
Essex Co. VA
At Fredericksburg, VA:
Lewis, Samuel

[57.543]
Billups, Robert:
Mathews Co. VA
At Fort Monroe, VA:
Carter, Polly
Carter, Sarah
Carter, Rebecca
Carter, Dick
Carter, Lucy
Carter, Ned

[57.514]
Billups, Susan:
Mathews Co. VA
At Fort Monroe, VA:

Armstead, Caroline
Armstead, Albert
Armstead, John
Armstead, Lucy

[57.562]
Bird, Dr:
Gloucester Co. VA
At Fort Monroe, VA:
Hews, Sally
Hews, Hews
Hews, John
Hews, William
Hews, Lizzie
Hews, Thomas

[57.502]
Bird, Henry:
Rockingham Co. VA
At Lynchburg Hospital,
Amherst Co. VA:
Scott, William: 23

[57.478]
Birds, Richard:
Caroline Co. VA
At Fredericksburg, VA:
Johnson, William
Johnson, Caroline
Johnson, Sarah

[57.571]
Bishoff, William:
Sussex Co. VA
At Fort Monroe, VA:
Wilkins, Mariah
Wilkins, Sandy

[57.576]
Bisker, Walter:
St. Mary's Co. MD
At Fort Monroe, VA:
Bennett, Eliza
Bennett, Rosa
Bennett, John

[57.475]
Black, William:
Fluvanna Co. VA
At Fluvanna Co. VA:
Ritchie, E: Old age

[57.535]
Blackman, Oscar:
Cumberland Co. VA
At Fort Monroe, VA:
Clark, Eliza
Clark, Eli

[57.542]
Blake, Benjamin:
King William Co. VA
At Fort Monroe, VA:
Turner, Sally
Turner, Dira
Turner, Nelsen
Turner, Steward

[57.546]
Turner, Sally
Turner, Phil
Turner, Dora
Turner, Stewart

[57.542]
Blake, James:
Mathews Co. VA
At Fort Monroe, VA:
Thomas, Lizzie
Thomas, Sarah
Thomas, Mary

[57.469]
Blakeley, E.:
Green Co. VA
At Fredericksburg, VA:
Unknown, Betsey: Child
Unknown, Hannah: Child
Unknown, John: Child
Unknown, Maria: Child

[57.470]
Blakey, Jane:
Green Co. VA
At Fredericksburg, VA
Slaughter, Madison: child
Slaughter, Betty
Slaughter, Marcus: Child
Slaughter, Angus: Child
Boras, Ro.: Child
Boras, John: Child
Boras, William
Slaughter, Charlotte

[57.555]
Bland, George: Prince George Co. VA
At Fort Monroe, VA:
Sweet, Margaret

[57.507]
Bland, Randall: (Maj.)
King & Queen Co. VA
At Fort Monroe, VA:
Chapman, Ann E.
Chapman, John

[57.515]
Hill, Catharine
[57.519]
Dickerson, Sarah
Dickerson, Eliza
Dickerson, Milly
Dickerson, Patsy

[57.550]
Bland, Reddick:
King & Queen Co. VA
At Fort Monroe, VA:
Robinson, Pheby
Robinson, Francis Ann
Robinson, Taura

[57.550]
Bland, Robert:
King & Queen Co. VA
At Fort Monroe, VA:
Toliver, Lucy
[57.566]
Graves, Mary
Toliver, Catharine
Toliver, Sarah

[57.509]
Bland, Rodrick:
King and Queen Co. VA
At Fort Monroe, VA:
Green, Francis

[57.528]
Bland, Rodward:
King & Queen Co. VA
At Fort Monroe, VA:
Cary, Rachael
Cary, John
Cary, Peter

[57.518]
Blare, John:
Prince George Co. VA
At Fort Monroe, VA:
Washington, Patsy

Washington, James
Washington, Sarah
Washington, Henry

[57.473]
Bleasan, A:
Fluvanna Co. VA
At Fluvanna Co. VA:
Unknown, Daniel:
Old Age
Unknown, Martha:
Old Age

[57.553]
Blend, John: Edenton, NC
At Fort Monroe, VA:
Blend, Harnett
Blend, Henry

[57.510]
Blunt, Thomas:
Sussex Co. VA
At Fort Monroe, VA:
Angrum, Eveline
Angrum, Rose
Angrum, Frank
Angrum, Henrietta
Masonberge, Polly
Masonberge, Eliza

[57.504]
Boardwright, Harvey:
Bedford Co. VA
At Bedford Co. VA
Boardwright, Robert: 30

[57.480]
Bogs, Lewis:
Stafford Co. VA
At Fredericksburg, VA:
Willis, Amelia

[57.562]
Bohanan, William:
Mathews Co. VA
At Fort Monroe, VA:
Lichfield, Fanny
Lichfield, Washington
Lichfield, John
Lichfield, Sarah

[57.505]
Bolt, H:
Bedford Co. VA
At Hospital Liberty,
Bedford Co. VA:
Unknown, America: 26
Unknown, Texanna: 1

[57.505]
Bond, Fanny:
Bedford Co. VA
At Hospital, Liberty,
Bedford Co. VA:
Unknown, Mary: 30
Unknown, Blucher: 2

[57.577]
Booker, A:
Elizabeth City Co. VA
At Downey Farm, VA:
Carey, Fanny
Carey, Maria
Carey, Sally

[57.570]
Booker, George:
Elizabeth City Co. VA
At Fort Monroe, VA:
Wallace, William

[57.527]
Booker, Richard:
Elizabeth City Co. VA
At Fort Monroe, VA:
Williams, Jane

[57.512]
Booker, Virginia:
Elizabeth City Co. VA
At Fort Monroe, VA:
Williams, Samuel

[57.476]
Boston, Dr:
Caroline Co. VA
At Fredericksburg, VA:
Stafford, Emanuel
Thomas, Delia
Stephens, Caroline
Stephens, Charoltte

[57.474]
Boston, F.C:
Fluvanna Co. VA
At Fluvanna Co. VA:
Boston, Charles:
Old age

Bower, Henry:
Fluvanna Co. VA
At Fluvanna Co. VA:
James, Rachel: Old age

[57.579]
Boyd, Dr: King
William Co. VA
At Downey Farm, VA:
Brown, Ellen

[57.509]
Boyden, A: (Dr.)
Smithfield Co. VA
At Fort Monroe, VA:
Jerdan, Margaret
Jerdan, George
Jerdan, Robert

[57.525]
Boykin, Dr:
Isle of Wight Co. VA
At Fort Monroe, VA:
Wilson, Millie
Jubilee, Sally
Jubilee, Benjamin

[57.511]
Boykin, John
Cherry Gutt, NC
At Fort Monroe, VA:
Brown, Matilda
Brown, John
Brown, Sarah
Brown, Henrietta
Brown, Peter

[57.555]
Boynton, Frank:
Isle of Wight Co. VA
At Fort Monroe, VA:
Jones, Ester
Jones, Byren
Jones, Jeff Davis
Jones, Walter

[57.580]
Brady, Thomas:
Gates Co. NC
At Downey Farm, VA:
Morris, Susan

[57.478]
Braid, Benjamin:
Essex Co. VA
At Fredericksburg, VA:
Tammy, Catharine
Samuel, Mary
Samuel, Abbey

[57.522]
Braks, William:
Mathews Co. VA
At Fort Monroe, VA:
Thomas, Susan
Thomas, Robert
Thomas, James

[57.472]
Branch, A: (Dr.)
Fluvanna Co. VA:
At Fluvanna Co. VA
Jones, William: Infirm
Johnson, Rose: Infirm
Miller, Katy: Infirm
Archer, Polly: Infirm

[57.468]
Brau[?]d, N.
Green Co. VA
At Fredericksburg, VA
Unknown, Gilbert: Child
Unknown, Thomas: Child

[57.471]
Briggs, Watson:
Fluvanna Co. VA
At Fluvanna Co. VA:
James, Daniel: Deranged

[57.585]
Bright, John:
Currituck Co. NC
At Downey Farm, VA:
Bolt, Betsey
Bolt, Mary Ann
Bolt, Victoria
Bolt, Hezekiah

[57.511]
Brighten, Ann:
Prince George Co. VA
At Fort Monroe, VA:
Lansin, Jessie
Lansin, Viene

[57.517]
Brokenberry, William:
Hanover Co. VA
At Fort Monroe, VA:
Griswell, Cecilia
Griswell, Mary
Griswell, Armstead

[57.569]
Brokenburg, Austin:
Essex Co. VA
At Fort Monroe, VA:
Fenton, Lucy A.

[57.560]
Bromley, Marshall:
Mathews Co. VA
At Fort Monroe, VA:
Brombley, Lucy

[57.480]
Brook, Jane:
Bowling Green, VA
At Fredericksburg, VA:
Harris, Hannah

[57.479]
Brooks, George:
Caroline Co. VA
At Fredericksburg, VA:
Coleman, Alice

Brooks, George:
Mathews Co. VA
At Fredericksburg, VA:
Brooks, Ann

[57.583]
Brountey, Mary:
Prince George Co. VA
At Downey Farm, VA:
Hubbard, Lucy Ann
Scott, Albert

[57.521]
Brown, Andrew:
Mathews Co. VA
At Fort Monroe, VA:
Hill, Nanny
Hill, William
Hill, Benjamin
Hill, Maltimor
Hill, Rolsy
Hill, Catharine

[57.515]
Brown, Christian J:
Mathews Co. VA
At Fort Monroe, VA:
Brown, Christian
Brown, Mary
[57.535]
James, Peter

[57.541]
Cooks, Nancy
Cooks, Mary
Cooks, Margaret
Cooks, Catharine

[57.517]
Brown, John:
Elizabeth City Co. VA
At Fort Monroe, VA:
Jasper, Phillips
Jasper, Adolphus

[57.473]
Bruce, Joseph:
Fluvanna Co. VA
At Fluvanna Co. VA:
Sauger, Lucy:
   Old Age
Saugon, W. Jane:
   Rheumatism

[57.472]
Bruce, William C:
Fluvanna Co. VA
At Fluvanna Co. VA:
Bruce, Rachel: Infirm

Bryan, John R.:
Fluvanna Co. VA
At Fluvanna Co. VA:
Gray, Dick: Invalid
Gray, Clara: Invalid
[57.474]
Texon, James: Infirm
Unknown, Winchester:
   Infirm

[57.480]
Bryan, Paul:
Spotsylvania Co. VA
At Fredericksburg, VA:
Johnson, Lucy

[57.471]
Bryan, William:
Fluvanna Co. VA
At Fluvanna Co. VA:
Morton, Jane: Infirm

[57.474]
Bryant, D.D:
Fluvanna Co. VA
At Fluvanna Co. VA:
Unknown, Maria: Old age
Bryant, Fanny
Bryant, John R.

[57.560]
Bryant, William:
New Bern, NC
At Fort Monroe, VA:
Bryant, Lucy
Bryant, Martha
Bryant, James

[57.519]
Bucket, William:
Eastern Shore, VA
At Fort Monroe, VA:
Johnson, Martha

[57.583]
Buckner, B: (Dr.)
Louisa Co. VA
At Downey Farm, VA:
Jones, Ann
Jones, Anna
Jones, Mary
Jones, Henry
Jones, Comoro

[57.519]
Bullock, Granville:
Louisa Co. VA
At Fort Monroe, VA:
Jones, Susan
Jones, Lucy
Jones, Martha
Jones, Overton
[57.549]
Bullock, Clara
Bullock, John
Bullock, Mary
[57.547]
Garrett, Sarah A.
Garrett, Thomas
Garrett, Eliza
[57.558]
Robinson, Esther

[57.526]
Bunkley, Edwin:
Smithfield Co. VA
At Fort Monroe, VA:
Andrews, Lucy

[57.563]
Burk, John:
Mathews Co. VA
At Fort Monroe, VA:
Litchfield, Armstead
Litchfield, Polly

[57.529]
Burkley, John:
Smithfield Co. VA
At Fort Monroe, VA:
Gross, Chasey

[57.578]
Burnham, William:
Warwick Co. VA
At Downey Farm, VA:
Washington, Lucy
Jones, William

[57.575]
Burr, Henry:
Nansemond Co. VA
At Fort Monroe, VA:
Wilson, Martha
Wilson, Abram

[57.584]
Burrows, T:
St. Mary's Co. MD
At Downey Farm, VA:
Sewall, Frank

[57.502]
Byers, Frank:
Washington Co. TN
At Lynchburg Hospital, Amherst Co. VA:
Byers, Jane: 21

[57.565]
Byron, William:
Huntville, NC
At Fort Monroe, VA:
Simonds, Margaret
Simonds, Henry

[57.473]
Caden, William:
Fluvanna Co. VA:
At Fluvanna Co. VA:
Banks, Isabella: Old

[57.501]
Calebee, James:
Bedford Co. VA:
At Lynchburg Hospital, Amherst Co. VA:
Calebee, Queen: 42

[57.582]
Calrit, Fred:
Nelson Co. VA
At Downey Farm, VA:
Smith, Nancy Ann

[57.477]
Cameron, Francis:
Caroline Co. VA
At Fredericksburg, VA:
Johnson, Wenna

[57.500]
Camp, Robert:
Amherst Co. VA
At Lynchburg Hospital, Amherst Co. VA:
Camp, Nancy: 45

Campbell, Samuel:
Nelson Co. VA
At Lynchburg Hospital, Amherst Co. VA:
Campbell, James: 80

[57.477]
Campbell, Thomas:
King George Co. VA
At Fredericksburg, VA:
Brown, Mary

[57.515]
Carey, Dr.:
Gloucester Co. VA
At Fort Monroe, VA:
Williams, Frank

[57.559]
Carey, John:
Elizabeth City Co. VA
At Fort Monroe, VA:
Patrick, Frank

[57.533]
Carrington, Thomas:
James City Co. VA
At Fort Monroe, VA:
Bryant, Fanny

[57.516]
Carrol, Henry:
St. Mary Co. MD
At Fort Monroe, VA:
Riley, Seleshie
Riley, James

[57.577]
Carter, Dr.:
Warwick Co. VA
At Downey Farm, VA:
Corben, Mary

[57.515]
Carter, Hill:
Charles City Co. VA
At Fort Monroe, VA:
Pride, Sarah
Christian, Julia A.
[57.519]
Christian, Sarah
Pride, Anthony

[57.536]
Christian, Julia
[57.543]
Christian, Joseph
Christian, Annie
Washington, Jane
[57.545]
Howard, Behannob
[57.552]
Howard, Virginia
Terrall, Elliza
[57.561]
Washington, Liddy
Jackson, Mary
[57.568]
Terrall, William
Morris, Betsey
Morris, Phillis
Morris, Lillie
Morris, Elijah
[57.574]
Jackson, Almina
Jackson, Jennie
Jackson, William
Jackson, Hill
Jackson, Amosan

[57.551]
Carter, Mrs.:
Charles City Co. VA
At t Fort Monroe, VA
Cooper, Mary
Cooper, Mary
Cooper, Louisa
Cooper, Betsey

[57.473]
Cary, R.M:
Fluvanna Co. VA
At Fluvanna Co. VA:
Randall, Biddie: Old age

[57.508]
Casey, William:
Isle of Wight Co. VA
At Fort Monroe, VA:
Andrews, Ann
Andrews, Rachael
Andrews, Thomas
Andrews, Soloman
Andrews, Martha
[57.543]
Billups, Fannie
Billups, Betsy
Billups, Ned
[57.560]
Davis, Mary
Davis, Ann

[57.479]
Chanclor, Thomas:
Caroline Co. VA
At Fredericksburg, VA:
Pendleton, Harriet
Pendleton, Beverly
Pendleton, Rose
Pendleton, Dudley
Pendleton, Fanny

[57.479]
Chapman, Fletcher: (Mrs.)
Isle of Wight Co. VA
At Fredericksburg, VA:
Chapman, Emma

[57.579]
Chauncy, Cary:
Charles City Co. VA
At Downey Farm, VA:
Clark, Rosetta
Clark, Robert

[57.527]
Cheesman, Samuel:
Elizabeth City Co. VA
At Fort Monroe, VA:
Davis, Sarah
Davis, Jane
Davis, Billy

[57.520]
Christian, Bat:
New Kent Co. VA
At Fort Monroe, VA:
Christian, Rosetta
Christian, Rosa
Christian, Jane

[57.526]
Christian, Benjamin:
Charles City Co. VA
At Fort Monroe, VA:
Braxtin, Fannie
Braxtin, Charlotte
Braxtin, Robert

[57.575]
Christian, David:
Gates Co. NC
At Fort Monroe, VA:
Christian, Mary
Christian, Mack
Christian, Francis

[57.578]
Christian, R.:
Charles City Co. VA
At Downey Farm, VA:
Allen, Betsy
Allen, Jesse

[57.540]
Christian, William C:
New Kent Co. VA
At Fort Monroe, VA:
Granton, Margaret
Granton, Fanny

[57.529]
Clark, Glotcher:
Gloucester Co. VA
At Fort Monroe, VA:
Gardnor, Mary
Gardnor, Sarah
Gardnor, Lettie
Gardnor, Lizzie

[57.475]
Clark, John W:
Fluvanna Co. VA
At Fluvanna Co. VA:
Key, Agnes: Old age

[57.507]
Clark, Mr:
Gloucester Co. VA
At Fort Monroe, VA:
Brooks, Ann

[57.473]
Clark, T.J:
Fluvanna Co. VA
At Fluvanna Co. VA:
Ware, Peter: Old age
Ware, Henry: Old age

[57.503]
Clarkson, Nelson:
Nelson Co. VA
At Lovington,
Nelson Co. VA:
Clarkson, Elv: 39

[57.501]
Clay, O.G:
Bedford Co. VA
At Lynchburg Hospital,
Amherst Co. VA:
Francis, Fanny: 30

[57.539]
Clayburn, John D:
(Maj.)
Williamsburg, VA
At Fort Monroe, VA:
Williams, Lina
Williams, Carter
Williams, John

[57.525]
Clayton, Jasper:
Surry Co. VA
At Fort Monroe, VA:
Moore, Betsey

[57.544]
Clement, Mr:
King William Co. VA
At Fort Monroe, VA:
Williams, Polly
Williams, Margaret
Williams, Elisha

[57.545]
Clements, Ira:
King William Co. VA
At Fort Monroe, VA:
Tompson, Eliza

[57.513]
Clemont, Judge:
King William Co. VA
At Fort Monroe, VA:
Holmes, Millie Ann

[57.566]
Clemonts, Phero:
Surry Co. VA
At Fort Monroe, VA:
Williams, Sarah A.
Williams, Bergy
Tolver, Lucy
Tolver, George
Tolver, Caroline

[57.558]
Cleyborn, J.D.:
York Co. VA
At Fort Monroe, VA:
Willams, Hellena
Willams, Carter
Willams, John
Willams, Fanny
Willams, Elec

[57.472]
Cock, John C:
Fluvanna Co. VA
At Fluvanna Co. VA:
Unknown, Robin:
Invalid

[57.473]
Cocks, Cary C:
Fluvanna Co. VA
At Fluvanna Co. VA:
Unknown, Nanny: Blind

[57.475]
Cocks, John W:
Fluvanna Co. VA
At Fluvanna Co. VA:
Decaton, C: Old age

[57.550]
Coe, Thomas:
King & Queen Co. VA
At Fort Monroe, VA:
Washington, Milly
Washington, Randall
Washington, Hellena

[57.525]
Cole, William:
Surry Co. VA
Thomas, Martha
Thomas, James
Thomas, Anderson

[57.563]
Colton, Henry:
King William Co. VA
At Fort Monroe, VA:
Nelson, Susan
Nelson, Manuel
Nelson, Kitty

[57.504]
Comer, William:
Bedford Co. VA
At Liberty Hospital,
Bedford Co. VA:
Comer, Emeline: 30
Comer, Thomas: 1

[57.565]
Conter, Charles:
Prince George Co. VA
At Fort Monroe, VA:
John, Sally

[57.470]
Conway, C:
Green Co. VA
At Fredericksburg, VA:
Unknown, Lewis: Male

[57.582]
Cooper, Fred:
Isle of Wight Co. VA
At Downey Farm, VA:
Brigham, Bina
Bowder, Nancy

[57.509]
Cooper, Henry:
Suffolk Co. VA
At Fort Monroe, VA:
Brewer, Hannah

[57.537]
Copeland, John:
Suffolk Co. VA
At Fort Monroe, VA:
Pierce, Martha

[57.560]
King, Mary J.

[57.558]
Cord, William:
St. Mary's Co. MD
At Fort Monroe, VA:
Brown, Ann
Brown, William

[57.510]
Cotten, John:
Sussex Co. VA
At Fort Monroe, VA:
Taylor, Michael A.
Taylor, Jacob
Taylor, Thomas
Taylor, John
Taylor, Mary
Taylor, Catharine

[57.535]
Covington, Thomas:
Charles City Co. VA
At Fort Monroe, VA:
Armstead, Eliza

[57.572]
Cox, Edward:
Henrico Co. VA
At Fort Monroe, VA:
Smith, Nancy

[57.547]
Cox, Harrison:
Prince George Co. VA
At Fort Monroe, VA:
[57.555]
Monk, Peggy
[57.568]
Ruffin, Maria
Marks, Sarah
Moody, Lucy
Moody, Nancy
King, Fanny
King, Sarah
King, George
King, Jennie
King, Ester
Young, Molly
Young, Edith
Young, Martha
Young, John
Young, Sarah

[57.580]
Cox, Henry:
York Co. VA
At Downey Farm, VA:
Thomas, Alice Adelier
Thomas, John

[57.544]
Cox, James B: Prince George Co. VA
At Fort Monroe, VA:
Morrison, Millie
Morrison, Soloman
[57.545]
Morrison, Caroline
Morrison, Mariah
Morrison, Bonton
[57.547]
Harvey, Hannah
Harvey, Lucinda
Harvey, Polly
[57.548]
Bolin, Nancy
Bolin, Andrew
[57.568]
Moore, Mariah
Moore, Boylan
Moore, Soloman
Moore, Miller
Moore, Caroline

[57.525]
Cox, Jefferson:
Richmond Co. VA
At Fort Monroe, VA:
Marshall, Robert:
Husband of Patsey
Marshall, Patsey:
  Wife of Robert

[57.543]

Cox, Virginia:
King William Co. VA
At Fort Monroe, VA:
Collins, Emeline
Collins, Charles
Collins, Rody

[57.519]
Craig, Charles:
Wilmington, NC
At Fort Monroe, VA:
Quince, Peggy
Quince, Lewis

[57.555]
Crandall, Thomas:
Elizabeth City Co. VA
At Fort Monroe, VA:
Hare, Francis

[57.579]
Crawken, Carey:
York Co. VA
At Downey Farm, VA:
Brown, Callifer
Brown, Rachell

[57.501]
Crea, Stephen:
Bedford Co. VA
At Lynchburg Hospital, Amherst Co. VA:
Crea, Smith: 23

[57.505]
Creesey, Thomas:
Bedford Co. VA
At Liberty Hospital
Bedford Co. VA:
Unknown, Willie: 21

[57.549]
Crenshaw, Agness:
Charles City Co. VA
At Fort Monroe, VA:
Robinson, Patsy
Robinson, William
Robinson, Joseph
Robinson, Archie

[57.505]
Crenshaw, Baldy:
Bedford Co. VA
At Liberty Hospital,
Bedford Co. VA:
Unknown, Eliza: 13
Unknown, Eliza: 25

[57.565]
Crocker, James:
Whiteford, NC
At Fort Monroe, VA:
Crocker, Lucy
Crocker, Lemin

[57.534]
Crocker, John:
St. Marys Co. MD
At Fort Monroe, VA:
Quintaine, Charles

[57.570]
Crockett, W:
York Co. VA
At Fort Monroe, VA:
Harmen, Richard
Harmen, Jacob
Harmen, George
Harmen, Charles
Harmen, Edward

[57.532]
Crockett, Wilet:
York Co. VA
At Fort Monroe, VA:
Bangs, Jerry

[57.524]
Crockston, Richard:
Essex Co. VA
At Fort Monroe, VA:
Loyd, Kitty

[57.481]
Cronin, James:
Caroline Co. Va.
At Fredericksburg, VA:
Ewing, Jane
Thompson, Sidney

[57.520]
Cross, William:
Gates Co. NC
At Fort Monroe, VA:
Cross, Sallie
Cross, John
Cross, Sally
Cross, Quinton
Cross, Dolphin

[57.501]
Crow, Thomas H:
Clarke Co. VA
At Lynchburg Hospital,
Amherst Co. VA:
Washington, Sally: 23

[57.554]
Crump, Harrison:
New Kent Co. VA
At Fort Monroe, VA:
Bolding, Caroline

[57.565]
Crump, John:
Pamunkey Co. VA
At Fort Monroe, VA:
Dandridge, Lavenia

[57.577]
Crump, Leonard: Dr.
New Kent Co. VA
At Downey Farm, VA:
Christian, Christiana
Christian, Isabella
Christian, Edward

[57.572]
At Fort Monroe, VA:
Samuel, Lucy

[57.545]
Crustine, James:
Northampton Co. VA
At Fort Monroe, VA:
Parker, Lucretia
Parker, Walker
Parker, James

[57.477]
Crutchfield:
Spotsylvania Co. VA
At Fredericksburg, VA:
Tolman, George

[57.580]
Cuder, Mills:
Nansemond Co. VA
At Downey Farm, VA:
Copeland, Jenny
Copeland, Hannah
Copeland, Joseph
Copeland, Andrew
Jackson

[57.516]
Custer, George: (Maj.)
At White House -
Washington D.C.
Custer, Jasper: in
Warwick Co. VA

[57.593]
Meredith, Rachel: At
Fort Monroe, VA

[57.538]
Custer, Joseph M:
Isle of Wight Co. VA
At Fort Monroe, VA:
Jerdon, Caroline
Jerdon, Johana
Jerdon, Emma

[57.550]
Tomlin, Almedia
Tomlin, Susana
Tomlin, Rose
Tomlin, Michael

[57.575]
Custine, Robert:
Northampton Co. VA
At Fort Monroe, VA:
Smith, Flora
Smith, Harriett
Smith, Sarah

[57.582]
Custis, (Major):
White Stone, VA
At Downey Farm, VA:
Jackson, Ann
Young, Jane
Brigham, Molly
Brigham, Charity

[57.513]
Custis, (Major):
Richmond, VA
At Fort Monroe, VA:
Weston, Louisa

[57.510]
Custis, William H:
Accomack Co. VA
At Fort Monroe, VA:
Wise, Rosetta
Wise, Sarah

[57.507]
Custis, William:
Surry Co. VA
At Fort Monroe, VA:
Baker, Charlotte
Baker, Thomas
Baker, Mary
Baker, Louisa

[57.567]
Dabney, William:
King William Co. VA
At Fort Monroe, VA:
Reed, Judy:

[57.503]
Davis, Arthur:
Amherst Co. VA
At Hospital,
Amherst Court House
Davis, Sarah J: 66
Davis, James: 70
Davis, Jacob: 37
Davis, Laura: 25
Davis, Sarah: 33
Davis, Mary: 41
Davis, Betsy: 27

[57.501]
Davis, Brown:
Bedford Co. VA
At Lynchburg Hospital,
Amherst Co. VA:
Hill, Amy: 80.

Davis, Cyrus:
Pittsylvania Co. VA:
At Lynchburg Hospital,
Amherst Co. VA:
Coleman, Bird: 55

Davis, Henry:
Lynchburg, VA
At Lynchburg Hospital,
Amherst Co. VA:
Davis, Molinda: 75

[57.522]
Davis, Marshall:
York Co. VA
At Fort Monroe, VA:
Williams, Phillis

[57.532]
Davis, Parlss:
King William Co. VA
At Fort Monroe, VA:
Jackson, Susan

[57.560]
Davis, Rheuben:
King William Co. VA
At Fort Monroe, VA:
Clasisen, Clary
Clasisen, James
Clasisen, Clara

[57.575]
Davis. R.B:
Louisa Co. VA
At Fort Monroe, VA:
Overton, Alexander

[57.500]
Dawson, Sidney:
Amherst Co. VA
At Lynchburg Hospital,
Amherst Co. VA:
Dawson, Sally: 37

[57.535]
Dawson, William:
Elizabeth City Co. VA
At Fort Monroe, VA:
Patrick, Lucretia
Patrick, Isaac
Patrick, Levi
Patrick, John
Patrick, Andrew

[57.468]
Deans, Louisa:
Green Co. VA
At Fredericksburg, VA:
Unknown, Frank: Child

[57.524]
Dennis, John: (Capt.)
Elizabeth City Co. VA
At Fort Monroe, VA:
Butts, Jane
Butts, Henry I.

[57.536]
Dennis, John:
York Co. VA
At Fort Monroe, VA:
Dennis, Millie

[57.504]
DeOde:
Bedford Co. VA
At Hospital in Liberty, Bedford Co. VA:
DeOde, Nelly: 60

[57.534]
Dexter, Jocklin:
New Kent Co. VA
At Fort Monroe, VA:
Williams, Mary
Williams, Joseph
Williams, Jerdon
Williams, Isabella

[57.521]
Difen, Dempsy:
Nansemond Co. VA
At Fort Monroe, VA:
Dexter, Hester
Dexter, Miles

[57.522]
Diggs, John:
Mathews Co. VA
At Fort Monroe, VA:
Tompkins, Charles
Tompkins, Harnett
Tompkins, Mary

[57.542]
Dillard, Jerry:
Franklin Co. NC
At Fort Monroe, VA:
Jones, Eliza
Jones, Puss
Jones, Cornelias
Jones, Hannah

[57.529]
Dillard, William:
Surry Co. VA
At Fort Monroe, VA:
Harrison, Martha
Harrison, Claresa
Harrison, Henrietta
Harrison, Jack

[57.560]
Dip, Albert:
Mathews Co. VA
At Fort Monroe, VA:
Hudgins, Harriett
Hudgins, Mary
Hudgins, Eliza

[57.562]
Dix, Albert:
Mathews Co. VA
At Fort Monroe, VA:
Furgain, Frances
Furgain, Isaac
Furgain, Jacob
Furgain, Robert

[57.520]
Dobson, Joseph:
Gloucester Co. VA
At Fort Monroe, VA:
Bowker, Mary
Bowker, Robert

[57.566]
Dorbson, William:
Gloucester Co. VA
At Fort Monroe, VA:
Kenny, Lucy
Kenny, Phil

[57.520]
Dorson, John:
Dinwiddie Co. VA
At Fort Monroe, VA:
Epps, Ned

[57.583]
Dougherty, Jacob:
Nansemond Co. VA
At Downey Farm, VA:
Copeland, Merider
Copeland, Lucy
Copeland, Lewis

[57.509]
Doves or Davis, John:
Gloucester Co. VA
At Fort Monroe, VA:
Smith, Gissie

[57.577]
Downey, J.W.:
Elizabeth City Co. VA
At Downey Farm, VA:
Smith, Miranda
Cyrus Cooper
Austin, Ann
Austin, Earl
Austin, Wealthy Ann
Thomas, Margaret
Thomas, Rose
Thomas, Dicy

[57.561]
Downman, John:
Sussex Co. VA
At Fort Monroe, VA:
Milkins, Lavina

[57.521]
Dukes, Abram:
Nansemond Co. VA
At Fort Monroe, VA:
Simonds, Matilda:

[57.537]
Dukes, Isaac:
Gates Co. NC
At Fort Monroe, VA:
Dukes, Mariah
Anderson, Sukie

[57.472]
Duncan, A.B:
Fluvanna Co. VA:
At Fluvanna Co. VA:
Unknown, Henry:
Asthma

[57.583]
Dundan, Edwin:
Isle of Wight Co. VA
At Downey Farm, VA:
Johnson, Priscilla

[57.541]
Dunn, Howard:
York Co. VA
At Fort Monroe, VA:
Bailey, Francis
Bailey, Matilda
Bailey, Rosa

Dunn, Thomas:
York Co. VA
At Fort Monroe, VA:
Carey, Francis

[57.502]
Edmonson, B:
Richmond, VA:
At Lynchburg Hospital,
Amherst Co. VA
Ranson, Louis, 27
Ranson, Marie: 25

[57.510]
Edmunds, Washington:
Surry Co. VA
At Fort Monroe, VA:
Harrison, Gilly
Harrison, Margaret
Harrison, Martha

[57.527]
Edwards, Butler:
King William Co. VA
At Fort Monroe, VA:
Paul, Emeline
Paul, Patsy
Paul, Lucy

[57.545]
Edwards, David:
Isle of Wight Co. VA
At Fort Monroe, VA:
Edwards, Louisa

[57.517]
Edwards, George:
King William Co. VA
At Fort Monroe, VA:
Lispan, Charles

[57.547]
Parker, Penny

[57.560]
Robinson, Ann

[57.547]
Edwards, Warner:
King William Co. VA
At Fort Monroe, VA:
Hickman, Emeline
Hickman, Charles
Hickman, Agness

[57.539]
Elliott, George: (Capt.)
Elizabeth City Co. VA
At Fort Monroe, VA:
Cam, Sally
Cam, Ellick
Cam, Cornelia
Cam, William
Cam, Georgetta
Cam, Silvey

[57.558]
Elliott, John:
Elizabeth City Co. VA
At Fort Monroe, VA:
Blue, Betsey:

[57.553]
Elliott, Logan:
New Kent Co. VA
At Fort Monroe, VA:
Quolls, Susan
Quolls, Isaac

[57.554]
Elliott, Temple:
Hanover Co. VA
At Fort Monroe, VA:
Ellis, Dilsey

[57.584]
Eppes, John:
Prince George Co. VA
At Downey Farm
Eppes, Jim

[57.510]
Epps, Dr.:
Charles City Co. VA
At Fort Monroe, VA:
Lewis, Margaret
Lewis, Charles
Lewis, Edmond
[57.527]
Smith, Susan
Smith, Rosa
Smith, Mary

[57.539]
Epps, Dr.:
James City Co. VA
At Fort Monroe, VA:
Booker, Jane
Booker, Ida
Booker, Fanny

[57.534]
Epps, Dr.:
Prince George Co. VA
At Fort Monroe, VA:
White, Catharine
White, Rosa
White, Louisa
White, Louisa

[57.521]
Epps, Dr.:
Richmond, VA
At Fort Monroe, VA:
Durgen, Sallie
Durgen, Mary

Durgen, Susan
[57.559]
Slaughter, Sarah

[57.571]
Epps, Edward:
Surry Co. VA
At Fort Monroe, VA:
Epps, Rosa
Epps, Temple
Epps, Alice
Epps, Henry

[57.536]
Epps, Richard: Dr.
Prince George Co. VA
At Fort Monroe, VA:
Holdon, Susan
Holdon, Robert
Holdon, Josaphine
Palister, Lucy
Palister, Simond
Palister, Benjamin
Palister, Harriet
[57.540]
Walker, Margaret A.
Walker, Charlotte
Walker, John
Walker, Richard
[57.553]
Slaughter, Susan
Slaughter, Peter
Slaughter, Louisa
Slaughter, Emma
[57.562]
Bell, Nancy
Bell, Sarah
Johnson, Silla
Johnson, Philip
Johnson, George

[57.546]
Epps, Richard:
Charles City Co. VA
At Fort Monroe, VA:
Henderson, Lucy
Henderson, Fanny
Henderson, Hannah
Henderson, Mary
Henderson, Albert
Henderson, Cornelius

[57.520]
Epps, Richard:
Chesterfield Co. VA
At Fort Monroe, VA:
Henderson, Millie
Henderson, Randall
Henderson, Alexander
Henderson, Matilda
Henderson, Hesekiah

[57.543]
Epsey, Dr.:
City Point,
Prince George Co. VA
At Fort Monroe, VA:
Bland, Nancy
Bland, Nancy

[57.524]
Epson, Dr.:
Prince George Co. VA
At Fort Monroe, VA:
Unknown, Randlie
Unknown, Eliza

[57.582]
Ercott, James:
Bertie Co. NC
At Downey Farm, VA:
Ercott, Elizabeth

[57.516]
Everett, Jassett:
Nansemond Co. VA
At Fort Monroe, VA:
Small, Margaret

[57.527]
Farren, Lyons:
Yorktown, VA
At Fort Monroe, VA:
Johnson, Emma
Johnson, Ella

[57.522]
Felter, Jasher:
Perquimmons Co. NC
At Fort Monroe, VA:
Rose, Charlotte

[57.560]
Felton, Richard:
Elizabeth City Co. VA
At Fort Monroe, VA:
Edney, Penny

[57.515]
Fenno, Thomas G:
Prince George Co. VA
At Fort Monroe, VA:
Glenfoot, Eliza

[57.532]
Fenny, John:
Amelia Co. VA
At Fort Monroe, VA:
Washington, Frank

[57.582]
Ferguson, Austin:
Charles City Co. VA
At Downey Farm, VA:
Jordan, Caroline
Jordan, Alexander
Jordan, Matilda
Jordan, Austin

[57.468]
Fishback, S:
Green Co. VA
At Fredericksburg, VA:
Unknown, George: Child

[57.555]
Fitchett. J.H:
Northampton Co. VA
At Fort Monroe, VA:
Fitchett, Carey
Fitchett, Nelson

[57.558]
Mosby, Elizabeth

[57.558]
Fitts Hew: {Fitzhugh?}
Northampton Co.VA
At Fort Monroe, VA:
Weston, Sarah

[57.475]
Flannagan, B.J:
Fluvanna Co. VA
At Fluvanna Co. VA:
Lyons, Nancy: Old age

[57.475]
Flannagan, J:
Fluvanna Co. VA
At Fluvanna Co. VA:
Prior, Matsey: Old age

[57.474]
Flannagan, William:
Fluvanna Co. VA
At Fluvanna Co. VA:
Burch, Reuben: Cripple

[57.469]
Fleming, J.B:
Green Co. VA
At Fredericksburg, VA:
Unknown, Harriet: Woman
Unknown, Rinda: Woman
Unknown, James: Child
Unknown, Eliza: Child
Unknown, Emma: Child

[57.500]
Flood, Henry:
Amherst Co. VA
At Lynchburg Hospital,
Amherst Co. VA:
Flood, Rhoda: 90

[57.500]
Floyd, Dr:
Campbell Co. VA
At Lynchburg Hospital,
Amherst Co. VA:
Floyd, Eliza: 30
Floyd, Martha: 34

[57.501]
Folks, E.J:
Lynchburg, VA
At Lynchburg Hospital,
Amherst Co. VA:
Edwards, Charles: 16

[57.558]
Foster, John:
Clark Co. VA
At Fort Monroe, VA:
Bright, Sallie

[57.560]
Foster, Warren:
Mathews Co. VA
At Fort Monroe, VA:
Smith, Leha

[57.476]
Foulas, Festus:
Fluvanna Co. VA
At Fluvanna Co. VA:
Ross, Jesse: 1 hand off

[57.471]
Fountain, William:
Fluvanna Co. VA
At Fluvanna Co. VA:
Howard, Stephen:
 Old Age

[57.537]
Fox, John:
Gloucester Co. VA
At Fort Monroe, VA:
Smith, Mary K.

[57.541]
Fox, John:
Northampton Co. VA
At Fort Monroe, VA:
Beach, Margaret

[57.473]
Fox, Joseph P:
Fluvanna Co. VA
At Fluvanna Co. VA:
Anderson, Ned: Invalid
Ferguson, Ed: Idiot

[57.581]
Franklin, J.N:
Nansemond Co. VA
At Downey Farm, VA:
Franklin, Mary

[57.501]
Franklin, Samuel:
Campbell Co. VA
At Lynchburg Hospital,
Amherst Co. VA:
Franklin, William: 60

[57.569]
Freeman, Joseph:
Norfolk, VA
At Fort Monroe, VA:
Malery, Lucy

[57.536]
Friend, Charles:
Prince George Co. VA
At Fort Monroe, VA:
Jackson, Vinnery

[57.521]
Gadrey, Samuel:
King & Queen Co. VA
At Fort Monroe, VA:
Robinson, Isabella
Robinson, Rhoda
Robinson, Ellie
Robinson, Benjamin
Robinson, Moses

[57.507]
Gaines, Dr:
Hanover Co. VA
At Fort Monroe, VA:
Keninton, Caroline
Keninton, Roy
Keninton, Johnson
Keninton, Michell
Keninton, Albert

[57.522]
James, Susan
[57.554]
Gaines, Catharine
Gaines, Peter
Gaines, Aaron
Gaines, Silvia
Gaines, Benjamin
[57.573]
Dudley, Alfred
[57.576]
Johnson, Peggy
Johnson, Betsy

[57.573]
Gaines, W.F: (Dr.)
Hanover Co. VA
At Fort Monroe, VA:
Grey, Dezzie

[57.524]
Gaines, Wm G: Dr.
Hanover Co. VA
At Fort Monroe, VA:
Govener, Caroline
Govener, Roy
Govener, Johnson
Govener, Albert
Govener, Bailey
[57.554]
Johnson, Eliza
Johnson, Patsey
Johnson, James
Johnson, Robert
Johnson, Washington
[57.557]
Grain, Harriet

[57.575]
Gallen, Thomas:
Albemarle Co. VA
At Fort Monroe, VA:
Marshall, Lucy
Marshall, Lizzie

[57.522]
Gallie, Braxton:
New Kent Co. VA
At Fort Monroe, VA:
More, Patsey
More, Sh[ ]
More, Daniel

[57.476]
Galt, James:
Fluvanna Co. VA
At Fluvanna Co. VA:
Crank, Housan: Infirm
Mosby, Malinda: Infirm
Achrell, Eliza: Infirm

Anderson, Eliza:
    Nearly blind
Fox, Mary: Deranged
Long, Jefferson: Infirm
Long, Letty: Scrofula.
Unknown, Nannie:
    Deranged
Unknown, Samuel:
    Infirm
Willis, Louisa: Infirm
Winney, Lucy: Infirm

[57.533]
Gamerell, Nat:
Elizabeth City Co. VA
At Fort Monroe, VA:
Allen, Patsey

[57.577]
Gamott, Richard:
Elizabeth City Co. VA
At Downey Farm, VA:
Booker, Emily
Booker, Janie
Smith, Charlote

[57.519]
Ganie, Madisen:
Southampton Co. VA
At Fort Monroe, VA:
Simond, Reno
Simond, James
Simond, Buck
Simond, Ellie

[57.565]
Ganroy, Samuel: Dr.
King & Queen Co. VA
At Fort Monroe, VA:
Bagby, Sarah

[57.554]
Garden, George:
Suffolk Co. VA
At Fort Monroe, VA:
Willis, Fanny

[57.532]
Garey, William:
King William Co. VA
At Fort Monroe, VA:
Robinson, Patsey
Robinson, Nancy
Robinson, William
Robinson, Susan

[57.511]
Garlic, Braxton:
New Kent Co. VA
At Fort Monroe, VA:
Fox, Hannah
Fox, Fanny
Stewart, Winnie
[57.537]
Nash, Kesiah
[57.567]
Fisher, Mary
Fisher, Eldridge

[57.523]
Garly, William:
King William Co. VA
At Fort Monroe, VA:
Bailey, Harriet
Bailey, Sarah

[57.524]
Garnett, James:
Mathews Co. VA
At Fort Monroe, VA:
Billups, Leach
Billups, Robert

Billups, Harriett
Billups, Charlott

[57.531]
Garrett, George:
Elizabeth City Co. VA
At Fort Monroe, VA:
Stevens, Liskie A.

[57.480]
Garrott, John:
Caroline Co. VA
At Fredericksburg, VA:
Jonnie, Susan
Jonnie, Lucy
Garner, Letha
Garner, James H.
Garner, Margaret

[57.523]
Gaskin, Capt.:
Nansemond Co. VA
At Fort Monroe, VA:
Bath, Nancy
Bath, Martha
Bath, Elizabeth
Bailey, Rebecca
Bailey, Nancy
Bailey, Laura
Bailey, Fannie

[57.549]
Gatlin, Reddick:
Gates Co. NC
At Fort Monroe, VA:
Gatlin, Anne
Gatlin, Rachel
[57.534]
Gatlin, Mary I.
Gatlin, Roxanne
Gatlin, Richard

[57.561]
Katlin, Lucy

[57.561]
Gatlin, Reduck:
Gates Co. NC
At Fort Monroe, VA:
Gulscom, Ann
Gulscom, Martha
Gulscom, Ann

[57.547]
Gay, Dr.:
King William Co. VA
At Fort Monroe, VA:
Gowens, Sarah

[57.474]
Gent, J.W:
Fluvanna Co. VA
At Fluvanna Co. VA:
Payne, Alley: Old age

[57.473]
George, R.F:
Fluvanna Co. VA
At Fluvanna Co. VA:
Fowler, Nelly: Old Age

[57.513]
Gett, Geret:
Elizabeth City Co. VA
At Fort Monroe, VA:
Jones, Sarah
Jones, Phillip
Jones, Hester
Jones, William
Jones, Indiana

[57.507]
Gidjet, William:
Northampton Co. VA
At Fort Monroe, VA:
Andrews, Eda
Andrews, Mary
Andrews, Eda
Andrews, John
Andrews, Julia

[57.503]
Giles, Rolls:
Nelson Co. VA
At Hospital, Lovington,
Nelson Co. VA:
Giles, Dessie J: age 44,
with 1 child
Giles, Philip: 50 yrs
Giles, Sarah: age 60,
with 1 child

[57.516]
Gilham, Maurice:
Prince George Co. VA
At Fort Monroe, VA:
Rice, Hannah
Rice, Darley
Rice, William
Rice, Robert

[57.521]
Glover, Jackson:
Edenton, NC
At Fort Monroe, VA:
White, Rebecca
White, Richard

[57.544]
Gofican, Edward:
Northampton Co. VA
At Fort Monroe, VA:

Savage, Peggy

[57.578]
Going, Edward:
Charles City Co. VA
At Downey Farm, VA:
Davis, Dianna
Brown, Alexander

[57.547]
Golden, James:
Gloucester Co. VA
At Fort Monroe, VA:
Young, Catharine

[57.585]
Golding, Simon:
Henrico Co. VA
At Downey Farm, VA:
Matthews, Betsey
Matthews, Dick

[57.535]
Gombley, Robert:
King William Co. VA
At Fort Monroe, VA:
Coleman, Sally

[57.577]
Goodall:
Portsmouth, VA
At Downey Farm, VA:
Rowe, Violet

[57.532]
Goodson, Thomas:
Isle of Wight Co. VA
At Fort Monroe, VA:
Robinson, Martha

[57.480]

Goodwin, Catharine:
Spottsylvania Co.VA
At Fredericksburg, VA:
Thomas, Nancy

[57.478]
Gordon, Andrew:
Spotsylvania Co. VA
At Fredericksburg, VA:
Gray, Minny
Unknown, Nancy
Unknown, Hannah

[57.477]
Gordon, Hiram:
Spotsylvania Co. VA
At Fredericksburg, VA:
Lewis, Louisa
Lewis, Edward
Lewis, Addison
Lewis, Charles
Lewis, Thomas

[57.543]
Gothican, Susan:
Northampton Co. VA
At Fort Monroe, VA:
Burras, Grace
Burras, Joshua

[57.567]
Gougin, Susan:
Northampton Co. VA
At Fort Monroe, VA:
Johnson, Ferby
Johnson, Joseph
Johnson, Millie

[57.501]
Graff, Thomas:
Campbell Co. VA
At Lynchburg Hospital,
Amherst Co. VA:
Jefferson, Frank: 18

[57.572]
Graham, John:
Richmond Co. VA
At Fort Monroe, VA:
Sidney, Winnie

[57.500]
Grant, Peter:
Campbell Co. VA
At Lynchburg Hospital,
Amherst Co. VA:
Grant, Charlotte: 23

[57.511]
Grasham, James:
Landcaster Co. VA
At Fort Monroe, VA:
Hawkins, Mary A.

[57.579]
Graves, Ben C:
Charles City Co. VA
At Downey Farm, VA:
Webb, Priscilla

[57.468]
Graves, J:
Green Co. VA
At Fredericksburg, VA:
Unknown, Frank: Child

[57.504]
Graves, William:
Bedford Co. VA
At Liberty Hospital,
Bedford Co. VA:
Graves, Anne: 27
Graves, Edward: 6
Graves, Bob Lee: 1

[57.474]
Gray, William: Dr.
Fluvanna Co. VA:
At Fluvanna Co. VA:
Brooks, Edmund:
    Old age

[57.567]
Green, Benjamin:
Henrico Co. VA
At Fort Monroe, VA:
Green, Lovly

[57.477]
Green, Captain:
Stafford Co. VA
At Fredericksburg, VA:
Robinson, Helen
Robinson, William
Robinson, Elizabeth
Robinson, Padda

[57.501]
Green, William:
Appomattox Co. VA
At Lynchburg Hospital,
Amherst Co. VA:
Green, Leander: 23

[57.593]
Gregory, (Judge):
Charles City Co. VA
At Warwick Co. VA:
Gregory, Brisse

[57.519]
Gregory, William:
Chesterfield Co. VA
At Fort Monroe, VA:
Hood, Ann
Hood, Mary
[57.566]
Good, Peggy
Good, Joseph
Good, John
Good, Sarah

[57.542]
Grey, (Dr.):
King William Co. VA
At Fort Monroe, VA:
Holmes, Mary

[57.557]
Grey, Peater:
King & Queen Co. VA
At Fort Monroe, VA:
Grimes, Nerry
Grimes, Ellen
Grimes, Emma

[57.584]
Grooms, J:
Goochland Co. VA
At Downey Farm, VA:
Boles, Caroline

[57.559]
Haldy, John:
Chesterfield Co. VA
At Fort Monroe, VA:
Sweet, Francis
Sweet, Stephen

[57.583]
Hall, J.:
Surry Co. VA
At Downey Farm, VA:
Clayborns, Mirander

[57.577]
Hall, James:
Surry Co. VA
At Downey Farm, VA:
Clayton, Lucy
Clayton, Archer

[57.512]
Hall, John:
Charles City Co. VA
At Fort Monroe, VA:
Hill, Aaron
Hill, Patsey

[57.530]
Hall, John:
Isle of Wight Co. VA
At Fort Monroe, VA:
Marshall, Charlotte
Marshall, Benjamin
Marshall, Collins

[57.501]
Halsey, Seth:
Campbell Co. VA
At Lynchburg Hospital,
Amherst Co. VA:
Blufort, Ned: 51

[57.506]
Hamilton, John:
Bristol TN:
At Liberty Hospital,
Bedford Co. VA:
Unknown, Mary: 25
Unknown, Kissy: 6
Unknown, Davy: 5

[57.480]
Hamphis?, Lawrence:
Spottsylvania Co. VA
At Fredericksburg, VA:
Williams, Sippy

[57.473]
Hanson, H.L:
Fluvanna Co. VA
At Fluvanna Co. VA:
Unknown, Ziddie: Infirm

[57.580]
Harbody, William:
Gloucester Co. VA
At Downey Farm, VA:
Rhone, Agnes

[57.577]
Harold, Moses:
Williamsburg, VA
At Downey Farm, VA:
Jones, Mary
Jones, Mary Eliza

[57.540]
Harold, Samuel:
Gates Co. NC
At Fort Monroe, VA:
Harold, Agness
Ballard, Martha

[57.549]
Harris, Robert:
Louisa Co. VA
At Fort Monroe, VA:
Trace, Walker

[57.501]
Harris, William:
Bedford Co. VA
At Lynchburg Hospital,
Amherst Co. VA:
Smith, Sarah: 23

[57.473]
Harris, William:
Fluvanna Co. VA
At Fluvanna Co. VA:
Harris, S: Old Age.

[57.513]
Harrison, George E:
Prince George Co. VA
At Fort Monroe, VA:
Davis, Rena

[57.581]
Harrison, John H:
Charles City Co. VA
At Downey Farm, VA:
Hunt, Judy
Hunt, Louisa
Churchill, Elizabeth
Rolin, Thomas
Hunt, Ben
Love, Caroline

[57.533]
Harrison, Richard:
Prince George Co. VA
At Fort Monroe, VA:
Jones, Mariah

[57.545]
Jones, Jane
Jones, Julia
[57.570]
Washington, Mariah
Washington, Peter
Washington, Charles
Washington, Lottie
Washington, Millie
Walker, Sarah
Walker, Ann
Walker, Sarah

[57.508]
Harrison, William B:
Prince George Co. VA
At Fort Monroe, VA:
Harrison, Angeline
Harrison, Nancy
[57.528]
Crumson, Sarah
Crumson, Nancy
Crumson, Napoleon
Harrison, Adeline
Harrison, Claresa
Harrison, Mariah
[57.548]
Shap, Caroline
Shap, Milley
Shap, Betsey
[57.569]
Williams, Lucy
Trusty, Hannah
Trusty, Alfred
Trusty, Susan
Trusty, Edmond
Trusty, William
[57.579]
At Downey Farm, VA:
Armistead, Cornelia
Armistead, Alice

Armistead, Henry
Armistead, Kitty
Carter, Eliza
Carter, Mary
Carter, Louisa
Carter, Eliza
Carter, Moses
Carter, Marion
Watkins, Amy
Harrison, Nancy
Trent, Elizabeth
Woodson, Lucy

[57.579]
Harrison, William M:
Charles City Co. VA
At Downey Farm, VA:
Williams, Eleanor

[57.537]
Harrison, Windfield:
Prince George Co. VA
At Fort Monroe, VA:
Riles, Daniel
[57.538]
Jones, Henry
Garly, Mary
Harrison, Ellen
Harrison, Louisa
Harrison, Walter
Harrison, Richard
[57.573]
Jackson, Betsey
Jackson, India
Jackson, Henry
Toliver, Sarah
Toliver, James
Jackson, Vinnery

[57.508]
Hart, Henry H:
Surry Co. VA
At Ft. Monroe, VA:
Spradley, Ann
Spradley, John

[57.500]
Harvey, Richard:
Campbell Co. VA
At Lynchburg Hospital,
Amherst Co. VA:
Harvey, Lucy: 24

[57.559]
Haskins, William:
King & Queen Co. VA
At Fort Monroe, VA:
Upture, Isabella
Upture, James
Upture, Eliza
Upture, Emma
Upture, Andrew
[57.559]
Upture, Isabella
Upture, James
Upture, Eliza
Upture, Emma
Upture, Andrew

[57.505]
Hatcher, J:
Bedford Co. VA
At Liberty Hospital,
Bedford Co. VA
Unknown, Peter: 70

[57.474]
Hawkins, C:
Fluvanna Co. VA
At Fluvanna Co. VA:
Unknown, Annaca:
Old age

[57.525]
Hawkins, John:
Surry Co. VA
At Ft. Monroe, VA:
Wilson, Joseph

[57.567]
Hawkins, John:
Warwick Co. VA
At Ft. Monroe, VA:
Hawkins, Jane
Hawkins, Anthony

[57.500]
Haydon, Emily:
Campbell Co. VA
At Lynchburg Hospital,
Amherst Co. VA:
Haydon, Ed: 70

[57.582]
Hayes, Joseph: Col.
Gloucester Co. VA
At Downey Farm, VA:
Cramp, Julia Ann
Thomas, James

[57.530]
Haynes, Richard:
Surry Co. VA
At Fort Monroe, VA:
Bailey, Caroline
Bailey, Mary

[57.479]
Henderson, John:
Caroline Co. VA
At Fredericksburg, VA:
Johnson, Emily
Johnson, William

[57.544]
Henly, Richard:
Hanover Co. VA
At Fort Monroe, VA:
Maison, Fanny

[57.511]
Hennican, Roland:
Surry Co. VA
At Fort Monroe, VA:
Harris, Peter
Harris, Millie

[57.548]
Herbert, John:
Elizabeth City Co. VA
At Fort Monroe, VA:
Jackson, Harmond

[57.523]
Herbert, Thomas:
Elizabeth City Co. VA
At Fort Monroe, VA:
Allen, Adeline
Allen, Matilda
Allen, Eli
Allen, Cornelius
Allen, Edwin
Allen, Charlotte
Allen, Nancy

[57.505]
Heston?, N:
Bedford Co. VA
At Liberty Hospital,
Bedford Co. VA
Unknown, Ellen: 22

[57.513]
Hickman, Charles
Elizabeth City Co. VA
At Fort Monroe, VA:
Robinson, Nancy

[57.558]
Hickman, William:
Elizabeth City Co. VA
At Fort Monroe, VA:
Shepherd, Eliza

[57.548]
Hill, James:
Caroline Co. VA
At Fort Monroe, VA:
Taylor, Benjamin
Taylor, Paul
Taylor, John
Taylor, Silas

[57.514]
Hill, Lucy:
Virginia
At Fort Monroe, VA:
Bailey, Semple
Bailey, William
Bailey, Virginia
Bailey, Louisa
Bailey, Tempy

Hill, William:
King William Co. VA
At Fort Monroe, VA:

Taylor, Caroline
Taylor, Major
Taylor, Emma
Taylor, Fleming
Taylor, Kennald
[57.523]
Bassa, Claresa
Bassa, Mariah
Bassa, Joseph
[57.566]
Grimes, Isaac

[57.481]
Hinds, John:
Stafford Co. VA
At Fredericksburg, VA:
Adamson, John
Adamson, Mary
Adamson, Seith

[57.546]
Hinebark, Richard:
King William Co. VA
At Fort Monroe, VA:
Mapp, Catharine
Mapp, Charlott
Mapp, Thomas

[57.582]
Hoag, Thomas:
York Co. VA
At Downey Farm, VA:
Pascoll, Susan

[57.513]
Hobdy, William:
Gloucester Co. VA
At Fort Monroe, VA:
Toliver, Hattie
Toliver, Agy
Toliver, Hattie

[57.552]
Hoget, Sherno:
Princess Ann Co. VA
At Fort Monroe, VA:
Delano, Lucy
Delano, Robert
Delano, Daniel

[57.562]
Hogg, Richard:
Gloucester Co. VA
At Fort Monroe, VA:
Carey, Lucy A
Carey, Emma
Carey, John

[57.507]
Hogg, Thomas:
Northampton Co. VA
At Fort Monroe, VA:
Barber, John

[57.472]
Holeman, George:
Fluvanna Co. VA
At Fluvanna Co. VA:
Eads, James: Infirm
Unknown, Ruth: Deaf

[57.564]
Holland, Edward:
Eastern Shore, VA
At Fort Monroe, VA:
Custer, Susan
Custer, John
Custer, William
Custer, Mary A.

[57.584]
Holland, J.H:
Nansemond Co. VA
At Downey Farm:
Cross, Judy
Williams, Fanny
Cross, Alice

[57.540]
Holland, Thomas:
Gloucester Co. VA
At Fort Monroe, VA:
Taylor, Lucy

[57.476]
Holman, George:
Fluvanna Co. VA
At Fluvanna Co. VA:
Unknown, Harriet: Infirm
Unknown, Clayborne: Infirm
Unknown, Betsy: Infirm

[57.480]
Holmes, [?]
Bowling Green,
Caroline Co. VA
At Fredericksburg, VA:
Washington, Caroline

[57.545]
Holt, F:
York Co. VA
At Fort Monroe, VA:
Jones, Sarah
Jones, Lucy
Jones, Jane
Jones, Lizzie

[57.504]
Holt, Joseph:
Bedford Co. VA
At Liberty Hospital,
Bedford Co. VA
Unknown, Nanda: 30
Unknown, Rachal: 4
Unknown, Washington: 1

[57.481]
Hooker, William:
Caroline Co. VA
At Fredericksburg, VA:
Ewing, Ann

[57.564]
Hoop, George:
Hampton, VA
At Fort Monroe, VA:
Andrews, Hannah
Andrews, John
Andrews, Eliza
Andrews, Mary J.

[57.475]
Hopkins, Ben:
Fluvanna Co. VA
At Fluvanna Co. VA:
Hopkins, Joshua: Infirm

[57.522]
Hopkins, Charles:
York Co. VA
At Fort Monroe, VA:
Thomas, Peter
Thomas, James
[57.578]
At Downey Farm, VA:
Cheeseman, Agnes

[57.500]
Hosely, Seth:
Campbell Co. VA
At Lynchburg Hospital,
Amherst Co. VA:
Hosely, Celia: 70

[57.500]
Hosler, Seth:
Campbell Co. VA
At Lynchburg Hospital,
Amherst Co. VA:
Johnson, Ready: 82

[57.476]
Howard, B:
Fluvanna Co. VA
At Fluvanna Co. VA:
Howard, Cary: Cripple

[57.564]
Howard, Dr.:
Isle of Wight Co. VA
At Fort Monroe, VA:
Brown, Matilda
Brown, Francis
Brown, Jack

[57.474]
Howard, P:
Fluvanna Co. VA
At Fluvanna Co. VA:
Johnson, Willis: Cripple

[57.543]
Howdy, Thomas:
Chesterfield Co. VA
At Fort Monroe, VA:
Cox, Marthy
Cox, Lucy
Cox, John
Cox, Martha
Cox, Jerdan
Cox, Mary

[57.541]
Howler, Thomas:
Chesterfield Co. VA
At Fort Monroe, VA:
Cogsnell, Betsey

[57.565]
Howlet, James:
Chesterfield Co. VA
At Fort Monroe, VA:
Sweet, Primus

[57.512]
Hubang, Richard:
King William Co. VA
At Fort Monroe, VA:
Recker, Julia

[57.593]
Hubbard, Dr.:
James City Co. VA
At Warwick Co. VA:
Evans, Phil
Evans, Kaziah

[57.471]
Huckstep, C.J:
Fluvanna Co. VA
At Fluvanna Co. VA:
Banks, Samuel:
   Old age & blind

[57.476]
Huckstep, Willis:
Fluvanna Co. VA
At Fluvanna Co. VA:
Unknown, Samuel: Blind
Unknown, Liloa: Infirm
Unknown, Jennie: Infirm

[57.530]
Hudgins, Archer:
Mathews Co. VA
At Fort Monroe, VA:
Chainey, Tompkins
Chainey, Mary
Chainey, Elizabeth
Chainey, Fridera
Chainey, Caroline

[57.578]
Hudgins, Delia:
Elizabeth City Co. VA
At Downey Farm, VA:
Reams, Minerva
Reams, Georgeanna

[57.566]
Hudgins, Elleck:
Mathews Co. VA
At Fort Monroe, VA:
Tabb, Robert

[57.552]
Hudgins, Holden:
Mathews Co. VA
At Fort Monroe, VA:
Johnson, Susan
Johnson, Rosetta
Johnson, John
Johnson, George
Johnson, James
Carlton, Laura
Carlton, Mary

[57.560]
Hudgins, Jessie:
Mathews Co. VA
At Fort Monroe, VA:
Hudgins, David

[57.578]
Hudgins, R:
Elizabeth City Co. VA
At Downey Farm, VA:
Grey, Lucy Ann:

[57.516]
Hudgins, Robert:
Elizabeth City Co. VA
At Fort Monroe, VA:
Wallace, William
Wallace, Eliza
[57.555]
Davis, Amanda
Davis, Indiana
Davis, Charity

[57.572]
Hudgins, Robert:
Mathews Co. VA
At Fort Monroe, VA:
Johnson, Mary
Johnson, Gussie
Johnson, Fanny
Johnson, Oliver

[57.508]
Hudsher, William:
King William Co. VA
At Fort Monroe, VA:
Stock, Mahaley

[57.471]
Hudson, William:
Fluvanna Co. VA:
At Fluvanna Co. VA:
Unknown, Eliza:
Old Age

[57.474]
Hughes, J:
Fluvanna Co. VA
At Fluvanna Co. VA:
Cary, Polly: Invalid

[57.472]
Hughes, John G:
Fluvanna Co. VA
At Fluvanna Co. VA:
Unknown, Grace: Infirm

[57.474]
Hughes, M.A: Mrs.
Fluvanna Co. VA
At Fluvanna Co. VA:
Hughes, Millie: Old age

Hughes, William:
Fluvanna Co. VA
At Fluvanna Co. VA:
Shelton, Charity:
Old age

[57.559]
Hunt, William:
Clark Co. VA
At Fort Monroe, VA:
Hunt, Francis
Hunt, Robert
Hunt, Henry
Hunt, Susan

[57.508]
Hunter, Robert:
Essex Co. VA
At Fort Monroe, VA:
Grimes, Benjamin

[57.556]
Grimes, Madison

[57.557]
Hunter, Robert:
King & Queen Co. VA
At Fort Monroe, VA:
Grimes, Benjamin

[57.533]
Huntley, Thomas:
Essex Co. VA
At Fort Monroe, VA:
Warren, Eliza
Warren, Lizzie
Warren, Elic
Warren, Cornelia
Warren, Magdaline

[57.509]
Huntly, Richard:
Hanover Co. VA
At Fort Monroe, VA:
Henry, Caroline
Henry, Lucy
Henry, Richard
Henry, Martha
Henry, Ann

[57.514]
Hynes, Richard:
Surry Co. VA
At Fort Monroe, VA:
Bailey, Jane

[57.500]
Irvin, Daniel:
Campbell Co. VA
At Lynchburg Hospital,
Amherst Co. VA:
Ervin, Daniel: 75

[57.569]
Ivey, William:
Elizabeth City Co. VA
At Fort Monroe, VA:
Tucker, Slara
Gillah, Delia

[57.516]
Jackson, Andrew:
Northampton Co. VA
At Fort Monroe, VA:
Gibbs, Susan
Gibbs, Joseph

[57.565]
Jacob, William:
Northampton Co. VA
At Fort Monroe, VA:
Jacob, Sarah
Jacob, Fanny
Jacob, Polly
Jacob, Horace
Jacob, Martha
Jacob, Lucy

[57.562]
Jacobs, Robert:
Northampton Co. VA
At Fort Monroe, VA:
Upture, Julia
Upture, Joseph

[57.508]
Jarget, Henry:
Sussex Co. VA
At Fort Monroe, VA:
Harrison, Matilda
[57.558]
Jarvis, Sally
Jarvis, Margaret
Jarvis, Lina

[57.539]
Jeffers, Dr.:
Essex Co. VA
At Fort Monroe, VA:
Brooks, Mariah
Brooks, Florence

[57.477]
Jenkins, Thomas:
King George Co. VA
At Fredericksburg, VA:
Lewis, Georgianna

[57.501]
Jenks, William:
Campbell Co. VA
At Lynchburg Hospital,
Amherst Co. VA:
Jenks, Mary: 80

[57.476]
Jennie, Mary F:
Fluvanna Co. VA
At Fluvanna Co. VA:
Burton, Julia A: Cripple

[57.564]
Jerdan, James:
Princess Ann Co. VA
At Fort Monroe, VA:
Brown, Ann
Brown, Elizabeth
Brown, Margarett

[57.507]
Jerdan, John:
Princess Ann Co. VA
At Fort Monroe, VA:
Simons, Matilda

[57.529]
Jerdan, Samuel P:
Smithfield Co. VA
At Fort Monroe, VA:
Hankins, Margarett
Hankins, Mary
Hankins, Edward
Hankins, Martha
Hankins, Henry
Hankins, Bobby

[57.563]
Jerdon, William:
Nansemond Co. VA
At Fort Monroe, VA:
Brown, Delia
Brown, Mary

[57.553]
Jessie, Lee:
East Tennessee
At Fort Monroe, VA:
Allen, Nancy
Allen, Catharine

[57.545]
Johnson, Ann:
New Kent Co. VA
At Fort Monroe, VA:
Allen, Margaret
Allen, Lavinia
Allen, Malinda
Allen, Emeline

[57.472]
Johnson, Dyer:
Fluvanna Co. VA
At Fluvanna Co. VA:
Johnson, Billy: Old Age

147

[57.471]
Johnson, George:
Fluvanna Co. VA
At Fluvanna Co. VA:
Unknown, Jennie: Infirm
Unknown, Willie: Infirm
Unknown, Hannah:. Infirm

[57.502]
Johnson, Harry:
Botetourt Co. VA
At Lynchburg Hospital,
Amherst Co. VA:
Harndall, Margaret: 40

[57.565]
Johnson, James:
King William Co. VA
At Fort Monroe, VA:
Henry, Charlott
Henry, Rosa
Henry, Lizzie

[57.473]
Johnson, John D:
Fluvanna Co. VA
At Fluvanna Co. VA:
Brown, Juda: Old Age

[57.475]
Johnson, Joseph:
Fluvanna Co. VA
At Fluvanna Co. VA:
Unknown, Hager:
    Old age

[57.559]
Johnson, Mary J:
Surry Co. VA
At Fort Monroe, VA:
Turner, Dolly

Turner, Ambelice
Turner, Frank
Turner, Cornelia
Turner, Sylvester

[57.582]
Johnson, Thomas:
Charles City Co. VA
At Downey Farm, VA:
Curtis, Sophia
Curtis, Ann
Curtis, Thomas Franklin

[57.474]
Johnson, W: Mrs.
Fluvanna Co. VA
At Fluvanna Co. VA:
Payne, Polly: Infirm

[57.502]
Joiner, Peter:
Amherst Co. VA
At Lynchburg Hospital,
Amherst Co. VA:
Joiner, Marie: 60

[57.571]
Jones, Burden:
Isle of Wight Co. VA
At Fort Monroe, VA:
Gorden, Serinda
Gorden, Martha
Gorden, Lizzie
Gorden, James
Gorden, Sarah

[57.513]
Jones, Caleb: Dr. :
St. Mary's Co. MD
At Fort Monroe, VA:
Langly, Susan

[57.532]
Jones, Carey:
Elizabeth City Co. VA
At Fort Monroe, VA:
Jones, Nancy
Jones, Ella
Jones, Margarett
Carter, Lizzie

[57.548]
Jones, Cleyborn:
Surry Co. VA
At Fort Monroe, VA:
Jefferson, Mary

[57.555]
Grey, William

[57.577]
Jones, George:
James City Co. VA
At Downey Farm, VA:
Smith, Agnes
Smith, Rebecca

[57.539]
Jones, Henry:
Surry Co. VA
At Fort Monroe, VA:
Branch, Susan
Branch, Mary
Branch, Thomas
Jones, Ida
Jones, William
Jones, Andrew

[57.502]
Jones, Jedediah:
North Carolina
At Lynchburg Hospital,
Amherst Co. VA:
Fields, Ann: 21

[57.578]
Jones, John D.W:
Charles City Co. VA
At Downey Farm, VA:
Lewis, Peggy

[57.541]
Jones, John P:
Elizabeth City Co. VA
At Fort Monroe, VA:
Pitchford, Caroline

[57.578]
Jones, John:
Warwick Co. VA
At Downey Farm, VA:
Smith, Susan
Smith, Louisa
Smith, Mary
Smith, Tom

[57.584]
Jones, Lewis:
Middlesex Co. VA
At Downey Farm, VA:
Bauks, Polly

[57.574]
Jones, Richard:
Prince George Co. VA
At Fort Monroe, VA:
Jones, Kersey
Jones, Alice

[57.474]
Jones, S.B:
Fluvanna Co. VA
At Fluvanna Co. VA:
Unknown, Maria: Nearly
   blind. 12 yrs old
Unknown, Lee:
Scrofula. 10 yrs old

[57.509]
Jones, Sarah:
Surry Co. VA
At Fort Monroe, VA:
Branch, Susan:

[57.544]
Jones, Thomas S:
King William Co. VA
At Fort Monroe, VA:
Harris, Jane
Harris, Millie

[57.570]
Jones, Thomas:
Essex Co. VA
At Fort Monroe, VA:
Wallace, Eliza

[57.515]
Jones, Warren:
Gloucester Co. VA
At Fort Monroe, VA:
Reed, Sarah

[57.531]
Bates, Annie
Bates, Henry
Bates, Ida

[57.500]
Jones, William:
Campbell Co. VA
At Lynchburg Hospital,
Amherst Co. VA:
Jones, Letty: 38

[57.580]
Jones, William:
Gates Co. NC
At Downey Farm, VA:
Savage, Celia A.

[57.581]
Harold, Mary

[57.551]
Jones, William:
Southampton Co. VA
At Fort Monroe, VA:
Jerdon, Hariett
Jerdon, Henry
Jerdon, Elizabeth
Jerdon, Lindy
Jerdon, Miles

[57.526]
Jones, William:
Surry Co. VA
At Fort Monroe, VA:
Carey, Ann
Carey, Manerva
Carey, Edith

[57.514]
Jones, Wilmot:
James City Co. VA
At Fort Monroe, VA:
Dennis, Nancy
Dennis, Lilley
Dennis, Seldun

[57.500]
Jordan, William:
Amherst Co. VA
At Lynchburg Hospital,
Amherst Co. VA:
Jordan, Moll: 70

[57.477]
Joyce, Hannah: (Miss)
Caroline Co. VA
At Fredericksburg, VA:
Minor, Polly

[57.574]
Kape, Jerry:
Elizabeth City Co. VA
At Fort Monroe, VA:
Weston, Elizabeth
Weston, John
Weston, Rachael
Weston, Lucy
Weston, Sally

[57.502]
Kees, James:
Amherst Co. VA
At Lynchburg Hospital,
Amherst Co. VA:
Keese, George: 53

[57.585]
Keetan, John:
Nansemond Co. VA
At Downey Farm, VA:
Keetan, Phillis

[57.548]
Kelley, Sylvestor:
Elizabeth City Co. VA
At Fort Monroe, VA:
Collins, Mahaley
Collins, Alice
Collins, Amelia
Collins, Sally

[57.584]
Kelly, M.H.:
Elizabeth City Co. VA

At Downey Farm, VA:
Armistead, Louisa
Armistead, Patty

[57.579]
Kemp, Austin:
Gloucester Co. VA
At Downey Farm, VA:
Christian, Allen

[57.585]
Kemp, H.:
Henrico Co. VA
At Downey Farm, VA:
Peyton, Eliza
Peyton, Ben
Peyton, Walker
Peyton, Clara
Peyton, Mary Alice

[57.556]
Kenny, Baldwin:
Lancaster Co. VA
At Fort Monroe, VA:
Yearby, Sharlett

[57.472]
Kent, William:
Fluvanna Co. VA
At Fluvanna Co. VA:
Kent, Turner:
Rheumatism

[57.474]
Kentage, John S:
Fluvanna Co. VA
At Fluvanna Co. VA:
Unknown, Polly

[57.476]
Key, E: Mrs.
Fluvanna Co. VA
At Fluvanna Co. VA:
Scott, India: Deaf &
    dumb

[57.473]
Kidd, B.V:
Fluvanna Co. VA
At Fluvanna Co. VA:
Unknown, Flora: Invalid

[57.475]
Kidd, W:
Fluvanna Co. VA
At Fluvanna Co. VA:
Unknown, Eliza: Old
age

[57.475]
Kidd, Walter J:
Fluvanna Co. VA
At Fluvanna Co. VA:
Unknown, Gracie:
    Old age

[57.537]
King, Edwin:
Nansemond Co. VA
At Fort Monroe, VA:
King, Louisa

[57.542]
King, Ned:
Elizabeth City Co. VA
At Fort Monroe, VA:
Selden, Jack
Selden, Eliza

[57.530]

King, Robert:
King William Co. VA
At Fort Monroe, VA:
Segor, Eli
Segor, Eliza
Segor, Lucinda

[57.545]
Knappe, Victor:
Northampton Co. VA
At Fort Monroe, VA:
Winder, Eddie
Winder, Nelson
Winder, Jack

[57.509]
Knight, Joseph:
Mathews Co. VA
At Fort Monroe, VA:
Knight, Ann

[57.559]
Knox, Lewis:
Isle of Wight Co. VA
At Fort Monroe, VA:
Pitt, Lucinda
Pitt, Wright
Pitt, Francis
Pitt, Caleb

[57.502]
Kyle, James:
Christiansburg, VA:
At Lynchburg Hospital,
Amherst Co. VA:
Kyle, Hannah: 30

[57.502]
Kyle, W:
Buchanan Co. VA
At Lynchburg Hospital,

Amherst Co. VA:
Russell, Elizabeth: 55

[57.522]
Lamb, John:
Surry Co. VA
At Fort Monroe, VA:
Price, Mary

[57.583]
Lancaster, A.:
Nansemond Co. VA
At Downey Farm, VA:
Gunn, Hetty
Gunn, Cherry
Gunn, Jack

[57.583]
Lane, Keziah:
Surry Co. VA
At Downey Farm, VA:
Harrison, Henrietta

[57.473]
Lane, William S:
Fluvanna Co. VA
At Fluvanna Co. VA:
Burks, George: Old Age

[57.550]
Langly, Waller:
St. Mary's, Maryland
At Fort Monroe, VA:
Davis, Ann
Davis, James

[57.569]
Lariby, Charles:
Charles City Co. VA
At Fort Monroe, VA:
Wilson, Sarah

[57.546]
Lawson, Barnes:
King & Queen Co. VA
At Fort Monroe, VA:
Roy, Rachael
Roy, Simon

[57.593]
Lee, Baker:
Warwick Co. VA
At Warwick Co. VA
Lee, Lucy

[57.584]
Lee, Henry:
Gates Co. NC
At Downey Farm, VA:
Lee, Manerva
Lee, Tom
Lee, Augustus
[57.585]
Lee, Malinda

[57.548]
Lee, Thomas:
Warwick Co. VA
At Fort Monroe, VA:
Robinson, Ellen

[57.571]
Lee, William:
Elizabeth City Co. VA
At Fort Monroe, VA:
Shune, Catharine

[57.531]
Leonard, Parce:
Elizabeth City Co. VA
At Fort Monroe, VA:
Wallace, Julia

[57.578]
Lewellyn, J:
Warwick Co. VA
At Downey Farm, VA:
Black, Sarah
Stetson, Ann

[57.477]
Lewis, Charles:
Spotsylvania Co. VA
At Fredericksburg, VA:
Davis, Tilly
Davis, Thomas

[57.531]
Lewis, Davis:
Elizabeth City Co. VA
At Fort Monroe, VA:
Smith, Patsy

[57.555]
Lewis, Hands:
Northumerland Co. VA
At Fort Monroe, VA:
Strong, Sarah

[57.532]
Lipscae?, John:
{Lipscombe?}
King William Co. VA
At Fort Monroe, VA:
Stired, Lettie
Stired, Emma
Stired, Jerry

[57.522]
Lipscomb, Capt.
King William Co. VA
At Fort Monroe, VA:
Lee, Margarett
Lee, Elizabeth

Lee, Samuel

[57.534]
Lipscon, John:
King William Co. VA
At Fort Monroe, VA:
Stewart, Lettie
Stewart, Emma
Stewart, Jerry

[57.507]
Lipsker, William:
King William Co. VA
At Fort Monroe, VA:
Burkley, Millie

[57.533]
Livingston, Martha:
Portsmouth, VA
At Fort Monroe, VA:
Moore, Annie
Moore, George

[57.523]
Livingston, Walter:
Nansemond Co. VA
At Fort Monroe, VA:
Brown, Claresa
Brown, Caledonia
Brown, George

[57.584]
Locke, W.H.:
St. Mary's Co. MD
At Downey Farm, VA:
Cassell, Margaret

[57.527]
London, Thomas:
Gloucester Co. VA
At Fort Monroe, VA:

Burrill, Polly

[57.515]
Looker, Thomas:
St. Mary's Co. MD
At Fort Monroe, VA:
Gough, Ann

[57.475]
Lovett, Richard:
Fluvanna Co. VA
At Fluvanna Co. VA:
Jackson, Millie: Infirm

[57.505]
Loving, Elliott:
Bedford Co. VA
At Liberty Hospital,
Bedford Co. VA
Unknown, Esther: 18

[57.584]
Lowry, Thomas:
Elizabeth City Co. VA
At Downey Farm, VA:
Marshall, Pleasant
Marshall, David
Marshall, Louisa
Marshall, William

[57.521]
Madery, Eldridge:
Surry Co. VA
At Fort Monroe, VA:
Connell, Amanda

[57.518]
Madway, Eldridge:
Elizabeth City Co. VA
At Fort Monroe, VA:
Green, Bob

Green, Catharine

[57.520]
Maggett, Chestine:
Southampton Co. VA
At Fort Monroe, VA:
Lightfoot, Agnes

[57.541]
Major, George:
Charles City Co. VA
At Fort Monroe, VA:
Bradley, Rachael

[57.508]
Malcott, Sylvester:
Elizabeth City Co. VA
At Fort Monroe, VA:
Tabb, Amy
Tabb, Laura
Tabb, Carey
Tabb, Willie

[57.501]
Marshall, Marie:
Appomattox Co. VA
At Lynchburg Hospital,
Amherst Co. VA:
Marshall, Anderson: 24

[57.578]
Marshall, Valentine:
Charles City Co. VA
At Downey Farm, VA:
Randall, Marshall
Randall, Frank
Randall, Amy

[57.565]
Martin, Dr.:
Williamsburg, VA
At Fort Monroe, VA:
Carter, Malinda
Carter, Henry

[57.506]
Martin, Dr:
Bedford Co. VA
Hospital At Liberty,
Bedford Co. VA:
Unknown, Milton: 7
Unknown, Ella: 5
Unknown, Betty: 2

[57.534]
Mason, Miles:
Middlesex Co. VA
At Fort Monroe, VA:
Washington, George

[57.575]
Mathews, James:
Prince George Co. VA
At Fort Monroe, VA:
Strong, Martha
Strong, Susan
Strong, James
Strong, John
Strong, Betsy

[57.500]
McCue, James:
Amherst Co. VA
At Lynchburg Hospital,
Amherst Co. VA:
McCue, Margaret: 24.

[57.502]
McFay, T:
Louden Co. VA
At Lynchburg Hospital,
Amherst Co. VA:
Williams, Mary: 25

[57.502]
Sullivan, Rachael:
Charlottesville, VA:
At Lynchburg Hospital,
Amherst Co. VA:
Anderson, Mary: 23

[57.474]
McGhee, W.S:
Fluvanna Co. VA
At Fluvanna Co. VA:
Unknown, Dolly: Old age

[57.541]
McGill, Benedict:
St. Mary's Co. MD
At Fort Monroe, VA:
Butler, Ann

[57.479]
McGorram, John:
Point End
At Fredericksburg, VA:
Evans, Jane
Evans, Billy
Evans, Milley
Evans, William
Evans, Catharine
Evans, Page
Evans, Donny

[57.473]
Melone, William P:
Fluvanna Co. VA
At Fluvanna Co. VA:
Baily, Caroline:
    Old Age

[57.472]
Melton, Gaines:
Fluvanna Co. VA
At Fluvanna Co. VA:
Abraham, Ben: Infirm

[57.521]
Middleton, James:
Wilmington, NC
At Fort Monroe, VA:
Murphy, William

[57.470]
Miller, Jack:
Green Co. VA
At Fredericksburg, VA:
Shirley, Reuben: Man.
    Aged, unable to
    support himself

[57.553]
Miller, Locken:
Mathews Co. VA
At Fort Monroe, VA:
Jarvis, Mariah

[57.473]
Miller, William:
Fluvanna Co. VA
At Fluvanna Co. VA:
Miller, Charles:
    Old Age

[57.509]
Minster, Martha:
Mathews Co. VA
At Fort Monroe, VA:
Todd, Daniel
Todd, John

[57.526]
Mitchell, James:
King & Queen Co. VA
At Fort Monroe, VA:
Corwin, Lennie
Corwin, Martha
Corwin, John
Corwin, Mary
Corwin, Nelson
Corwin, Isabella

[57.550]
Mocks, Julas:
Prince George Co. VA
At Fort Monroe, VA:
Jones, Patience

[57.567]
Monks, Edward :
Prince George Co. VA
At Fort Monroe, VA:
Jones, Anthony

[57.574]
Moody, Mr:
Chesterfield Co. VA
At Fort Monroe, VA:
Chapman, Emma
Chapman, Sarah
Chapman, Joseph

[57.477]
Moor, Richard:
Richmond, VA
At Fredericksburg, VA:
Evans, Alice
Evans, George
Evans, John

[57.478]
Evans, William
Evans, Marsha
Evans, Wallace

[57.577]
Moore, John:
Elizabeth City Co. VA
At Downey Farm, VA:
Moore, Jerrie

[57.501]
Mormon, Louis:
Bedford Co. VA
At Lynchburg Hospital,
Amherst Co. VA:
Morman, Samuel: 70

[57.536]
Morral, William:
Elizabeth City Co. VA
At Fort Monroe, VA:
Hope, Fanny
Hope, Charles
Hope, Merritt
Hope, Lucy
Hope, Jane

[57.474]
Morris, E:
Fluvanna Co. VA
At Fluvanna Co. VA:
Minor, Matilda: Invalid

[57.537]
Morrison, Edmund:
Isle of Wight Co. VA
At Fort Monroe, VA:
Garden, Emmie

[57.500]
Mosby, William:
Amherst Co. VA
At Lynchburg Hospital,
Amherst Co. VA:
Anthony, Nancy: 30

[57.501]
Moss, Henry:
Greenbrier Co. VA
At Lynchburg Hospital,
Amherst Co. VA:
Moss, Emma: 20

[57.500]
Munday, Marie:
Amherst Co. VA
At Lynchburg Hospital,
Amherst Co. VA:
Munday, Arohy: 54

[57.513]
Munday, Robert:
King William Co. VA
At Fort Monroe, VA:
Wilson, Ann

[57.584]
Murphy, Josiah:
Nansemond Co. VA
At Downey Farm, VA:
Williams, James
[57.583]
Gath, Mary J.
Gath, Kitty

Gath, Lucy

[57.530]
Murphy, Thomas A:
West-Millum Co. VA
{Westmoreland?}
At Fort Monroe, VA:
Armstrong, Ann
Armstrong, Joseph

[57.554]
Murry, Dr.:
Suffolk Co. Va
At Fort Monroe, VA:
Murry, Matilda
Murry, John
Murry, Henry

[57.546]
Myers, Gilbert:
Elizabeth City Co. VA
At Fort Monroe, VA:
Randall, Bridget
Randall, Mary
Randall, Abram
Randall, Henry
Randall, Solomon

[57.533]
Myers, William:
Elizabeth City Co. VA
At Fort Monroe, VA:
Booker, Eda

[57.549]
Neal, Leonard:
St. Mary's Co. MD
At Fort Monroe, VA:
Watts, Adeline
Watts, George
Watts, Mary

Watts, William

[57.584]
Nelson, William:
Virginia Co. VA
At Downey Farm, VA:
Sykes, Laura

[57.556]
Nelson, Joseph:
Nansemond Co. VA
At Fort Monroe, VA:
Nelson, Toney

[57.517]
Newman, Sarah:
Isle of Wight Co. VA
At Fort Monroe, VA:
Tabb, Mary
Tabb, Jake
Tabb, Lizzie

[57.506]
Nickolis, A.B:
Bedford Co. VA
At Lynchburg Hospital,
Amherst Co. VA:
Unknown, Betty: 25

[57.516]
No owner listed.
North Carolina
At Fort Monroe, VA:
Bell, Mary
Bell, Marthy

[57.543]
Nodingham, Leonard:
Eastern Shore,
Northampton Co. VA
At Fort Monroe, VA:

Carpenter, Julia
[57.558]
Roberts, Lydia

[57.520]
Norfleet, Elisha:
Suffolk Co. VA
At Fort Monroe, VA:
Russell, Maria
[57.544]
Rose, Dilem
Scott, Lucinda
Scott, Clarence

[57.512]
Norrill, William:
Elizabeth City Co. VA
At Fort Monroe, VA:
Jackson, Lavina
Jackson, Martha

[57.579]
Nottingham, William:
York Co. VA
Smith, Molly: At Downey Farm, VA:
[57.593]
Smith, Mary: At Warwick Co. VA

[57.580]
Oldhern, Leroy:
Eastville, E. Shore VA
At Downey Farm, VA:
Knight, Leah
Knight, Francis

[57.502]
Openchain, Samuel:
Rockbridge Co. VA
At Lynchburg Hospital,

Amherst Co. VA:
Irvin, Ellen: 30

[57.514]
Organ, Mary:
Grassins Co. VA
At Fort Monroe, VA:
Carrol, Rachael:

[57.539]
Orphan from:
Prince George Co. VA
At Fort Monroe, VA:
Johnson, Ann

[57.539]
Orphans from Williamsburg, VA
At Fort Monroe, VA:
Warden, Fanny
Warden, Ellick

[57.528]
Osborn, Montgomery:
Prince George Co. VA
At Fort Monroe, VA:
Bailey, Margaret
Bailey, Virginia
Bailey, William
Bailey, Mariah
Bailey, Peter
Bailey, Lucy
Bailey, Sarah

[57.544]
Osborne, Dr.:
Prince George Co. VA
At Fort Monroe, VA:
Ruffin, Sarah

[57.555]

Oulds, William:
Princess Anne Co. VA
At Fort Monroe, VA:
Oulds, Dinah

[57.577]
Outland, Augustus:
Isle of Wight Co. VA
At Downey Farm, VA:
Outland, Winnie

[57.506]
Owen, Louis:
Jefferson Co. VA:
At Liberty Hospital,
Bedford Co. VA
Unknown, Mary: 26.
Unknown, Jim: 16

[57.475]
Pace, Jesse:
Fluvanna Co. VA
At Fluvanna Co. VA:
Moss, Elizabeth:
Old age

[57.474]
Pace, Lucy: Mrs.
Fluvanna Co. VA
At Fluvanna Co. VA:
Vest, Thomas: Old age
Johnson, Franklin:
Old age

[57.532]
Paden, Jerome:
Charles City Co. VA
At Fort Monroe, VA:
James, David

[57.567]
Page, Charles:
Charles City Co. VA
At Fort Monroe, VA:
Phillips, Ann
Phillips, Delia
Phillips, Richard
Shepard, Rena

[57.531]
Page, Edward:
King William Co. VA
At Fort Monroe, VA:
Durgee, Elizabeth

[57.501]
Paris, George:
Giles Co. VA
At Lynchburg Hospital,
Amherst Co. VA:
Paris, Sally: 18
Smith, Emma: 24

[57.474]
Parish, C.M: Mrs.
Fluvanna Co. VA
At Fluvanna Co. VA:
Jackson, Sarah: Infirm

[57.568]
Parish, John:
Elizabeth City Co. VA
At Fort Monroe, VA:
Webster, Mary

[57.569]
Parker, George W:
Accomac Co. VA
At Fort Monroe, VA:
Upher, Louisa
Upher, Hellen
Upher, Georgiania
Upher, Nat

[57.574]
Parker, George:
Isle of Wight Co. VA
At Fort Monroe, VA:
Parker, Ester
Parker, James

[57.585]
Parker, H.D.:
Gates Co. NC
At Downey Farm, VA:
Parker, Penelope
Parker, Samuel

[57.580]
Parker, James:
Sussex Co. VA
At Downey Farm, VA:
Jones, Robert

[57.583]
Jackson, Hannah

[57.580]
Parker, John W:
Nansemond Co. VA
At Downey Farm, VA:
Goodman, Mahala

[57.523]
Parker, John:
Eastern Shore,
Northampton Co. VA
At Fort Monroe, VA:
Allen, Lucy
Allen, Mary

[57.543]
Carter, Delia
Carter, Windfield

[57.553]
Parker, William:
Chesterfield Co. VA
At Fort Monroe, VA:
Boykin, Elizabeth
Boykin, Charlett
Boykin, Agness
Boykin, Charles
Boykin, Robert

[57.583]
Parker, William:
Sussex Co. VA
At Downey Farm, VA:
Daugherty, Fanny

[57.510]
Parris, Jackson:
Elizabeth City Co. VA
At Fort Monroe, VA:
Buckers, Nettie
Buckers, Nancy
Buckers, Esaae {Esau?}

[57.533]
Paterson, C: Mr.:
Buckingham Co. VA
At Fort Monroe, VA:
Mitchell, Eliza
Mitchell, Samuel
Mitchell, Sophia

[57.502]
Payne, Philip:
Cameron Co. VA
At Lynchburg Hospital,
Amherst Co. VA:
Payne, Tom: 23

[57.472]
Payne, R.B:
Fluvanna Co. VA
At Fluvanna Co. VA:
Unknown, York: Idiot

[57.473]
Payne, R:
Fluvanna Co. VA
At Fluvanna Co. VA:
Unknown, David:
Old Age

[57.472]
Payne, William:
Fluvanna Co. VA
At Fluvanna Co. VA:
Cooper, John: Cripple

[57.569]
Payton, Henry:
Charles City Co. VA
At Fort Monroe, VA:
Henderson, Mary
Henderson, Isaac
Henderson, Moses

[57.500]
Pedigore, James:
Campbell Co. VA
At Lynchburg Hospital, Amherst Co. VA:
Pedigore, Martha: 31

[57.581]
Penn, John:
Calvert Co. MD
At Downey Farm, VA:
Gladden, Sopia
Spriggs, Eleanor

[57.537]
Percil, Boardman:
King William Co. VA
At Fort Monroe, VA:
Grimes, Ella

[57.472]
Perkins, Isaac:
Fluvanna Co. VA
At Fluvanna Co. VA:
Bowlers, Stephen:
Infirm

[57.473]
Perkins, J:
Fluvanna Co. VA
At Fluvanna Co. VA:
Perkins, Henry: Old Age

[57.479]
Peters, John C:
Spottsylvania Co. VA
At Fredericksburg, VA:
Crump, Ann
Crump, Mary
Crump, Georgianna
Crump, Edward
Crump, Harris

[57.475]
Pettit, Samuel:
Fluvanna Co. VA
At Fluvanna Co. VA:
Parish, J: Infirm
Parish, Lydia: Infirm

[57.561]
Phetty, William:
Hanover Co. VA
At Fort Monroe, VA:
Brey, Claresa

[57.540]
Phillips, James:
Charles City Co. VA
At Fort Monroe, VA:
Gower, Sarah
Gower, Ellick
Gower, Sarah
Gower, Joseph
Gower, Maria

[57.525]
Phillips, Jefferson:
Elizabeth City Co. VA
At Fort Monroe, VA:
Baker, Rachael
Baker, Susan
Baker, Indiana

[57.536]
Phillips, Thomas:
Elizabeth City Co. VA
At Fort Monroe, VA:
Hope, Jane
Hope, Mary

[57.566]
Picket, Nathaniel:
James City Co. VA
At Fort Monroe, VA:
James, Caroline
James, Sally

[57.502]
Pierce, Jacob:
Amherst Co. VA
At Lynchburg Hospital, Amherst Co. VA:
Pierce, Charlotte: 24
Pierce, Virginia: 29

Pierce, Laura: 35
Pierce, Emily: 42
Pierce, Clara: 67
Pierce, James: 49

[57.533]
Pierson, Richard:
Prince George Co. VA
At Fort Monroe, VA:
Harris, Ellen
Harris, Indiana
Harris, Julia
Harris, James

[57.532]
Pinia, Fanny:
King William Co. VA
At Fort Monroe, VA:
Jackson, Rebecca

[57.563]
Pollard, Benjamin:
King William Co. VA
At Fort Monroe, VA:
Seldon, Emily
Seldon, Marshall
Seldon, Fannie

[57.537]
Pollard, James
King William Co. VA
At Fort Monroe, VA:
Reddick, Sarah
[57.564]
Braxton, Harriett

[57.538]
Pollard, Thomas:
King William Co. VA
At Fort Monroe, VA:
Armstead, Nancy

[57.544]
Druge, Peter
[57.545]
Sherman, Anna
[57.572]
White, Armstead

[57.528]
Pollard, William:
King William Co. VA
At Fort Monroe, VA:
Brandis, Malinda
[57.541]
Anderson, Rosetta
Anderson, Susan
Anderson, Pinkie
Anderson, Charles

[57.544]
Pondexter, Dabne:
Lynchburg, VA
At Fort Monroe, VA:
Tanner, Amand

[57.504]
Powell, Thomas:
Bedford Co. VA
At Liberty Hospital,
Bedford Co. VA:
Unknown, Neilly: 60

[57.578]
Pressey, Calvin:
York Co. VA
At Downey Farm, VA:
Howard, Chole

[57.517]
Pretty, William:
Hanover Co. VA
At Fort Monroe, VA:

Grey, Clarisey

[57.469]
Price, G.W:
Green Co. VA
At Fredericksburg, VA:
Unknown, Robert: Child
Unknown, Fanny: Woman
Unknown, Bettie: Child
Unknown, Netty: Woman
Unknown, Nelly: Child
Unknown, Amanda: Child

[57.534]
Price, John:
Cumberland Co. VA
At Fort Monroe, VA:
Jeofers, Jenott
Jeofers, George H.
Jeofers, Henry

[57.468]
Pritchet, R:
Green Co. VA
Former owner deceased,
and the Estate insolvent.
At Fredericksburg, VA:
Unknown, Millie: Woman
Unknown, Nell: Woman
Unknown, Lua: Child
Unknown, Emily: Child
Unknown, Mary: Child
Unknown, Gabriel: Child
Unknown, Moses: Child
Unknown, Betsy: Child
Unknown, William: Child
Unknown, Thornton: Man
Unknown, Fanny: Child
Unknown, Amy: Child
Unknown, Benjamin:
Child
Unknown, Sarah: Child

[57.542]
Pritchett, David:
Deep Creek,
South End, NC
At Fort Monroe, VA:
McCoy, Surmelia
McCoy, Mariso?
McCoy, Angeline
McCoy, Edith

[57.471]
Raglin, W.P:
Fluvanna Co. VA:
At Fluvanna Co. VA:
Cousins, Evalena: Infirm
Caruthers, William
McFettis, Rebecca: Blind

[57.580]
Rand, Charles:
Isle of Wight Co. VA
At Downey Farm, VA:
Good, Elizabeth
Good, Robert

[57.581]
Randall, George: Maj.
Charles City Co. VA
At Downey Farm, VA:
Randall, Delia
Randall, Lavina
Randall, Judy
Randall, Katy
Randall, Julia
Randall, Ida

[57.529]
Randall, William:
Nelson Co. VA
At Fort Monroe, VA:
Rankle, William

[57.556]
Randall, William

[57.505]
Rasey?, Thomas:
Bedford Co. VA
At Liberty Hospital,
Bedford Co. VA
Unknown, Mary Ann: 10

[57.581]
Reddick, Alvin:
Whitford Co. NC
At Downey Farm, VA:
Pinier, Priscilla

[57.581]
Reddick, Jeptha
At Downey Farm, VA:
Smith, Awander

[57.584]
Reddick, Richard:
Nansemond Co. VA
At Downey Farm, VA:
Johnson, Joseph
Johnson, Anne
Johnson, Joseph Henry
Johnson, John T.
Johnson, Mary Catherine

[57.582]
Reddick, Widow:
Bertie Co. NC
At Downey Farm, VA:
Doles, Adeline

[57.549]
Reddick, Wiley:
Gates Co. NC
At Fort Monroe, VA:

Gregory, Phania
Gregory, Rebecca

[57.561]
Reduck, William:
Gates Co. NC
At Fort Monroe, VA:
Price, Ester
Price, John
Price, Charles

[57.569]
Reed, Hawkins:
York Co. VA
At Fort Monroe, VA:
Jones, Paul

[57.503]
Reevs, Robert:
Nelson Co. VA
At Hospital at Lovington,
Nelson Co. VA:
Johnson, Agnes

[57.503]
Reevs, William:
Nelson Co. VA
Hospital at Lovington,
Nelson Co. VA:
Reevs, Phebe: 60
Bartlett, Daniel: 29

[57.501]
Reid, J:
Campbell Co. VA
At Lynchburg Hospital,
Amherst Co. VA:
Jackson, Jimy: 25

[57.500]
Rice, Patterson:
Campbell Co. VA
At Lynchburg Hospital,
Amherst Co. VA:
Rice, Booker: 23

[57.515]
Riddick, Richard:
Suffolk, VA
At Fort Monroe, VA:
Gorden, Mary

[57.518]
Riddick, William H:
Gates Co. NC
At Fort Monroe, VA:
Riddick, Harriet
Riddick, Edward
Riddick, Alfred
Riddick, Molly
Riddick, Nancy

[57.503]
Robertson, Hugh:
Nelson Co. VA
At Hospital at
Lovington, Nelson Co.
Robertson, Veelsonnus:
age 37

[57.503]
Robertson, William:
Nelson Co. VA
Hospital at Lovington,
Nelson Co. VA:
Sampson, Samuel: 29

[57.502]
Robinson, John:
Albermarle Co. VA

Lynchburg Hospital,
Amherst Co. VA:
Robinson, Robert: 16

[57.554]
Robinson, John:
Henrico Co. VA
At Fort Monroe, VA:
Marshall, Franky

[57.511]
Rodringham, Josaphene:
York Co. VA
At Fort Monroe, VA:
Westen, Susan
Westen, Martha

[57.583]
Ronds, William:
Louisa Co. VA
At Downey Farm, VA:
Jackson, Eliza

[57.573]
Ronett, John P:
Charles City Co. VA
At Fort Monroe, VA:
Julias, Francis

[57.502]
Ross, Peter:
North Carolina:
At Lynchburg Hospital,
Amherst Co. VA:
Ross, Temple: 40

[57.500]
Rosser, Pleasant:
Campbell Co. VA
At Lynchburg Hospital,
Amherst Co. VA:

Rosser, Selina: 40

[57.478]
Rowan, [ ]:
Spotsylvania Co. VA
At Fredericksburg, VA:
Gallary, Sarah
Gallary, Margaret
Gallary, Mary
Gallary, Linnia
Gallary, Idia
Slaughter, Helen
Thornton, Millia
Thornton, George
Thornton, Ro.

[57.556]
Rowe, Benjamin:
Gloucester Co. VA
At Fort Monroe, VA:
Tabb, Elizabeth
Tabb, William

[57.569]
Rowe, Edward:
Gloucester Co. VA
At Fort Monroe, VA:
Cook, Susan

[57.578]
Rowell, Widow:
York Co. VA
At Downey Farm, VA:
Pressey, Mary
Pressey, William
Pressey, Maria Susan

[57.551]
Roy, John P:
Charles City Co. VA
At Fort Monroe, VA:

Carter, Mary

[57.525]
Ruffin, Edmund:
Prince George Co. VA
At Fort Monroe, VA:
Prophit, Ebrie
Prophit, Rose
Prophit, Alda
[57.527]
Washington, Rebecca
Washington, Richard
Washington, Milly
Washington, Julia
Washington, Randall
Washington, Richard
Washington, Sarah
Locklin, Fanny
[57.572]
Tolver, Spriggs
Tolver, Eliza

[57.548]
Ruffin, Edward:
Prince George Co. VA
Reed, Peggy
Reed, Augustes
Reed, Henry
Reed, Indiana
Reed, Lewis
Reed, Clara A.

[57.578]
Ruffin, Maj:
Prince George Co. VA
At Fort Monroe, VA:
Dillard, Lucretia

[57.560]
Ruffin, Thomas:
Surry Co. VA

At Fort Monroe, VA:
Barker, Mary E
Barker, William

[57.531]
Ruffin, William:
Surry Co. VA
At Fort Monroe, VA:
Jones, Nancy
Jones, Alice
Jones, Edward
Jones, Charles[57.557]
Morris, Agness
[57.564]
Cox, Ellis

[57.501]
Rust, G.W:
Bedford Co. VA
At Lynchburg Hospital,
Amherst Co. VA:
Sidney, Louisa: 35

[57.473]
Salad, George W:
Fluvanna Co. VA
At Fluvanna Co. VA:
Sauger, Samuel: Old Age

[57.505]
Sanderded, Dr:
Bedford Co. VA
At Liberty Hospital,
Bedford Co. VA
Unknown, Sarah: 22
Unknown, Jeffries: 60
Unknown, Betty: 60
Unknown, Sam: 70
Unknown, Marie: 65
Unknown, Mary: 21
Unknown, Edward: 10

Unknown, James: 45
Unknown, Almus: 45
Unknown, Israel: 60
Unknown, Nanda: 34
Unknown, Ellen: 10
Unknown, Emma: 1
[57.506]
Unknown, Dorcas: 70
Unknown, Minerva: 30
Unknown, Margaret
Unknown, Francis: 7
Unknown, Ann: 5
Unknown, William: 3
Unknown, Virginia: 28

[57.502]
Saunders, Cloyd:
South Carolina:
At Lynchburg Hospital,
Amherst Co. VA:
Genoa, Ella: age 16

[57.479]
Saunders, John:
Spottsylvania Co. VA
At Fredericksburg, VA:
Lewis, Luie
Lewis, Charlon
Lewis, Edward

[57.540]
Savage, Edward:
Elizabeth City Co. VA
At Fort Monroe, VA:
Thomas, Nelly

[57.513]
Savage, Fanny:
Elizabeth City Co. VA
At Fort Monroe, VA:
Dunn, Lockey

[57.583]
Savage, Jesse:
Nansemond Co. VA
At Downey Farm, VA:
Savage, Mary

[57.576]
Savage, Mr:
Sussex Co. VA
At Fort Monroe, VA:
Moody, Cherry

[57.511]
Scott, John:
Isle of Wight Co. VA
At Fort Monroe, VA:
Jerdan, Eliza
Jerdan, Henrietta
Jerdan, Ellie
Jerdan, Emily

[57.479]
Scott, Mrs:
Hanover Co. VA
At Fredericksburg, VA:
Williams, Silvia

[57.501]
Scott, Samuel:
Campbell Co. VA
At Lynchburg Hospital,
Amherst Co. VA:
Scott, Benjamin: 80.

[57.500]
Screggs, John:
Nelson Co. VA
At Lynchburg Hospital,
Amherst Co. VA:
Screggs, Dick: 60

[57.515]
Searber, Charles H:
Prince George Co. VA
At Fort Monroe, VA:
Taylor, Jane
Taylor, Adeline
Taylor, Francis
Taylor, Joseph
Taylor, Jacob

[57.512]
Seasber, George:
Accomac Co. VA
At Fort Monroe, VA:
Jerson, Laurance

[57.473]
Seay, Austin:
Fluvanna Co. VA
At Fluvanna Co. VA:
Unknown, Sally: Infirm

[57.471]
Seay, B.W:
Fluvanna Co. VA
At Fluvanna Co. VA:
Beaver, Dosby: Infirm
McCary, Maria: Infirm

[57.473]
Seay, George G:
Fluvanna Co. VA
At Fluvanna Co. VA:
Kingston, J.B: Cripple

[57.546]
Selden, John:
Charles City Co. VA
At Fort Monroe, VA:
Douglass, Philis
Douglass, Lucy
Douglass, Agness
Douglass, Margarett
[57.547]
Jones, Margaret
Jones, Mary
[57.573]
Carter, Patience

[57.571]
Selden, Robert:
Gloucester Co. VA
At Fort Monroe, VA:
Ray, Lucretia
Ray, Dick
Ray, Moseby
Ray, Lucretia
Ray, Thomas
[57.524]
Braxton, Eliza
Braxton, Rose

[57.584]
Shaw, J.I: (Dr.)
St. Mary's Co. MD
At Downey Farm, VA:
Crawley, Jane

[57.556]
Shelley, Frank:
Isle of Wight Co. VA
At Fort Monroe, VA:
Wilson, Pauline
Wilson, Sam
Wilson, George

[57.516]
Shepard, Ellie:
Mathews Co. VA
At Fort Monroe, VA:
Dickson, Mary
Dickson, Sarah

[57.475]
Shepherd, J.A:
Fluvanna Co. VA
At Fluvanna Co. VA:
Jones, Polly: Old age

[57.474]
Shepherd, William D:
Fluvanna Co. VA
At Fluvanna Co. VA:
Flowers, Malinda:
    Old age

[57.511]
Sherman, Ballard:
New Kent Co. VA
At Fort Monroe, VA:
Page, Lucy
Megins, Louisa

[57.522]
Sherman, Benjamin:
New Kent Co. VA
At Fort Monroe, VA:
Mickens, Louisa
Christian, Lucy

[57.574]
Sherman, Benjamin:
New Kent Co. VA
In New Kent Co. VA
Mickens, Louisa
Christian, Lucy

[57.501]
Sherman, James A:
Lynchburg, VA:
At Lynchburg Hospital,
Amherst Co. VA:
Henry, Nancy: 85

[57.517]
Sherman, Mastin:
New Kent Co. VA
At Fort Monroe, VA:
Taylor, Elizabeth

[57.539]
Robinson, Julia

[57.574]
Sherman. Headley:
New Kent Co. VA
At Fort Monroe, VA:
Meekes, Caroline
Meekes, Fleming
Meekes, Littleton
Meekes, Elle E.
Meekes, Caroline

[57.578]
Shields, S: Dr.
Elizabeth City Co. VA
At Downey Farm, VA:
Shields, Ricard
Shields, Polly

[57.549]
Simonds, Joshua:
Nansemond Co. VA
At Fort Monroe, VA:
Carson, Lourice

[57.526]
Simonds, William:
Goochland Co. VA
At Fort Monroe, VA:
Boyden, Rosey
Boyden, Delia
Boyden, Joseph
Boyden, Manuel
Boyden, Maria

[57.468]
Sims, Robert:
Green Co. VA
Following persons:
Former owner unable
to support:
At Fredericksburg, VA:
Unknown, Susan: Child
Unknown, Louisa: Child
Unknown, Mary: Child
Unknown, Rose: Woman
Lewis, John: Child
Unknown, Emily: Child
Unknown, Martha: Child.
Unknown, Jennie: Child.

[57.469]
Unknown, Nelly: Woman
Unknown, Charlotte:
    Woman
Unknown, Moses: Man
Unknown, Milly: Child
Unknown, William: Child
Unknown, Caroline: Child.
Unknown, Columbia:
    Child.

[57.533]
Sinclair, John:
Gloucester Co. VA
At Fort Monroe, VA:
Henry, Fanny
Henry, Eliza
Henry, Alice
Henry, Jennie

[57.515]
Sinclare, Jefferson:
Elizabeth City Co. VA
At Fort Monroe, VA:
Bright, Eliza
Bright, Phillip

[57.517]
Skinner, Joseph:
Newbern, NC
At Fort Monroe, VA:
Kinsey, Ann

[57.502]
Slaughter, Fickling:
Albermarle Co. VA
At Lynchburg Hospital,
Amherst Co. VA:
Perkins, Amy: 70.

[57.512]
Slocum, John:
Cumberland Co. VA
At Fort Monroe, VA:
Jackson, Fanny
Jackson, Walter
Jackson, Emily
Edmonds, Agness
Smith, Francis
Green, Betty Ann
Gates, Hester Jane
Gates, Dotty
Gates, Lewis

[57.524]
Smith, Frank:
York Co. VA
At Fort Monroe, VA:
Cook, Dafney

[57.542]
Smith, George:
York Co. VA
At Fort Monroe, VA:
Gales, Susan

[57.577]
Smith, Henry:

York Co. VA
At Downey Farm, VA:
Pressey, Tom

[57.524]
Smith, John:
Charles City Co. VA
At Fort Monroe, VA:
Bailey, Sally
Bailey, Jackson

[57.581]
Smith, John:
Charles City Co. VA
At Downey Farm, VA:
Taylor, Martha Ann
Crosly, Lavina
Crosly, Wilbur
Crosly, Clemma
Crosly, Sandy
Crosly, Edward
Parker, Mary

[57.557]
Smith, John:
Edenton, NC
At Fort Monroe, VA:
Taylor, Louisa
Taylor, Elijah
Taylor, Sally Ann

[57.519]
Smith, Mortimore:
King & Queen Co. VA
At Fort Monroe, VA:
Bagby, Lucy

[57.560]
Smith, Mr:
Norfolk, VA
At Fort Monroe, VA:

Judon, Amand

[57.593]
Smith, Nelson:
Warwick Co. VA
At Warwick Co. VA:
Hill, Fanny
Hill, Millie

[57.518]
Smith, Owen:
Elizabeth City Co. VA
At Fort Monroe, VA:
Smith, Johnson
Smith, Hannah
Smith, Rosa
Smith, Luck
Smith, Abram
Smith, Rachael

[57.562]
Smith, Samuel:
Mathews Co. VA
At Fort Monroe, VA:
Coltin, Emily

[57.530]
Smith, Sand:
Mathews Co. VA
At Fort Monroe, VA:
Colter, Emily
Colter, Joseph

[57.578]
Smith, Tom:
York Co. VA
At Downey Farm, VA:
Purlieu, Lucy Ann

[57.530]

Smith, W.S:
Elizabeth City Co. VA
At Fort Monroe, VA:
Patrick, Ellen
Patrick, Sella
Patrick, Peter

[57.519]
Smith, William S:
Charles City Co. VA
At Fort Monroe, VA:
Booker, Ann

[57.508]
Smith, William:
Elizabeth City Co. VA
At Fort Monroe, VA:
Booker, Matilda

[57.548]
Smith, William:
Gloucester Co. VA
At Fort Monroe, VA:
Williams, Betsey

[57.545]
Smith, William:
Prince George Co. VA
At Fort Monroe, VA:
Harnett, Charlett
Harnett, Emma

[57.570]
Smith, William:
Prince Edward Co. VA
At Fort Monroe, VA:
Miller, Lilley

[57.472]
Snead, Ben:
Fluvanna Co. VA

At Fluvanna Co. VA:
Unknown, Wilson:
Blind

[57.516]
Snell, Henry:
St. Mary's Co. MD
At Fort Monroe, VA:
Berry, Laurice
Berry, George

[57.475]
Snotty, Mrs:
Fluvanna Co. VA
At Fluvanna Co. VA:
Jackson, Lydia: Infirm
Snows, Washington:
Unknown, Isabella:
Old Age

[57.529]
Southhould, Stephen:
Isle of Wight Co. VA
At Fort Monroe, VA:
Nichols, Emma
Nichols, Jennie
Nichols, Mary
Nichols, Kate
Nichols, Henry

[57.569]
Southold, William H:
Charles City Co. VA
At Fort Monroe, VA:
Rogister, Nancy

[57.501]
Spelter, James:
Campbell Co. VA
At Lynchburg Hospital,
Amherst Co. VA:

Sheer, Frank: 40

[57.480]
Spindas?, Benjamin:
Spottsylvania Co. VA
At Fredericksburg, VA:
Thompson, John

[57.563]
Spradley, Punch:
Surry Co. VA
At Fort Monroe, VA:
Spradley, Charlott
Spradley, Emma
Spradley, Cherry
Spradley, Gilbert
Spradley, Tirgers?

[57.563]
Spradley, Thomas:
Surry Co. VA
At Fort Monroe, VA:
Pierce, Adaline
Pierce, Polly
Pierce, Agness

[57.572]
Randall, Hannah
Randall, Lewis
Randall, David
Randall, Lucy
Randall, Archie

[57.550]
Spradly, Richard:
Surry Co. VA
At Fort Monroe, VA:
Nozery, Dinah
Nozery, William
Nozery, Catharine

[57.524]
Spratley, Thomas:
Surry Co. VA
At Fort Monroe, VA:
Bailey, Margaret
Bailey, Susan
Bailey, Patsey
Bailey, Miles

[57.540]
Spruell, Hesekiah:
Plymouth, NC
At Fort Monroe, VA:
Spruell, Chloe Ann

[57.475]
Staples, A: Mrs.
Fluvanna Co. VA
At Fluvanna Co. VA:
Unknown, Malinda:
    Old age

[57.471]
Staples, I: Mrs.
Fluvanna Co. VA
At Fluvanna Co. VA:
Lucas, Fanny: Old Age
Unknown, Fanny:
    Old Age

[57.500]
Staten, Ruben:
Campbell Co. VA
At Lynchburg Hospital,
Amherst Co. VA:
Brooks, Thomas: 33

[57.581]
Stedgt, Merrit:
Surry Co. VA
At Downey Farm, VA:

Coker, Caroline

[57.560]
Stephens, John:
King William Co. VA
At Fort Monroe, VA:
Thomas, Mariah
Thomas, Nancy

[57.501]
Stine, J.W:
Lynchburg, VA:
At Lynchburg Hospital,
Amherst Co. VA:
Matthews, Jim: 18

[57.518]
Stock, Dr:
Charles City Co. VA
At Fort Monroe, VA:
Harrison, Braxton
Harrison, Edmond

[57.573]
Stocks, Dr.
Charles City Co. VA
At Fort Monroe, VA:
Harrison, Millie
Harrison, Armstead

[57.516]
Stocks, P:
Charles City Co. VA
At Fort Monroe, VA:
Thornton, Clara
Thornton, Thomas

[57.544]
Stocks, Potan:
Charles City Co. VA
At Fort Monroe, VA:

Robinson, Carter
Robinson, Lucy
Robinson, Rachel
Robinson, Mariah
Robinson, Fannie
Robinson, Isham

[57.584]
Stokeley, Franklin:
Elizabeth City, NC
At Downey Farm, VA:
Granger, Warren
Granger, Mary

[57.501]
Stone, Elizabeth:
Pittsylvania Co. VA
At Lynchburg Hospital,
Amherst Co. VA:
Stone, Amelia: 35

[57.584]
Stovel, W:
York Co. VA
At Downey Farm, VA:
Chatman, Susan

[57.475]
Stowe, Fanny:
Fluvanna Co. VA:
At Fluvanna Co. VA:
Strong, G: Blind

[57.474]
Strange, Ed:
Fluvanna Co. VA
At Fluvanna Co. VA:
Unknown, Woman:
    Old age

[57.475]
Strange, Ned:
Fluvanna Co. VA
At Fluvanna Co. VA:
Friday, Clary: Blind

[57.472]
Stratton, M: Mrs.
Fluvanna Co. VA
At Fluvanna Co. VA:
White, Thomas: Infirm
White, Hannah: Infirm

[57.477]
Sudon, John:
Spotsylvania Co. VA
At Fredericksburg, VA:
Lewis, Hiram
Lewis, Thomas

[57.525]
Sulivan, Christian:
Dinwiddie Co. VA
At Fort Monroe, VA:
Murry, Ann
Murry, Fannie
Murry, Jennie

[57.512]
Sutton, Catharine:
Edenton, NC
At Fort Monroe, VA:
Spence, Martha

[57.547]
Syke, Benjamin:
Georgia
At Fort Monroe, VA:
Stewart, Fanny

[57.584]

Sykes, Michael:
Virginia Co. VA
At Downey Farm, VA:
Sykes, Eliza

[57.558]
Symons, John:
Bertie, NC
At Fort Monroe, VA:
Newell, Patsey

[57.547]
Tabb, John:
Gloucester Co. VA
At Fort Monroe, VA:
Jackson, Louisa
Jackson, Robert
Jackson, Ellen

[57.579]
Tabb, William: Mrs.
York Co. VA
At Downey Farm, VA:
Hardgrove, Francis
Hardgrove, Robert Henry

[57.477]
Talber, Thomas:
Fredericksburg VA
At Fredericksburg, VA:
Jones, Mary
Williams, Selina

[57.583]
Talley, Sam:
Louisa Co. VA
At Downey Farm, VA:
Bottey, George
Bottey, Agnes

[57.561]
Tayler, George:
King William Co. VA
At Fort Monroe, VA:
Lambert, Susan
Lambert, Fanny
Lambert, Edward
Lambert, Charles

[57.517]
Taylor, Curren:
Gloucester Co. VA
At Fort Monroe, VA:
Lambert, Nelly
Lambert, Hellen
Lambert, Susie
Lambert, Allice
Lambert, Andrew
[57.528]
Brooks, Mary
Brooks, Martha
Brooks, Mary

[57.519]
Taylor, George:
King William Co. VA
At Fort Monroe, VA:
Henry, Charlotte
[57.559]
White, Iras

[57.480]
Taylor, James:
Bowling Green, VA
At Fredericksburg, VA:
Johnson, Timmy

[57.473]
Taylor, James:
Fluvanna Co. VA
At Fluvanna Co. VA:
Bowers, Reuben:
    Old Age

[57.530]
Taylor, John:
York Co. VA
At Fort Monroe, VA:
Washington, Sally
Washington, Nace
Dickerson, Nace:
    Orphan

[57.581]
Taylor, R:
Surry Co. VA
At Downey Farm, VA:
Brigham, Jesse
Brigham, Pocahontas

[57.531]
Taylor, W.P:
York Co. VA
At Fort Monroe, VA:
Baker, Betsey:
Baker, William

[57.521]
Taylor, William P:
York Co. VA
At Fort Monroe, VA:
Minkin, Malinda
Minkin, Amy

[57.531]
Taylor, William:
Gloucester Co. VA
At Fort Monroe, VA:

Carey, Lucy Ann
Carey, Emma
Carey, John

[57.556]
Taylor, David:
Sussex Co. VA
At Fort Monroe, VA:
Gray, Ann
Gray, Richmond
Gray, George
Washington
Gray, Susan

[57.582]
Temple, James:
Prince George Co. VA
At Downey Farm, VA:
Still, Eliza

[57.566]
Tennis, John:
York Co. VA
At Fort Monroe, VA:
Johnson, Sarah Ann
Johnson, William

[57.480]
Terry, Richard:
Spottsylvania Co. VA
At Fredericksburg, VA:
Nelson, James

[57.502]
Thil[ ], Charles:
Greensboro NC:
At Lynchburg Hospital,
Amherst Co. VA:
Whiting, Hannah: 40.

[57.585]

Thomas, Billy:
St. Mary's Co. MD
At Downey Farm, VA:
Hawkins, Eliza

[57.556]
Thomas, John E:
Isle of Wight Co. VA
At Fort Monroe, VA:
Thomas, Silvey
Thomas, John
Thomas, Mary
[57.584]
At Downey Farm, VA:
Thomas, Corey
Thomas, Mary

[57.475]
Thomas, M:
Fluvanna Co. VA
At Fluvanna Co. VA:
Carr, Madison: Crippled

[57.474]
Thoma , P T: (Mrs.)
Fluvanna Co. VA
At Fluvanna Co. VA:
Unknown, Fanny:
Infirm & blind

[57.546]
Thomas, Richard:
Isle of Wight Co. VA
At Fort Monroe, VA:
Thomas, Lucy

[57.572]
Thomas, Spradley:
Surry Co. VA
At Fort Monroe, VA:
Randall, Hannah

Randall, Lewis
Randall, David
Randall, Lucy
Randall, Archie

[57.516]
Thompson, C:
Elizabeth City Co. VA
At Fort Monroe, VA:
Watts, Nancy
Watts, Robin

[57.527]
Thompson, Taswell:
Gloucester Co. VA
At Fort Monroe, VA:
Bundy, Hardy
Bundy, Betsy
wife of Hardy

[57.555]
Thornton, Richard:
Surry Co. VA
At Fort Monroe, VA:
Vaughn, Jane
Vaughn, Emily

[57.539]
Thurston, James:
King & Queen Co. VA
At Fort Monroe, VA:
Bundley, Fanny
Bundley, Ranson
Bundley, William
Bundley, Minnie
Bundley, Jennie

[57.468]
Timbro, Polly:
Green Co. VA
At Fredericksburg, VA:

Unknown, Fleming:
Child

[57.529]
Todd, Robinson:
Smithfield Co. VA
At Fort Monroe, VA:
Clarey, Ester
Clarey, Sarah
Clarey, Fanny
Clarey, Edwin

[57.536]
Toland, William:
Hanover Co. VA
At Fort Monroe, VA:
Johnson, Louisa

[57.558]
Toller, Henry:
New Kent Co. VA
At Fort Monroe, VA:
Gaines, Ann
Gaines, Michell

[57.571]
Tolliver, John:
Hanover Co. VA
At Fort Monroe, VA:
Fukes, Sarah
Fukes, Isader
Fukes, Sephy

[57.538]
Tolliver, John:
Henrico Co. VA
At Fort Monroe, VA:
Norris, Mary
Norris, Anna
Norris, Thomas
Norris, Sally

[57.475]
Toucy, John W:
Fluvanna Co. VA
At Fluvanna Co. VA:
Baker, Millie: Infirm

[57.513]
Trower, John:
Northampton Co. VA
At Fort Monroe, VA:
Trower, Mary A.
Trower, Butler
Trower, Jerry
Trower, Wadora
Trower, Sarah

[57.480]
Tulliver, William:
King George Co. VA
At Fredericksburg, VA:
Taplet, Anna

[57.475]
Turner, James H:
Fluvanna Co. VA
At Fluvanna Co. VA:
Minor, Richard:
Ruptured

[57.520]
Turner, John:
Nansemond Co. VA
At Fort Monroe, VA:
Clay, Almedra
Clay, Josephine

[57.477]
Turner, William:
Spotsylvania Co. VA
At Fredericksburg, VA:
Hale, Millie

[57.536]
Twine, M:
Elizabeth City Co. VA
At Fort Monroe, VA:
Henton, Noah

[57.558]
Twine, Sarah:
Elizabeth City Co. VA
At Fort Monroe, VA:
Goodman, Mary

[57.512]
Twine, Thomas:
Elizabeth City Co. VA
At Fort Monroe, VA:
Taylor, Judy
Taylor, Marthia
Taylor, Cornelius
Taylor, Margaret
Taylor, Mary Ann
Foster, Margaret
Foster, Thomas
Foster, George
[57.559]
Johnson, Catharine

[57.537]
Tyler, Hiram:
Charles City Co. VA
At Fort Monroe, VA:
Johnson, Betsy

[57.535]
Tyler, John:
Charles City Co. VA
At Fort Monroe, VA:
Black, Eliza
Black, Thadious
Black, Ellen
Black, Mary

Black, Joseph

[57.571]
Tyler, John:
Hanover Co. VA
At Fort Monroe, VA:
Sails, Mary
Sails, Martha
Sails, William
Sails, James
Sails, Killis

[57.540]
Tyler, Thomas:
Hanover Co. VA
At Fort Monroe, VA:
Quarrels, Charlett

[57.504]
Former Owners & residence unknown:
At Liberty Hospital, Bedford Co. VA:
Unknown, W. Henry: 7
Unknown, Frazer: 6
[57.505]
Unknown, Sukey: 60
Unknown, Davy: 30
Unknown, Robert: 20

[57.506]
Former Owner unknown:
Former residence Rappahannock Co. VA:
At Liberty Hospital, Bedford Co. VA:
Unknown, Henry: 16
Unknown, John: 1
Unknown, Susan Mary: 5
Unknown, Louisa: 1

[57.528]
Unknown former owner: Former residence in Prince George Co. VA:
At Fort Monroe, VA:
Wilkins, Ester
Wilkins, Patience
Wilkins, James
Wilkins, Washington
Wilkins, Henry

[57.507]
Unknown former owner: Former residence: Northampton Co. VA
At Fort Monroe, VA:
Addison, John
Colwell, Annie
Unknown, Martha:
Unknown, Georgianna: Child
Unknown, Columba: Child

[57.541]
Upcher, Ann:
Maryland
At Fort Monroe, VA:
Brown, Alice
Brown, Robert

[57.534]
Upshure, William:
Northampton Co. VA
At Fort Monroe, VA:
White, Ann
White, John
White, Mary
White, Leren

[57.563]
Upture, William:
Charles City Co. VA
At Fort Monroe, VA:
Green, Malinda

[57.593]
Van Bullock, Grant:
Louisa Co. VA
At Warwick Co. VA
Jackson, Esther
Jackson, Robert
Jackson, Elsie

[57.538]
Vanten, Robert:
Charles City Co. VA
At Fort Monroe, VA:
Shepard, Morris
Shepard, Ella

[57.575]
Vaughn, Dr:
Elizabeth City Co. VA
At Fort Monroe, VA:
Jones, Jennie

[57.518]
Vaughn, Jacob:
Elizabeth City Co. VA
At Fort Monroe, VA:
Smith, Hannah
Smith, Abram
Smith, Rosa
Smith, Rachael

[57.577]
Vaughn, Robert:
Elizabeth City Co. VA
At Downey Farm, VA:
Vaughn, Eliza

[57.579]
Vaughn, Rosetta

[57.557]
Vaughn, Thomas:
Edenton, NC
At Fort Monroe, VA:
Vaughn, Elsie

Vaughn. R:
Elizabeth City Co. VA
At Downey Farm, VA:
Rowe, William

[57.502]
Waldron, Captain:
Rappahannock Co. VA
At Lynchburg Hospital,
Amherst Co. VA:
Waldron, Aaron: 66

[57.480]
Walker, Alexander:
Fredericksburg, VA
At Fredericksburg, VA:
Thornton, Antony
Slean, Margaret

[57.474]
Walker, J.W:
Fluvanna Co. VA
At Fluvanna Co. VA:
Unknown, Hampton:
Old age
Unknown, Laura:
Old age

[57.553]
Walker, W.B:
Charles City Co. VA
At Fort Monroe, VA:

Marrell, Hanan

[57.581]
Wallace, A:
Stafford Co. VA
At Downey Farm, VA:
Jones, Amanda

[57.478]
Wallace, Richard:
Spottsylvania Co. VA
At Fredericksburg, VA:
Wagensworth, Melina
Wagensworth, Mary
Wagensworth, Lucy
Wagensworth, Moriah
Wagensworth, Henry

[57.502]
Walls, William:
Amherst Co. VA
At Lynchburg Hospital,
Amherst Co. VA:
Davenport, John: 45
Davenport, Matilda: 37

[57.534]
Ward, Georgeana:
New Kent Co. VA
At Fort Monroe, VA:
Webb, Catharine

[57.593]
Warden, Mr.:
Warwick Co. VA
At Warwick Co. VA
Lightfoot, Henry
Lightfoot, Rachael

[57.519]
Waren, Moses:
Williamsburg, VA
At Fort Monroe, VA:
Ellis, Everett:
Ellis, Lizzie

[57.539]
Warren, Edwin P:
Prince George Co. VA
At Fort Monroe, VA:
Brown, Catharine
Brown, William Henry

[57.538]
Warren, Michael:
James City Co. VA
At Fort Monroe, VA:
Douglass, Matilda
Douglass, Matilda
Douglass, Fanny
Douglass, Lucy
Douglass, Betsy

[57.524]
Warren, Mr:
Surry Co. VA
At Fort Monroe, VA:
Harrison, Gally
Harrison, Sarah
Harrison, Rose

[57.555]
Warren, Thomas:
North Carolina
At Fort Monroe, VA:
Keely, Sarah
Keely, Laura

[57.477]
Washington, John:
Caroline Co. VA
At Fredericksburg, VA:
Coats, Benjamin

[57.480]
Johnson, Lissy
Jones, Alvena
Jones, William
Johnson, Harrity
Jones, Georgiana

[57.565]
Washington, William:
Hurtville, NC
At Fort Monroe:
Washington, Jane
Washington, Charles
Washington, Francis

[57.579]
Watkins, E.O:
Chesterfield Co. VA
At Downey Farm, VA:
Good, Maria

[57.552]
Watkins, Edward:
Chesterfield Co. VA
At Fort Monroe, VA:
Williams, Betsey
Williams, Lizzie
Williams, Fanny
Williams, Peter

[57.556]
Williams, Patsey
Williams, Fanny
Williams, Lizzie:
Williams, Peache

[57.515]
Watkins, Henry:
Elizabeth City Co. VA
At Fort Monroe, VA:
Adams, Mary
Adams, Edward
Adams, Diza

[57.580]
Wattes, Catherine:
Elizabeth City Co. VA
At Downey Farm, VA:
Parker, Mary Eliza
Parker, Isaac
Johnson, Amelia Ann
Johnson, Alice
Gatewood, Aaron
Gatewood, Esther

[57.516]
Watts, Thomas:
Elizabeth City Co. VA
At Fort Monroe, VA:
Watts, Robin

[57.542]
Webb, Henry:
New Kent Co. VA
At Fort Monroe, VA:
Robinson, Sally
Slate, Clarisa
[57.574]
Smith, Louisa
Smith, Ellen
Smith, Henry
Webb, Jane

[57.507]
Webb, Mr:
Nottoway Co. VA
At Fort Monroe, VA:

173

Ball, Betsey
Ball, Ella
Ball, Charlott
Ball, Lewis

[57.583]
Webb, S: Dr.
New Kent Co. VA
At Downey Farm, VA:
Lewon, Winnie
Lewon, Mary

[57.514]
Webb, Samuel: Dr.
New Kent Co. VA
At Fort Monroe, VA:
King, Amy
King, Nelson
[57.518]
Brown, Millie
[57.540]
King, Caroline
King, Polly
King, Logan
King, Dinah
King, Mary

[57.585]
Webster, L:
Charles Co. MD.
At Downey Farm, VA:
Slater, Sarah Ann
Slater, Lewis
Slater, Ann
Slater, Robert

[57.528]
Weed, Joseph:
New Kent Co. VA
At Fort Monroe, VA:
Webb, Jane

Webb, Burrell
Webb, Jackson

[57.542]
Wescott, William:
Northampton Co. VA
At Fort Monroe, VA:
Risby, Jennie
Risby, Frances

[57.501]
Whalen, S:
Appomattox Co. VA
At Lynchburg Hospital,
Amherst Co. VA:
Buckey, Linsey: 25

[57.561]
Wheeler, Robert:
Elmont, VA
{Note: Elmont is in Hanover Co.}
At Fort Monroe, VA:
Battles, Mary
James, Mariah
James, Thomas

[57.527]
White, Ambrose:
King William Co. VA
At Fort Monroe, VA:
Henderson, Sarah

[57.472]
White, David:
Fluvanna Co. VA
At Fluvanna Co. VA:
Unknown, Sophia Ann: Nearly blind

[57.564]

White, Edwin:
Surry Co. VA
At Fort Monroe, VA:
Boykin, Millie
Boykin, Nancie
Boykin, Arther
Boykin, Louisa

[57.475]
White, James P:
Fluvanna Co. VA
At Fredericksburg, VA:
Unknown, Uncle Jack: One leg off
Unknown, Jacob: Blind
Unknown, John: Nearly Blind

[57.472]
White, John W:
Fluvanna Co. VA
At Fluvanna Co. VA:
Unknown, Squire: Old Age
Unknown, Mason: Invalid

[57.514]
White, Samuel:
Isle of Wight Co. VA
At Fort Monroe, VA:
Wilson, Nellie

[57.468]
White, W:
Green Co. VA
At Fredericksburg, VA:
Unknown, Nelson: Child

[57.509]
White, William:
Mathews Co. VA
At Fort Monroe, VA:
Washington, Kittie
Washington, Hunter
Washington, Brooks

[57.565]
Whiten, Canon:
Elizabeth City Co. VA
At Fort Monroe, VA:
Morris, Kitty
Morris, Patsy
Morris, Moses

[57.512]
Whiting, Canen:
Elizabeth City Co. VA
At Fort Monroe, VA:
Williams, Margaret
Williams, Frank
Williams, Dabney

[57.557]
Whiting, Henry:
Elizabeth City Co. VA
At Fort Monroe, VA:
Howard, Pheby

[57.521]
Whitney, Carter:
Richmond, VA
At Fort Monroe, VA:
Jupee, Amanda
Jupee, Alice

[57.529]
Whitney, Sterrit:
Smithfield, VA
At Fort Monroe, VA:

Smith, Robert
Smith, Ann

[57.581]
Wickham, William:
Hanover Co. VA
At Downey Farm, VA:
Drew, Susan

[57.554]
Wilcox, Dr:
Charles City Co. VA
At Fort Monroe, VA:
Jefferson, Annie
Jefferson, Maria
Jefferson, Allen

[57.536]
Wilcox, Dr:
Elizabeth City Co. VA
At Fort Monroe, VA:
Wilson, Christian
Wilson, Benjamin
Wilson, Frederick

[57.550]
Wilcox, Jackson:
Prince George Co. VA
At Fort Monroe, VA:
Willis, Hannah
Willis, Aaron
Willis, Samuel
Willis, Eda
Willis, Marshall

[57.538]
Wilcox, Jacob:
Prince George Co. VA
At Fort Monroe, VA:
Marshall, David

[57.522]
Wilcox, Jacob:
Petersburg, VA
At Fort Monroe, VA:
Willis, Lucretia

[57.560]
Wilcox, Westmore:
Charles City Co. VA
At Fort Monroe, VA:
Edlay, Martha
Edlay, Fleming

[57.572]
Wilcox, William: Dr.
Charles City Co.
At Fort Monroe, VA:
Hall, Patsey
Hall, Hatty
Hall, Patsy
Hall, Sarah

[57.558]
Wild, Richard:
Albemarle Co. VA
At Fort Monroe, VA:
Anderson, Lavenia
Anderson, Lucy
Anderson, Fanny

[57.525]
Wiley, Thomas:
Richmond, Co. VA
At Fort Monroe, VA:
Washington, Saderfield
Washington, Daniel

[57.545]
Wilkins, William:
Northampton Co. VA
At Fort Monroe, VA:
Gidget, Rachael

[57.508]
Williams, Billy:
Mathews Co. VA
At Fort Monroe, VA:
Jones, Martha

[57.472]
Willis, A.G: Dr.
Fluvanna Co. VA
At Fluvanna Co. VA:
Nelson, Peter: Old Age

[57.565]
Wilson, Ashby:
Nansemond Co. VA
At Fort Monroe, VA:
Garrett, Nancy

[57.535]
Wilson, Ashfille:
Nansemond Co. VA
At Fort Monroe, VA:
Camford, Clarisa

[57.512]
Wilson, Henry:
Western VA
At Fort Monroe, VA:
Wilson, Amy

[57.514]
Wilson, James S:
Surry Co. VA
At Fort Monroe, VA:
Crump, Sally

[57.568]
Page, Jennie

[57.566]
Wilson, James:
York Co. VA
At Fort Monroe, VA:
Dennis, D.

[57.579]
Wilson, John P:
Prince George Co. VA
At Downey Farm, VA:
Robinson, Daniel
Robinson, Eliza

[57.533]
Wilson, John: Dr.
Charles City Co. VA
At Fort Monroe, VA:
Scott, Jessey
[57.579]
At Downey Farm:
Jackson, Caroline
Jackson, Edmund
Jackson, Christiana
Jackson, Elvey
Jackson, Cornelius
Jackson, Henry Moler

[57.555]
Wilson, Mr:
Amelia Co. VA
At Fort Monroe, VA:
Wilson, General

[57.525]
Wilson, R: Dr.
Isle of Wight Co. VA
At Fort Monroe, VA:
Young, Francis A.

[57.519]
Wilson, Robert:
Isle of Wight Co. VA
At Fort Monroe, VA:
Wilson, Ben
Wilson, Matilda
[57.570]
Wilson, Lucy
Wilson, Jordan
Wilson, William
Wilson, Nellie
[57.477]
Wilson, W:
Fredericksburg VA
At Fredericksburg, VA:
Jackson, Jennett

[57.553]
Wilson, Willis:
Isle of Wight Co. VA
At Fort Monroe, VA:
Tynes, Lilly

[57.562]
Winder, John:
Eastern. Shore,
Northampton Co. VA
At Fort Monroe, VA:
Winder, Ann
Winder, Frank
Winder, Lehae

[57.531]
Winder, John:
Elizabeth City Co. VA
At Fort Monroe, VA:
Winder, Harry
Winder, Dolly

[57.578]
Winder, Lewis:
Elizabeth City Co. VA
At Downey Farm, VA:
Rodgers, Fred
Rodgers, Jim
Rodgers, Charey
[57.577]
Taylor, Peggy

[57.520]
Winn, Edmond:
York Co. VA
At Fort Monroe, VA:
Russell, Lucy
Russell, George
Russell, Hanah
Russell, Laura
Russell, Lizzie

[57.520]
Winn, Edmond:
York Co. VA
At Fort Monroe, VA:
Gatens, Polly

[57.474]
Winn, P.J:
Fluvanna Co. VA
At Fluvanna Co. VA:
Mutter, George: Infirm

[57.552]
Winston, Mackin:
King William Co. VA
At Fort Monroe, VA:
Harris, Claben

[57.544]
Winston, Phillip:
Hanover Co. VA

At Fort Monroe, VA:
Lewis, Matilda
Lewis, Denice

[57.551]
Winston, William:
Hanover Co. VA
At Fort Monroe, VA:
Crane, Thomas

[57.536]
Wobb?, John:
Prince George Co. VA
At Fort Monroe, VA:
Green, Ann
Green, James

[57.472]
Wood, H:
Fluvanna Co. VA
At Fluvanna Co. VA:
Unknown, Betsy:
Old Age

[57.554]
Wood, William:
Elizabeth City Co. VA
At Fort Monroe, VA:
Marshall, Charlotte
Marshall, Jacob
Marshall, Susan

[57.471]
Woods, Henry:
Fluvanna County VA
At Fluvanna Co. VA:
Unknown, Jacob:
Old Age.
Unknown, Jolly:
Deranged

[57.475]
Woodson, F: Mrs.
Fluvanna Co. VA
At Fluvanna Co. VA:
Decaton, Dilsa: Old age
Unknown, Dilsey:
Old age

[57.510]
Wren, Albert:
Isle of Wight Co. VA
At Fort Monroe, VA:
Cole, Rose
Cole, Annie

[57.476]
Wren, Gilchrist:
Essex Co. VA
At Fredericksburg, VA:
Fields, Benjamin
Fields, Margaret

[57.477]
Brooks, Samuel

[57.520]
Wren, Thomas:
Surry Co. VA
At Fort Monroe, VA:
Wardy?, Cherry

[57.538]
Wren, Thomas:
Isle of Wight Co. VA
At Fort Monroe, VA:
Wren, Eda

[57.585]
Wright, Sylvester:
Nansemond Co. VA
At Downey Farm, VA:
King, Louisa

[57.470]
Wright, W:
Green Co. VA
At Fredericksburg, VA:
Slaughter, John: Man

[57.555]
Wright, William:
Essex Co. VA
At Fort Monroe, VA:
Thomas, Mary

[57.575]
Haskins, Matilda
Braxton, Fannie
Braxton, Anderson

[57.557]
Yates, John:
Nansemond Co. VA
At Fort Monroe, VA:
Savage, Eliza

[57.541]
Young, Nathan:
Isle of Wight Co. VA
At Fort Monroe, VA:
Coe, Richard

[57.593]
Young, William G:
Warwick Co. VA
At Warwick Co. VA:
Taylor, Lucy

FREE BORN PERSONS AT FORT MONROE, VA:
{Listed under their pre-war Residences.}

[57.549]
Charles City Co. VA
Johnson, Margaret
Johnson, John
Johnson, James

[57.546]
Childs, Betsey
Childs, Milly
Childs, Amanda

[57.562]
Chesterfield Co. VA
Dungy, William

[57.527]
Elizabeth City Co. VA
Washington, Eliza
Washington, Sarah
Washington, Rose
Washington, William

[57.537]
King, Betsy

[57.531]
Gloucester Co. VA
Jones, Elizabeth

[57.547]

Hayes, Caroline
Hayes, Rose
Hayes, John
Hayes, Henry

[57.508]
Isle of Wight Co. Va
Lawrence, Emily
Lawrence, Ellen
Lawrence, Allice

[57.509]
Dix, Eliza
Dix, Sarah

[57.517]
Dix, Eliza
Dix, Mary

[57.530]
Bailey, Oriaden
Bailey, Amelia

[57.531]
Smith, Lizzie
Smith, Ida
Smith, Mariah
Smith, Cheny
Smith, George
Smith, Eliza

[57.540]

Gale, Mary L
Gale, John

[57.548]
Tynes, Angeline
Tynes, Mary

[57.549]
Bailey, Polly
Bailey, Thomas

[57.553]
Williams, Delia
Williams, Susie
Robinson, Marthy

[57.573]
Jones, Victoria
Jones, Susan
Jones, Julia A
Jones, Elizabeth
Jones, Margaret:
Jones, Eliza

[57.578]
Scott, Martha
Scott, Margarett
Scott, Caroline
Scott, John

[57.572]
Williams, Rhoda
Williams, James

Williams, John
Williams, Hannah
Williams, George

[57.514]
Nansemond Co. VA
Jerdan, Nancy
Jerdan, Amy
[57.523]
Copeland, Richard
Copeland, Lindey
Copeland, Harriett
[57.532]
Fladden, Jane
Fladden, James
Fladden, George
[57.540]
Reddick, Armassa
Reddick, Wealthy:
Reddick, Willis
[57.570]
Richards, Precilla
Richards, Julia
Richards, Mary
[57.573]
Johnson, Elizabeth
Johnson, Martha
Johnson, Peter

[57.522]
Norfolk, VA
Sawyer, W.H

[57.535]
Petersburg, VA
Bundy, Elizabeth
Tyler, Lucy A
Tyler, Thomas
Tyler, William

[57.517]
Portsmouth, VA

Wilson, Mary A.
Wilson, John
Wilson, Henry
[57.518]
Scott, Patience
[57.542]
Sawyer, Fanny
Sawyer, Arphenia
[57.544]
Epps, Adeline

[57.526]
Richmond, VA
Barns, Ann Eliza
Barns, John
Barnes, Mary
Barnes, Nathan
Barnes, Ames
[57.575]
Moore, Nancy
Moore, Rebecca
Moore, Jane

[57.566]
Smithfield, VA
Smith, Georgean
Smith, Josephine
Smith, Mary Francis

[57.554]
Suffolk, VA
Spencer, Lizzie
Spencer, Johana
Spencer, Gertrude
Spencer, William

[57.524]
Surry Co. VA
Barnes, Eliza
Barnes, John
[57.525]

Shepard, Rebecca
Shepard, Lucy
Shepard, George
[57.537]
Hill, Nelly
[57.561]
Barnes, Mary
[57.567]
Hasket, Ellick
Hasket, Lavinia
Harrison, Indiana
Harrison, Adeline
[57.573]
George, Eliza
George, Woodland

[57.535]
Winchester, VA
Burrace, Lucy

[57.511]
York Co. VA
Thomas, Martha
Thomas, Mary
Thomas, Levi
Thomas, Soloman

FREE BORN AT DOWNEY FARM:
{Listed under pre-war residence.}

[57.567]
Unknown pre-war residence:
Copeland, Rhoda
Copeland, Isam
Copeland, Mary
[57.580]
Johnson, Allen
Johnson, Francis Ann
Johnson, Leuender
Johnson, Elizabeth
Johnson, Charity
Johnson, Octavia
Johnson, Christopher
Johnson, Martha Jane
Johnson, Mary Eliza
Johnson, James Austin
Johnson, Sarah Eliza
Holland, Sally
Holland, Eliza
Holland, Elizabeth
Holland, Peter
Copeland, Sarah
Copeland, William
Copeland, Wright
Copeland, Mary E
Ellis, Betsey

[57.583]
Lewis, Eliza
Lewis, Oliveer Ann
Goodwin, Margaret Ann
Norfleet, Mary
Daugherty, Pautriome

Daugherty, Jackson
Daugherty, Betty
Simpson, Mary
Simpson, Lizzie

[57.581]
New Kent Co. VA:
Dandridge, Elsie
Dandridge, Martha
Dandridge, Charlotte
Johnson, Nellie

[57.577]
Sussex Co. VA:
Buster, Eliza
Buster, Mary Ann

[57.473]
Fluvanna Co. VA:
Gadding, Betty: deaf & dumb

[57.477]
Fredericksburg, VA
Lewis, William
Buckner, Sally:
        Bought her freedom
Curtis, Charlotte
King, Fillia
King, Thomas

[57.593]
Warwick Co. VA:
Johnson, Emeline: 4 children

SURNAME INDEX - FREEDMEN

Achrell: 66, 137
Acket: 101, 115
Ackin: 30
Adams: 66, 86, 87, 98, 115, 116, 173
Adamson: 68, 143
Addison: 46, 67, 70, 81, 139, 171
Adney: 55
Aikins: 4
Akin: 31
Akins: 4
Alfriend: 32
Allen: 2-4, 10, 11, 30, 40, 45, 52, 59, 60, 76, 77, 81, 82, 88, 96, 99, 103, 106, 109, 110, 114, 116, 126, 137, 143, 147, 150, 157, 175, 180
Allis: 44
Alston: 54
Ambler: 73, 117
Amon: 16
Ampey: 28
Ampy: 28
Anams: 82, 117
Anderson: 23, 24, 30, 39, 45, 47, 52, 55, 61, 64, 65, 67, 71-73, 80, 83, 85, 86, 103, 105, 111, 114, 117, 128, 133, 136, 137, 153, 159, 175, 178
Andrews: 81, 82, 85, 89, 95, 117, 124, 126, 138, 144
Angrum: 92, 121

Archer: 27, 29, 36, 40, 43-45, 54, 57, 62, 64, 93, 108, 123, 140, 145
Archy: 15, 36
Armstead: 4, 27, 34, 36, 38, 39, 77, 83, 84, 88, 93-95, 97, 117, 118, 120, 123, 124, 128, 159, 167
Armstrong: 4, 16, 103, 155
Ash: 4
Askey: 17, 106, 118
Augurn: 95, 118
Austin: 30, 33, 55, 65, 85, 107, 110, 123, 132, 135, 150, 163, 180
Bacon: 108, 118
Badden: 86, 118
Bagby: 79, 137, 165
Bagley: 57
Bailey: 4, 23, 24, 50, 51, 55, 57, 77, 80, 83-86, 90, 95, 97, 98, 100, 103, 118, 133, 137, 138, 142, 143, 146, 156, 165, 167, 178
Baily: 65, 154
Baines: 4
Baird: 32
Baker: 1, 4, 17, 18, 38, 41-43, 55, 59, 60, 66, 77, 79, 88, 97, 118, 131, 151, 158, 169, 170
Baldwin: 26, 97, 150
Ball: 81, 174
Ballard: 86, 98, 112, 118, 141, 164
Banister: 20

Bank: 44
Banks: 14, 30, 31, 33, 55, 56, 64, 65, 112, 125, 145
Barber: 1, 28, 81, 144
Barden/Bardon: 76, 116
Barley: 95, 100, 119
Barn: 84, 119
Barnard: 71
Barns/Barnes: 24, 79-81, 99, 151, 179
Barnet/Barnett: 50, 71
Barrett: 15, 16
Barrow: 80, 119
Bartem: 47
Bartlett: 10, 45-47, 74, 160
Baskerville: 37, 38
Bates: 10, 37, 43, 61, 64, 78, 87, 119, 149
Bath: 100, 138
Battles: 77, 174
Bauks: 111, 149
Baxter: 15, 22
Bayley: 11
Baylor: 85, 119
Bean/Beans: 88, 112, 119
Bearch: 91, 119
Beard: 49
Beaver: 64, 163
Beemun: 32
Beesley: 10
Bell: 1, 4, 7, 10, 13, 18, 32, 34, 37, 42, 45, 71, 89, 91, 102, 105, 119, 120, 134, 155
Bellew: 22, 26
Benisonk: 101, 120

181

SURNAME INDEX - FREEDMEN

Bennett: 23, 24, 104, 120
Bensen: 5
Benton: 74
Berry: 5, 16, 104, 166
Beverly: 19, 24, 38, 67, 70, 126
Billups: 88, 89, 93, 114, 119, 120, 126, 137, 138
Bilyard: 49, 52, 53
Bingsley: 31
Bird: 10, 42, 53, 55, 71-74, 78, 120, 131
Birdewell: 115
Bishoff: 92, 120
Bishop/Bishops: 31, 49, 52
Bisker: 104, 120
Bivins: 10
Blackman: 99, 120
Blackwell: 52
Blake: 21, 83, 84, 93, 120, 121
Blanch: 57
Blanchester: 5
Bland: 1, 43, 49, 51, 54, 56, 79, 91, 102, 121, 134
Blanks: 25
Blare: 90, 121
Blend: 105, 121
Blue: 89, 133
Bluford/Blufort: 35, 71, 140
Blunt: 5, 36, 76, 92, 116, 121
Boardwright: 74, 121
Boats: 28
Bodyd: 55
Bogg: 71
Bohanan: 94, 122

Bolding: 99, 130
Boles: 111, 140
Bolew: 56
Bolin: 60, 91, 129
Bolling: 31, 32, 34, 43
Bolt: 18, 74, 75, 112, 122, 123
Bond: 15, 75, 122
Bonner: 20, 21, 42, 49, 51
Booker(s): 45-48, 57, 72, 87-89, 95, 100, 107, 122, 134, 137, 155, 161, 166
Boon: 49, 51
Boots: 71
Boras: 64, 121
Bostick: 27
Boston: 65, 67, 122
Bottey: 111, 168
Botts: 46
Boulon: 44
Bounce: 41
Bowder: 108, 128
Bowers: 65, 169
Bowker: 78, 132
Bowlers: 64, 158
Bowles: 62
Bowman: 50-52
Bows: 56
Bowser: 17
Boyd: 30, 31, 35, 110, 122
Boyden: 95, 103, 122, 164
Boykin: 81, 85, 101, 104, 122, 157, 174
Boynton: 86, 122
Bracy: 5, 6
Bradley: 20, 31, 96, 153
Bradshaw: 1

Braks: 93, 123
Bramm: 74
Branagan: 1
Branch: 10, 28, 30, 32, 39, 40, 42, 44, 47, 64, 65, 79, 80, 123, 148, 149
Brander: 28
Brandis: 83, 159
Brandit: 54
Branton: 60
Braxton/Braxtin: 53, 78, 84, 85, 95, 98, 99, 114, 115, 126, 137, 159, 163, 167, 178
Bray: 15
Breadlove: 55, 57
Brent: 10
Brewer: 94, 128
Brey: 77, 158
Bricks: 44
Bridley: 30
Bridway: 30
Briggs: 10, 32, 33, 44, 64, 123
Brigham: 108, 111, 128, 130, 169
Bright: 5, 9, 87, 103, 112, 123, 136, 164
Brighten: 90, 123
Brightesley: 31
Brightwell: 30
Brimer: 57
Brindle: 47
Brinkley: 8, 18
Brister: 12
Britcher: 19
Brock: 15, 70
Brokenberry: 77, 123
Brokenburg: 85, 123

SURNAME INDEX - FREEDMEN

Bromley/Brombley: 94, 123
Brookins: 115
Brooks: 40, 56, 65, 67, 68, 71, 78, 85, 93, 123, 127, 140, 147, 167, 168, 175, 177
Brothers: 8
Brountey: 110, 123
Brown: 2, 5, 10, 16, 20, 21, 27, 29-31, 33-35, 41-43, 45, 47, 49-57, 59, 60, 62, 65, 68, 72, 81, 86, 87, 91, 93, 98, 100, 102, 104, 108-110, 119, 122-125, 128, 129, 131, 139, 145, 147, 148, 152, 171, 173, 174
Bruce: 14, 44, 45, 64, 65, 124
Bryant: 64 -66, 99, 106, 124, 125
Buchanan: 20, 72, 151
Bucker/Buckers: 51, 87, 157
Bucket: 101, 124
Buckey: 72, 174
Buckner: 68, 93, 111, 117, 124, 180
Buford: 32
Bullivant: 49
Bullock: 102, 124, 172
Bumel: 112
Bundley: 79, 170
Bundy: 78, 102, 170, 179
Bunkley: 95, 124
Bunnill: 21

Burch: 65, 135
Burchard: 38
Burk: 94, 124
Burke: 21, 58
Burkes: 44
Burks: 65, 151
Burkley: 82, 95, 124, 152
Burl: 1
Burnett: 51, 112
Burnham: 109, 125
Burr: 37, 38, 100, 125
Burrace: 103, 179
Burras: 82, 139
Burrell/Burrill/Burrel: 5, 8, 11, 15, 98, 78, 152, 174
Burrows: 112, 125
Burton: 21, 60, 66, 147
Bush: 51, 85, 119
Buster: 108, 180
But: 16, 55, 63
Butcher: 112
Butlar/Butler: 1, 61, 71, 81, 83, 104, 133, 153, 170
Butt: 2, 15, 18, 26
Butts: 88, 131
Byers: 72, 125
Byron: 106, 125
Cacine: 21
Calebee: 72, 125
Calhoun: 8
Callis: 114
Calrit: 111, 125
Cam: 88, 89, 133
Camel: 30, 56
Cameron: 53, 67, 73, 125, 157 **Camford:** 100, 176
Camp: 71, 125

Campbell: 35, 68, 71, 117, 125, 135, 136, 139, 140, 142, 145-147, 149, 158, 160, 161, 163, 166, 167
Candar: 28
Candy: 23
Canter: 14
Capps: 5
Carber: 20
Carey: 6, 18, 24, 26, 27, 55, 78, 80, 82, 86-89, 98, 107, 108, 112, 118, 122, 125, 129, 133, 135, 144, 148, 149, 153, 169
Cargan: 21
Carpenter: 82, 156
Carr: 2, 21, 54, 66, 169
Carrington: 38, 99, 125
Carrol: 104, 125, 156
Carson: 100, 164
Carter: 5, 10, 15, 32, 44, 45, 52, 55, 56, 58, 61, 67, 69, 71, 82, 89, 93-99, 109, 114, 117, 120, 125-127, 142, 148, 153, 157, 162, 163, 167, 175
Cary: 8, 9, 25, 30, 65, 66, 79, 109, 112, 121, 126, 127, 145, 146
Casey: 7, 85, 86, 126
Cason: 14
Cassell: 43, 112, 152
Cassen: 16
Cassey: 89

SURNAME INDEX - FREEDMEN

Chainey: 93, 145
Chambers: 41
Chandler: 69, 71
Chaplin: 19
Chapman: 13, 79, 86, 102, 121, 126, 154
Chappee: 49
Chappel: 52
Charity: 1, 2, 8, 12, 14, 47, 52, 55, 62, 65, 89, 110, 111, 130, 146, 180
Chaterfield: 45
Chatman: 108, 167
Chauncy: 109, 126
Chaycon: 28
Cheatham: 31
Cheens: 114
Cheesman: 88, 126
Cheny: 3, 85, 178
Cherer: 36
Chetham: 30
Childs: 96, 178
Chimes: 5
Christian: 18, 19, 48, 55, 88, 93, 95, 96, 98, 99, 102, 105, 107, 109, 110, 123, 125-127, 130, 150, 164, 168, 175
Churchill: 109, 112, 141
Civil/Civils: 5, 7
Claiborne: 26, 30, 33
Clary/Clarey: 66, 76, 84, 95, 116, 131, 168, 170
Clark: 5, 25, 30, 35, 43, 45, 47, 53, 54, 65, 66, 78, 99, 103, 109, 120, 126, 127, 136, 146

Clarkson: 74, 127
Clasisen: 84, 131
Clay: 72, 100, 127, 170
Claybon/Clayburn: 44, 94, 127
Clayman: 76, 116
Clayton: 80, 108, 127, 140
Clement: 26, 84, 127
Clements: 84, 127
Clemont: 83, 127
Clemonts: 81, 127
Clowet: 29
Cloyd: 42, 73, 162
Coats: 67, 69, 173
Coe: 79, 86, 128, 178
Cogsnell: 101, 145
Coker: 108, 167
Colding: 8
Cole: 20, 37, 80, 85, 128, 177
Colefield: 8
Coleman: 9, 33, 35, 43, 67, 69, 72, 83, 113, 123, 131, 139
Coles: 34, 38, 61
Coley: 24, 30
Collin/Colins: 3, 16, 21, 51
Collins: 5, 10, 23, 48, 83, 85, 89, 93, 117, 129, 140, 150
Collier/Colier: 28, 50, 55
Colter: 31, 93, 165
Coltin: 94, 165
Colton: 43, 84, 128
Colwell: 81, 171
Combs: 1
Comer: 74, 76, 116, 128

Connell: 80, 152
Conquest: 11
Conter: 91, 128
Cooh: 61
Cook: 42, 44, 67, 78, 97, 112-115, 117, 161, 165
Cooke: 69
Cooks: 93, 124
Cooley: 31
Cooper: 5, 8, 62, 64, 94-96, 107, 108, 118, 126, 128, 132, 158
Copeland: 2, 3, 84, 94, 100, 108, 110, 128, 130, 132, 179, 180
Copland: 8
Copper: 3
Corben: 109, 125
Cord: 104, 128
Cormick: 5, 8, 14
Corporal: 16
Corprew: 3, 5
Corwin: 79, 154
Cosby: 23, 44
Costin: 10
Cotten: 5, 92, 128
Couch: 14, 38
Coulborn: 11
Couley: 10
Council: 8
Cousins: 40, 64, 160
Covington: 95, 128
Cox: 41, 51, 54, 77, 81, 83, 91, 92, 101, 102, 107, 108, 128, 129, 145, 162
Craig: 60, 105, 129
Cramp: 110, 142
Crandall: 89, 129
Crane: 77, 177

SURNAME INDEX - FREEDMEN

Crank: 66, 137
Cranshaw: 37
Cratlock: 23
Crawford: 34, 42, 72
Crawken: 108, 129
Crawley: 52, 112, 163
Crayton: 35
Crea: 72, 129
Crenshaw: 30, 75, 96, 129
Creppen: 10
Criar: 49
Crick: 41
Crickman: 18
Crier: 51
Crigwell: 1
Crocker: 104, 106, 129
Crockett: 97, 98, 129, 130
Crockston: 84, 130
Crosby: 12
Crosly: 109, 165
Cross: 3, 5, 13, 105, 111, 130, 144
Crowley: 29
Crudey: 29
Crump: 67, 80, 99, 104, 107, 130, 158, 176
Crumson: 90, 141
Crustine: 82, 130
Cuder: 110, 130
Cuffee: 18
Cuffey: 2, 3, 5
Cunningham: 62
Curtis: 8, 68, 109, 110, 112, 148, 180
Custer: 86, 101, 104, 130, 144
Custine: 82, 130

Custis: 79, 97, 99, 111, 130, 131
Dabney: 54, 62, 84, 87, 115, 131, 175
Daly: 21
Dandridge: 58, 104, 107, 113, 130, 180
Danson: 26
Danville: 56, 57
Davenport: 7, 29, 73, 172
Davis: 1, 5, 11, 32, 37-39, 45, 47, 57-60, 67, 69, 72, 73, 78, 83, 84, 86, 88-90, 97, 102, 104, 109, 112, 122, 126, 131, 132, 139, 141, 146, 151, 152
Dawson: 37, 71, 88, 131
Day: 10, 42
Dean: 3, 8
Deane: 17
Decaton: 66, 127, 177
DeFord: 3
Delano: 81, 144
DeOde: 74, 132
Derdan: 5
Derriga: 76, 116
Dexter: 98, 100, 132
Dickens: 1
Dickenson: 9
Dickerson: 48, 79, 97, 121, 169
Dickinson: 60
Dicks: 36
Dickson: 93, 163
Didley: 47
Difen: 100, 132
Diggs: 22, 93, 112, 113, 132

Dillard: 80, 106, 110, 132, 162
Dilson: 31, 45
Dip: 94, 132
Discon: 56
Dix: 85, 94, 114, 132, 178
Dobson: 78, 132
Dock: 20
Dodge: 59
Doherty: 5
Doles: 112, 160
Donan: 10
Donel: 77, 118
Dorbson: 78, 132
Dorson: 102, 132
Doss: 23
Dotson: 30
Dougherty: 110, 132
Douglas: 57
Douglass: 16, 46, 53, 96, 100, 163, 173
Doves: 132
Downer: 69
Downman: 92, 132
Downs: 10
Dozier: 14, 16, 22
Draper: 41
Drew: 16, 33, 111, 175
Druge: 83, 159
Drummon: 42
Duck: 15
Dudley: 24, 62, 67, 77, 126, 136
Dukes: 100, 105, 133
Duly: 69
Dundan: 109, 133
Dungy: 101, 178
Dunn: 87, 97, 98, 133, 162
Durden: 16
Durgee: 83, 157

SURNAME INDEX - FREEDMEN

Durgen: 99, 134
Eads: 64, 144
Easley: 24
Ebbs: 56
Edlar: 40
Edlay: 96, 175
Edler: 49, 51
Edmonds: 23, 34, 99, 165
Edmonson: 42, 73, 133
Edmunds: 5, 23, 79, 80, 133
Edney: 43, 89, 135
Edwards: 5, 8, 24, 33, 40, 58, 72, 83, 84, 86, 133, 136
Egaton: 47
Eggins: 30
Egleston: 41
Eldridge: 58, 80, 88, 99, 137, 152
Ellett: 30
Elliot: 52
Elliott: 2, 3, 5, 8, 10, 12, 17, 75, 77, 88, 89, 99, 133, 152
Ellis: 32, 40, 49, 51-53, 69, 77, 81, 94, 108, 133, 162, 173, 180
Ely: 2, 17
Ennis: 55
Eoler: 33
Epeys: 29
Eppes: 49, 52, 91, 110, 134
Epps: 29, 30, 32, 33, 40, 51, 81, 90, 91, 94-96, 99 -102, 132, 134, 179
Epson: 90, 134

Ercott: 112, 134
Ervin: 48, 72, 146
Este: 23
Evans: 24, 25, 48, 49, 52, 60, 68, 145, 153, 154
Everedge: 5
Everett: 16, 56, 94, 100, 135, 173
Evin/Ervin: 48
Ewing: 68, 130, 144
Fairford: 11
Farmer: 24, 25, 30
Farquer: 25
Farren: 98, 135
Fautrod: 69
Felter: 105, 135
Felton: 89, 135
Fenley: 20
Fenno: 90, 135
Fenny: 103, 135
Fenton: 85, 123
Fenwick: 20, 21
Fereby: 12, 14, 16, 17
Ferguson: 65, 110, 135, 136
Ferris: 31
Field: 28, 114, 115
Fields: 31, 32, 38, 68, 72, 114, 148, 177
Fig: 47
Filds: 43
Fin: 44
Findum: 47
Finks: 60
Finney: 11
Firoled?: 44
Fisher: 10, 42, 45, 50, 53, 59, 99, 137
Fitchett: 82, 135
Fitzgerald: 29
Fitzhugh: 1, 82, 135

Fladden: 100, 179
Fleming: 22, 27, 52, 63, 83, 96, 99, 135, 143, 164, 170, 175
Flood: 46, 71, 74, 135
Flowers: 65, 164
Floyd: 72, 135
Fobs: 3
Fogg: 3
Folger: 86, 117
Folley: 40
Forbes: 3, 7
Ford: 44
Foreman: 1 -3, 5, 18
Fortune: 5
Foster: 5, 23, 25, 45, 60, 87, 94, 103, 136, 171
Fountain: 21, 46, 64, 69, 136
Fourqurean: 25
Fowler: 36, 65, 138
Fox: 64, 65, 69, 78, 82, 98, 113, 136, 137
Franklin: 7, 11, 12, 21, 44, 65, 72, 106, 107, 110, 132, 136, 148, 156, 167
Frayser: 69
Frazer: 1, 32, 54, 55, 75, 171
Frazier: 113
Free born: 65, 72, 78, 80, 81, 84-88, 94-97, 99-103, 107, 108, 110, 178, 180
Freeland: 76, 116
Freeman: 102, 136
Friday: 66, 119, 168
Friend: 31, 90, 136
Frost: 18

186

SURNAME INDEX - FREEDMEN

Fukes: 77, 170
Fulford: 3
Fuller: 3
Furgain: 94, 132
Furtress: 7
Gable: 28
Gadding: 65, 180
Gadline: 17
Gadrey: 79, 136
Gaines: 15, 64, 77, 99, 114, 136, 137, 154, 170
Gale: 13, 57, 86, 178
Gales: 26, 98, 165
Gallagher: 55
Gallary: 67, 161
Gallen: 103, 137
Gallie: 98, 137
Gamerell: 88, 137
Games: 15
Gamott: 107, 137
Ganes: 41
Ganet: 41
Ganie: 101, 137
Ganroy: 79, 137
Garden: 86, 94, 137, 155
Gardner: 113, 114
Gardnor: 78, 127
Garey: 83, 137
Garlic: 98, 99, 137
Garly: 83, 91, 137, 142
Garner: 15, 20, 68, 138
Garnett: 84, 93, 118, 137
Garney: 20
Garo: 76, 116
Garret: 21

Garrett: 1, 25, 35, 88, 100, 102, 124, 138, 176
Gaskin: 100, 138
Gatens: 97, 177
Gatewood: 107, 173
Gath: 110, 155
Gatlin: 105, 138
Gatter: 103, 118
Gay: 84, 138
Geary: 49, 52
Gee: 36
Genoa: 73, 162
Gerst: 24
Gett: 87, 138
Gibbs: 82, 113, 147
Gibson: 28
Gidget: 82, 176
Gidjet: 81, 138
Gilchrist: 50, 52, 68, 177
Giles: 41, 42, 44, 54, 72, 74, 138, 157
Gilham: 90, 138
Gillan: 46
Gillem: 54
Gillet: 10
Gilley: 53
Gilliam: 28, 35
Girsh: 27
Gladden: 112, 158
Gladdox: 1
Glenfoot: 90, 135
Glover: 32, 52, 105, 138
Godfrey: 56
Godwin: 17
Goffigan: 10
Gofican: 82, 138
Going: 109, 139
Golden: 78, 139
Golding: 111, 139

Goldsmith: 60
Goldston: 41
Gombley: 83, 139
Goney: 69
Good: 30, 40, 41, 44, 54, 102, 108, 110, 140, 160, 173
Goodall: 108, 139
Goodin: 15
Goodman: 3, 8, 19, 24, 76, 77, 89, 110, 116, 157, 171
Goods: 46
Goodsend: 16
Goodwin: 28, 42, 67, 108, 139, 180
Gorden: 32, 87, 94, 148, 161
Gordon: 13, 16, 55, 67, 69, 113, 139
Gothican: 82, 139
Gough: 35, 104, 152
Gougin: 82, 139
Gould: 28
Govener: 77, 137
Gowens: 84, 138
Gower: 96, 158
Graham: 102, 113, 139
Grain: 77, 137
Graindier: 86, 115
Gramby: 71
Grammar: 49, 53
Grammer: 42
Granett: 35
Grange: 42
Granger: 107, 167
Grant: 43, 72, 139, 172
Granton: 99, 127
Grantum: 114
Grasham: 97, 139

SURNAME INDEX - FREEDMEN

Gratcher: 24
Grautein: 60
Grave: 29
Graves: 13, 30, 31, 42, 63, 74, 79, 109, 114, 121, 139, 140
Gray: 38, 61, 64, 65, 67, 69, 92, 124, 139, 140, 169
Greasy: 64, 117
Greaves: 50
Green: 1, 2, 5, 21, 28, 31, 33, 36, 37, 42, 44, 46, 49, 60, 62, 68, 72, 76, 79, 88, 90, 96, 110, 121, 123, 128, 131, 135, 139, 140, 144, 152-154, 159, 164, 165
Grees: 29
Gregory: 14, 15, 17, 30, 101, 102, 105, 114, 140, 160
Grey: 1, 77, 79, 80, 83, 107, 136, 140, 146, 148, 159
Griffin: 10, 114
Grigg: 39
Grimes: 79, 83 -85, 140, 143, 146, 158
Grimm: 44
Grisly: 34
Griswell: 77, 123
Grooms: 111, 140
Gross: 95, 124
Groton: 10
Guerson: 115
Guilford: 36
Gulscom: 105, 138
Gunn: 111, 151
Gunnell: 20

Gurley: 16
Guss: 55
Guthrie: 23
Haden: 69
Haines: 19
Haldy: 140
Hall: 3, 12, 20, 25, 54, 56, 85, 95, 97, 108, 114, 140, 175
Hamilton: 75, 115, 141
Hamlin: 49, 51, 52
Hamod: 113
Hams: 60, 113
Hancock: 30
Hand: 66, 113, 136
Handley: 25
Hankins: 95, 147
Hansen: 42
Harbody: 110, 141
Harburn: 58
Harden: 47
Hardgrove: 108, 168
Hardy: 15, 17, 38, 61, 78, 170
Hare: 89, 129
Harndall: 72, 148
Harner: 17
Harnett: 4, 91, 93, 105, 121, 132, 166
Harper: 56
Harrad: 113
Harrelton: 54
Harris: 11, 19-21, 28-30, 32, 35, 42, 44, 50, 56, 59, 60, 65, 67, 68, 71, 72, 76, 80, 84, 90, 102, 115, 116, 123, 141, 143, 149, 158, 159, 177

Harrison: 3, 5, 8, 12, 20, 29, 32-35, 41, 42, 48, 49, 51, 52, 54, 57, 62, 69, 79-81, 90-92, 95, 97, 99, 108, 109, 113, 128, 130, 132, 133, 141, 142, 147, 151, 167, 173, 179
Harrod: 113
Harsin: 43
Hart: 79, 142
Harvey: 32, 72, 74, 91, 121, 129, 142
Hase: 38
Hasket: 81, 179
Haskins: 38, 40, 57, 79, 85, 142, 178
Hatch: 20, 49, 52
Hatcher: 29, 42, 75, 142
Hatchett: 36
Hawkins: 65, 80, 97, 98, 104, 112, 115, 139, 142, 160, 169
Haydon: 72, 142
Hayes: 78, 110, 113, 142, 178
Haynes: 80, 142
Haze: 28
Hedgely: 23
Height: 54
Heinger: 9
Hembrick: 31
Henderson: 40, 42, 61, 67, 83, 96, 97, 101, 120, 134, 143, 158, 174
Hendrick: 25
Hendricks: 37, 38
Henly: 77, 143
Hennican: 80, 143

SURNAME INDEX - FREEDMEN

Henning: 114
Henton: 88, 171
Herbert: 5, 45, 88, 89, 143
Herring: 22
Hew: 82, 135
Hews: 78, 120
Hickman: 84, 87, 89, 133, 143
Hicks: 31, 36, 56
Hill: 21, 28, 41, 56, 58, 72, 79, 80, 83, 84, 93, 95-97, 103, 104, 121, 123, 125, 126, 131, 140, 143, 165, 179
Hinebark: 84, 143
Hines: 49, 53
Hinton: 15, 17
Hoag: 108, 143
Hobdy: 78, 143
Hobson: 47
Hocker: 35
Hocks: 69
Hodges: 3, 5
Hoe: 2
Hoffman: 3
Hogard: 58
Hoget: 81, 144
Hogg: 78, 81, 144
Holden: 10, 93, 94, 145
Holdon: 90, 134
Holland: 10, 44, 78, 86, 101, 110, 111, 118, 144, 180
Hollman: 3
Holloway: 49, 52
Holly: 9
Holman: 66, 109, 118, 144

Holmes: 5, 11, 22, 26, 30, 31, 43, 68, 69, 83, 114, 127, 140, 144
Holt: 49, 52, 57, 75, 98, 144
Homes: 31
Honeycutt: 54
Hood: 101, 140
Hoop: 89, 144
Hooper: 47, 61
Hope: 21, 88, 154, 158
Hopkins: 3, 5, 16, 18, 21, 66, 97, 108, 144
Hopper: 5
Hornes: 37
Hosely: 72, 145
Hoskins: 57
House: 35, 40, 73, 74, 130, 131
How: 34
Howard: 23, 27, 64-66, 86, 89, 96-98, 108, 113, 126, 133, 136, 145, 159, 175
Howdy: 101, 145
Howe: 34
Howler: 101, 145
Howlet: 101, 145
Hubang: 82, 145
Hubbard: 35, 76, 110, 116, 123, 145
Hudgins: 20, 22, 87, 89, 93, 94, 107, 132, 145, 146
Hudsher: 82, 146
Huggins: 26
Hughes: 12, 24, 29, 65, 114, 146
Humphrey: 14, 21

Hunt: 24, 42, 49, 53, 103, 109, 141, 146
Hunter: 5, 7, 14, 79, 84, 85, 93, 146, 175
Huntley: 84, 146
Huntly: 77, 146
Hurtson: 47
Hutchinson: 49, 51
Hutson: 46
Hyde: 56
Hynes: 80, 146
Irvin: 72, 146, 156
Isaaks: 30, 31
Ivey: 89, 147
Jackson: 2-3, 10, 12, 23-24, 26, 27, 29, 34-35, 37, 40, 42-52, 55-57, 60, 65-66, 68-73, 78, 82, 83, 87, 89-92, 95, 97-99, 102, 105, 108-111, 113, 117-118, 126, 130-131, 136, 138, 142- 143, 147, 152, 156-157, 159-161, 165-166, 168, 172, 174-176, 180
Jacobs: 18, 82, 147
Jarget: 92, 147
Jarrett: 43
Jarvis: 94, 147, 154
Jasper: 80, 87, 104, 124, 127, 130
Jeffers: 37, 41, 76, 85, 116, 147
Jefferson: 15, 26, 58, 60, 64, 71, 72, 75, 80, 87, 88, 96, 102, 129, 137, 139, 148, 156, 158, 164, 175
Jeffries: 42, 75, 162
Jeffs: 30

SURNAME INDEX - FREEDMEN

Jenkins: 42, 44, 68, 147
Jenks: 72, 147
Jennings: 1, 25
Jeofers: 99, 159
Jeran: 48
Jerdan: 81, 85, 95, 100, 101, 122, 145, 147, 163, 179
Jermai?: 30
Jerson: 97, 163
Jessie: 28, 77, 90, 94, 100, 106, 118, 119, 123, 146, 147
Jinning: 46
John: 115
Johns: 20, 29, 49, 52
Johnson: 2, 3, 6, 8, 16, 17, 19, 26, 28-30, 32, 35, 37, 38, 42, 43, 45, 50, 51, 54, 60-62, 64-70, 72, 74, 77, 80, 82, 84, 88, 89, 91, 93-96, 98-101, 107, 109-111, 114, 115, 119, 120, 123-125, 133-137, 139, 143, 145-148, 156, 160, 165, 168-171, 173, 178-180
Johnston: 18, 55, 57-59
Joiner: 73, 148
Jolly: 6, 64, 177
Jones: 1, 6, 12, 20, 21, 27, 29-33, 35, 36, 38, 41-43, 45, 47-53, 55-58, 60, 65, 66, 68, 69, 71, 72, 76-81, 84-93, 96, 98, 99, 101, 102, 104, 106, 108, 109, 111-114, 116, 119, 122-125, 132, 138, 141, 142, 144, 148, 149, 154, 157, 160, 162-164, 168, 172, 173, 176, 178
Jonnie: 68, 138
Jordan: 32, 45, 48, 50, 51, 71, 86, 110, 135, 149, 176
Joyner: 10
Jubilee: 85, 122
Judge: 58, 83, 127, 140
Judkins: 6, 55
Judon: 102, 165
Juleford: 58
Julias: 97, 161
Jupee: 99, 175
Kain: 8
Kape: 89, 150
Kaser: 30
Katlin: 105, 138
Kearney: 45
Keasey: 29
Keaton: 37
Keeller: 71
Keely: 106, 173
Keen: 37, 38
Keese: 73, 150
Keetan: 111, 150
Kelley: 89, 150
Kellum: 10
Kelly: 40, 107, 150
Kemp: 110, 111, 150
Keney: 52
Keninton: 77, 136
Kennedy: 49
Kenny: 78, 97, 132, 150
Keny: 41
Key: 1, 57, 66, 127, 150
Kidd: 20, 65, 66, 115, 150
Kier: 43
Kimbro: 26
Kimpt: 42
Kingston: 65, 163
Kinsey: 106, 165
Kirby: 23
Knappe: 82, 151
Knight: 3, 43, 93, 111, 151, 156
Knox: 86, 151
Kyle: 72, 151
Lacey: 26
Lack: 27
Lacy: 26, 27
Lafayette: 6
Lambert: 83, 84, 168
Lancaster: 97, 111, 150, 151
Land: 3, 7, 9, 43, 48
Landrum: 74
Lane: 48, 65, 108, 151
Lang: 45
Langdon: 46
Langley: 6
Langly: 104, 148, 151
Lansin: 90, 123
Larden: 56
Lariby: 97, 151
Lashley: 35, 36
Laster: 7
Lawford: 6

SURNAME INDEX - FREEDMEN

Lawrence: 47, 62, 67, 71, 76, 85, 116, 141, 178
Lawson: 42, 79, 151
Laydon: 21
Lease: 35
Lee: 12, 19, 23, 28, 38, 42, 60, 63, 66, 70, 74, 83, 89, 104, 106, 112, 114-116, 140, 147, 149, 151, 152
Lendsey: 55
Leonard: 11, 82, 88, 99, 104, 130, 151, 155
Lester: 19
Lewellyn: 109, 152
Lewis: 1, 4, 11, 16, 18, 21, 25-27, 29-32, 37, 38, 40, 41, 47-49, 51, 59-61, 63, 64, 67, 68, 70, 77, 81, 86, 88, 91, 95, 104, 105, 107-113, 116-118, 120, 121, 128, 129, 132, 134, 139, 147, 149, 151, 152, 162, 164-166, 168, 170, 174, 177, 180
Lewon: 107, 174
Lichfield: 94, 122
Liddleton: 113
Liggin: 45
Liggins: 8, 46
Lightfoot: 57, 101, 115, 153, 172
Ligon: 47
Lild: 28
Lilds: 29
Lincoln: 14, 21
Lipscae: 83, 152

Lipscomb: 29, 83, 152
Lipscon: 83, 152
Lipsker: 82, 152
Lispan: 83, 133
Litchfield: 94, 124
Livingston: 100, 101, 152
Locke: 112, 152
Locket: 29
Locklin: 92, 162
Logan: 23-25, 44, 51, 99, 133, 174
Loisa: 55
Lon: 42
London: 78, 152
Loney: 55
Long: 35, 64, 137
Looker: 104, 152
Loomis: 114
Loper: 31
Louis: 34, 57, 72, 73, 75, 133, 154, 156
Louns: 38
Lousey: 41
Love: 14, 58, 109, 141
Lovis: 2, 3
Lownes: 38
Lowns: 37, 38
Lowry: 107, 152
Loyd: 84, 130
Lucas: 1, 2, 50, 51, 53, 60, 64, 167
Luckes: 30
Lunder: 54
Lundy: 36
Lunford: 6
Lynch: 44, 62
Lynn: 46
Lyons: 59, 66, 98, 135
Machin: 19
Mack: 26, 42, 45, 105, 126

Macus: 56
Madery: 80, 152
Madock: 42
Madray: 8
Madway: 88, 152
Maggett: 101, 153
Mago: 44
Magruder: 3
Maisen: 103, 116
Maison: 77, 143
Major: 21, 22, 41, 57, 83, 96, 109, 111, 130, 131, 143, 153
Malcott: 87, 153
Malery: 102, 136
Malone: 57
Manford: 29
Manning: 6
Mansfield: 28
Mapp: 10, 84, 143
March: 12
Mardell: 57
Marks: 49, 50, 52, 92, 128
Marrell: 96, 172
Marsh: 55, 114
Marshal: 8, 32
Marshall: 2, 6, 9, 14, 35, 43, 47, 58, 60, 72, 76, 84, 85, 89, 91, 94, 97, 102, 103, 107, 109, 112, 119, 123, 129, 131, 137, 140, 152, 153, 159, 161, 175, 177
Marthan: 41
Martin: 42, 43, 56, 67, 71, 74, 75, 94, 117, 153
Masin: 10

SURNAME INDEX - FREEDMEN

Mason: 10, 13, 15, 32, 33, 35-37, 41, 49-51, 53, 54, 56, 57, 61, 65, 103, 114, 153, 174
Masonberge: 92, 121
Masters: 28, 71, 115 11 154, 163, 165, 175, 176
Matthews: 7, 61, 72, 74, 111, 139, 167
Maune: 55
Mayo: 30
McAllister: 61
McCann: 50
McCargo: 27
McCary: 64, 163
McClennan: 9
McCoy: 8, 9, 14, 105, 106, 160
McCraw: 25
McCray: 30
McCue: 71, 153
McFettis: 64, 160
McGee: 45
McGill: 104, 153
McKennsy: 6
McPherson: 15, 26
Meade: 49, 53
Meekes: 99, 164
Megins: 98, 164
Mekins: 57
Mercer: 6, 70
Meredith: 130
Merrit: 30, 108, 167
Merritt: 36, 88, 154
Meus: 29
Meyor: 1
Micel: 47
Michel: 45
Mickens: 98, 164

Middleton: 43, 105, 154
Miegs: 114
Milborn: 11, 98, 116
Miles: 3, 7, 23, 70, 71, 76, 80, 100, 101, 103, 116, 132, 149, 153, 167
Milkins: 92, 132
Mill: 44
Miller: 1, 3, 6, 27, 42, 43, 45-47, 60, 64, 65, 92, 94, 104, 114, 123, 129, 154, 166
Milliner: 57
Mills: 5, 8, 9, 12, 47, 110, 130
Milsey: 113
Mims: 31, 35
Mindeth: 20
Miner: 60
Minga: 51
Mingo: 3, 10, 39, 46
Minister: 45
Miniver: 3
Minkin: 97, 169
Minor: 32, 65-67, 69, 70, 150, 154, 170
Minster: 93, 154
Mirsells: 2
Mitchell: 14, 29, 42, 79, 103, 154, 157
Mocks: 91, 154
Modest: 42
Mody: 46
Monday: 1, 9, 31
Mondon: 19
Monk: 91, 128
Monks: 91, 154
Montacue: 114
Montague: 113

Moody: 30, 42, 92, 93, 102, 128, 154, 163
Moon: 43
More: 46, 98, 137
Moreby: 60
Morgan: 7, 32, 54, 61
Morman: 62, 72, 154
Morral: 88, 154
Morris: 6, 11, 35, 55, 65, 80, 89, 96, 112, 113, 122, 126, 154, 162, 172, 175
Morrison: 49, 52, 86, 91, 129, 155
Morse: 60
Morton: 64, 124
Mosby: 41, 42, 66, 71, 82, 135, 137, 155
Moseby: 3, 79, 163
Moss: 54, 66, 72, 155, 156
Mother: 1
Moxley: 2
Munday: 71, 83, 155
Munden: 15
Murphy: 103, 105, 110, 111, 154, 155
Murry: 94, 102, 155, 168
Muse: 115
Mutter: 65, 177
Myers: 88, 89, 155
Mynick: 29
Nash: 6, 28, 46, 47, 53, 98, 114, 137
Neal: 104, 155
Nealy: 114
Neely: 55
Neilson: 71

SURNAME INDEX - FREEDMEN

Nelson: 1, 8, 11, 12, 15, 16, 18, 20, 21, 23, 26, 30, 31, 41, 44, 59, 63, 65, 67, 71, 74, 79, 82, 84, 98, 100, 103, 111, 114, 125, 127, 128, 135, 138, 151, 154, 155, 160, 161, 163, 165, 169, 174, 176
Nero: 34
Newby: 8, 13
Newell: 106, 168
Newfelt: 13
Newman: 85, 155
Nibby: 36
Nichols: 54, 85, 166
Nicholson: 3
Nickys: 30
Nodingham: 82, 155
Noel: 18
Nomux: 70
Norfelt: 18
Norfleet: 59, 108, 111, 117, 156, 180
Norlet: 100
Norrill: 87, 156
Norris: 76, 170
Northam: 11
Northington: 38
Nottingham: 11, 108, 156
Nozery: 80, 166
Nunley: 23
Oflin: 7
Oldhern: 111, 156
Olds: 6, 14
Oliver: 37, 38, 40, 48, 94, 108, 113, 146
Olmsted: 60
Olston: 32
Orange: 50, 52

Orcutt: 19
Organ: 104, 156
Osborn: 37, 90, 156
Oulds: 81, 156
Outland: 108, 156
Overstreet: 15
Overton: 102, 124, 131
Owen: 6, 14, 15, 25, 29, 54, 75, 88, 156, 165
Owens: 13, 27, 35
Paden: 95, 156
Page: 1, 11, 26, 42, 57, 58, 81, 83, 96, 98, 113, 114, 153, 157, 164, 176
Palister: 90, 134
Palmer: 11, 14, 26, 32
Pamels?: 8
Parham: 31, 54
Paris: 1, 17, 72, 157
Parish: 65, 66, 89, 157, 158
Parker: 6, 10, 11, 23, 25, 27, 40, 43, 54, 58, 59, 71, 80, 82, 84, 87, 97, 100, 101, 107-110, 112, 119, 130, 133, 157, 165, 173
Parramore: 11
Parris: 87, 157
Parsens: 6
Parsons: 11, 14
Pascoll: 108, 143
Paterson: 103, 157
Pates: 70
Paton: 22
Patrick: 23, 26, 27, 30, 34, 46, 88, 89, 125, 131, 166

Patten: 14
Patterson: 29, 43, 47, 72, 161
Payne: 1, 55, 56, 59, 64, 65, 73, 138, 148, 157, 158
Payton: 13, 22, 97, 158
Peadon: 55
Pearl: 70
Pedigore: 72, 158
Pegram: 6, 19, 30, 42
Peirce: 3
Peldia: 3
Pendleton: 67, 68, 113, 126
Penn: 112, 158
Penne: 113
Pennington: 54
Pennock: 23, 24, 26, 27
Percil: 83, 158
Perkins: 21, 42, 51, 56, 64, 65, 73, 158, 165
Perry: 10, 17, 41
Person: 2, 3
Persons: 29, 31, 73, 74, 76, 164, 178
Peters: 27, 57, 67, 158
Pettice: 37
Peyton: 111, 150
Phantroy: 56
Phetty: 77, 158
Phillips: 3, 17, 18, 21, 26, 49, 53, 87, 88, 96, 115, 124, 157, 158
Phylo: 20
Picket: 100, 158

SURNAME INDEX - FREEDMEN

Pierce: 73, 81, 94, 113, 128, 158, 159, 166
Pierson: 90, 159
Pimeni: 42
Pinia: 83, 159
Pinier: 112, 160
Pisan: 28
Pitchford: 89, 149
Pitt: 3, 4, 58, 86, 151
Pittman: 60
Pleasant: 2, 4, 5, 7, 14, 16, 22, 23, 27, 43, 56, 57, 72, 107, 152, 161
Poindexter: 25
Pollard: 37, 46, 83, 84, 159
Pollid: 56
Pollock: 46
Pondexter: 104, 159
Pool: 4, 38
Pope: 15
Portriss: 52, 53
Posen: 4
Powell: 11, 15, 30, 31, 54, 75, 159
Pressey: 108, 159, 161, 165
Preston: 43, 49, 62
Pretty: 77, 159
Price: 45, 46, 55, 63, 80, 99, 105, 113, 151, 159, 160
Pride: 95, 125
Pridly: 30
Prior: 38, 46, 66, 135
Pritchet: 63, 70, 159
Pritchett: 16, 64, 105, 106, 160
Proctor: 9
Prophit: 90, 162
Pryor: 41

Purlieu: 108, 165
Quarles: 24, 31
Quarrels: 77, 171
Quince: 105, 129
Quintaine: 104, 129
Quolls: 99, 133
Raby: 8
Ragland: 24, 43
Ragsdale: 28
Rainey: 28, 29
Ramsay: 19
Rand: 108, 160
Randal: 34
Randall: 8, 12, 18, 22, 30, 51, 52, 56, 65, 76, 79, 81, 89, 90, 101, 103, 108, 109, 113, 116, 118, 121, 126, 128, 134, 153, 155, 160, 162, 166, 169, 170
Randle: 103
Randol: 44, 46
Randolph: 6, 32, 45, 66, 115
Rankle: 103, 160
Ransdell: 1
Ransom: 21
Rauke: 59
Rawles: 6
Rawls: 6, 7
Ray: 9, 55, 78, 79, 163
Read: 11
Ream: 43
Reams: 42, 107, 145
Recker: 82, 145
Red: 62
Reddick: 12, 79, 83, 100, 105, 110-112, 121, 138, 159, 160, 179
Redman: 113, 115

Reduck: 105, 138, 160
Reed: 4, 6, 8, 9, 11, 16, 18, 45, 46, 78, 84, 91, 98, 114, 131, 149, 160, 162
Reems: 28
Reeves: 32
Reevs: 74, 160
Reid: 57, 72, 160
Revel: 70
Reynolds: 61
Rhone: 110, 141
Rice: 34, 72, 84, 90, 119, 138, 161
Richards: 100, 179
Richardson: 30, 32, 42, 56, 58, 71
Richtell: 44
Rickes: 50
Ricks: 51, 115
Riddick: 4, 6, 8-10, 17, 19, 40, 94, 105, 161
Riddin: 16
Ridley: 49, 53
Riggins: 55
Riles: 91, 142
Riley: 104, 114, 125
Rillups: 61
Rind: 42
Risby: 82, 174
Ritchie: 50, 53, 66, 120
Rivers: 11, 57
Roberts: 4, 12, 29, 42, 82, 156
Robertson: 51, 52, 74, 113, 161
Robins: 114

SURNAME INDEX - FREEDMEN

Robinson: 13, 15, 25, 31-33, 35, 40-43, 47, 55-57, 59, 68, 73, 76, 79, 83, 84, 86, 87, 91, 95, 96, 98, 99, 102, 104, 110, 113, 114, 121, 124, 129, 133, 136, 137, 139, 140, 143, 151, 161, 164, 167, 170, 173, 176, 178
Rock: 58
Rodgers: 107, 177
Rodringham: 97, 161
Rogers: 6
Rogister: 97, 166
Rolin: 109, 141
Romey: 9
Rone: 60
Ronett: 97, 161
Roots: 55
Roper: 57
Ross: 29, 44, 57, 58, 60, 66, 73, 136, 161
Rosse: 31
Rosser: 72, 161
Rowe: 78, 107, 108, 114, 139, 161, 172
Rowell: 108, 161
Rowlett: 31
Roxam: 25
Roy: 77, 79, 96, 113, 136, 137, 151, 161
Royal: 49, 52
Rud: 6
Ruffin: 31, 33, 40, 76, 80, 81, 90-92, 110, 116, 128, 156, 162
Ruggen: 44
Rush: 50
Russell: 72, 97, 100, 115, 151, 156, 177

Rynnall: 57
Sachel: 11
Saidferro: 70
Sails: 77, 171
Salad: 31, 65, 162
Sampson: 22, 26, 27, 43, 73, 74, 118, 161
Samson: 46, 47
Sanders: 13, 17
Sandy: 22, 24, 27, 36, 41, 49, 92, 109, 120, 165
Sanford: 18
Sanlin: 16, 22
Sauger: 65, 124, 162
Saugon: 65, 124
Saunders: 11, 67, 73, 162
Savage: 11, 82, 87, 89, 93, 100, 111, 112, 139, 149, 162, 163, 178
Sawyer: 12, 17, 94, 102, 179
Schuchins: 7, 8
Schuckons: 4
Scott: 2, 4, 6, 11, 14, 29, 32, 33, 36, 41, 46, 49, 51, 52, 54, 55, 60, 66, 67, 72, 73, 82, 85, 86, 94, 95, 110, 113, 114, 120, 123, 150, 156, 163, 176, 178, 179
Screggs: 71, 163
Scutching: 15, 17
Seaborn: 54
Searber: 90, 163
Seasber: 97, 163
Seddon: 38
Segor: 83, 151

Selden: 78, 79, 89, 96, 97, 150, 163
Seldon: 78, 84, 159
Senley: 50
Sergeant: 49, 51, 52
Sewall: 112, 125
Seward: 36, 50, 51
Sewell: 17
Seymore: 21, 114
Shafford: 6
Shands: 43
Shanklins: 2
Shap: 91, 141
Shatten: 11
Shaw: 112, 163
Sheer: 72, 166
Shelley: 86, 163
Shelton: 59, 65, 146
Shepard: 34, 80, 93, 96, 157, 163, 172, 179
Sheperson: 34
Shephard: 4, 8
Sherman: 72, 84, 98, 99, 159, 164
Sherrard: 58
Shields: 20, 37, 107, 113, 164
Shiff: 1
Shins: 6
Shirley: 64, 154
Shoe: 10, 29, 82, 101, 111, 124, 144, 155-157, 176
Shores: 55
Shune: 89, 151
Sidney: 6, 10, 68, 69, 71, 72, 102, 130, 131, 139, 162
Siler: 51
Silvey: 26, 47, 54, 86, 89, 133, 169

195

SURNAME INDEX - FREEDMEN

Simmons: 6, 14, 19
Simond: 84, 90, 101, 118, 134, 137
Simonds: 100, 101, 103, 106, 115, 125, 133, 164
Simons: 40, 42, 81, 147
Simpson: 55, 85, 180
Sinclair: 78, 164
Sinclare: 87, 164
Singleton: 9, 55, 113
Sinton: 18
Skinner: 106, 165
Slate: 99, 173
Slater: 112, 174
Slaughter: 64, 67, 73, 91, 99, 121, 134, 161, 165, 178
Slean: 68, 172
Slocum: 99, 165
Small: 1, 11, 17, 100, 135
Smallwood: 6
Smaugh: 11
Smith: 1, 2, 4, 6, 9-11, 17, 27-29, 32, 33, 35, 40, 45, 47, 48, 50, 52, 53, 55-60, 70-72, 77-79, 82, 85, 87, 88, 91, 93-95, 97-99, 102, 104, 105, 107-111, 113, 114, 125, 128-130, 132, 134, 136, 137, 141, 148, 149, 152, 156, 157, 160, 165, 166, 172, 173, 175, 178, 179
Snead: 6, 10, 65, 166
Snell: 104, 166
Sninners: 10
Snowden: 15

Southall: 6, 17, 49, 52
Southhould: 85, 166
Southold: 7, 97, 166
Spadey: 11
Sparks: 113
Sparrow: 4
Spence: 4, 105, 168
Spencer: 21, 31, 34, 45, 48, 57, 62, 70, 94, 114, 179
Spires: 54
Spooner: 39
Spotman: 15
Spradley: 79, 81, 142, 166, 169
Spradly: 80, 166
Spragon: 48
Spratley: 10, 80, 167
Sprattley: 21
Spriggs: 92, 112, 158, 162
Spruell: 105, 167
Spurlock: 113
Stanard: 70
Stansfield: 57
Statesman: 21
Stearns: 6
Stedgt: 108, 167
Steers: 15
Stephens: 67, 70, 84, 113, 122, 167
Steptson: 109
Stevens: 17, 23, 88, 138
Stevenson: 27, 34
Steward: 22, 83, 120
Stewart: 10, 22, 42, 70, 71, 83, 84, 98, 106, 120, 137, 152, 168
Sticker: 45
Still: 110, 169

Stired: 83, 152
Stitch: 40
Stith: 54
Stock: 15, 82, 91, 95, 146, 167
Stocks: 95 -97, 167
Stokeley: 107, 167
Stokes: 43, 113, 114
Stone: 6, 21, 72, 111, 130, 167
Stong: 70
Stoveall: 23
Stovel: 108, 167
Strong: 48, 52, 66, 92, 104, 152, 153, 167
Stubbs: 113
Sulivan: 102, 168
Sullivan: 61, 73, 153
Sutton: 105, 168
Swan: 21, 30
Sweet: 91, 101, 121, 140, 145
Syke: 106, 168
Sykes: 42, 49-51, 111, 155, 168
Symons: 106, 168
Syner: 86, 118
Tabb: 60, 78, 85, 87, 94, 108, 114, 145, 153, 155, 161, 168
Taliaferro: 33
Talley: 70, 111, 168
Tally: 38
Tammy: 67, 123
Tannel: 11
Tanner: 104, 159
Taplet: 68, 170
Tatum: 6, 54

SURNAME INDEX - FREEDMEN

Taylor: 1, 4, 13, 15, 20, 22, 26, 30, 43-45, 47, 49, 52, 54-56, 59, 61, 65, 68, 70, 78, 83, 84, 87, 90, 92, 97, 98, 104, 105, 107-109, 128, 143, 144, 163-165, 168, 169, 171, 177, 178
Tazewell: 11
Temple: 37, 73, 77, 81, 110, 133, 134, 161, 169
Temples: 6
Templeton: 41
Tennis: 98, 169
Terrall: 96, 126
Terry: 36, 46, 67, 70, 169
Texon: 65, 124
Theat: 42
Thom: 26
Thompson: 6, 11, 19, 26, 67, 68, 78, 87, 130, 166, 170
Thorn: 70
Thornton: 32, 56, 60, 64, 67-69, 80, 95, 115, 159, 161, 167, 170, 172
Thurston: 11, 79, 113, 170
Tiler: 51
Tillman: 32
Tillor: 70
Tisdell: 43
Titchet: 11
Toast: 60
Toavers: 11
Todd: 54, 70, 93, 95, 113, 154, 170
Toland: 77, 170

Toler: 58
Toliver: 78, 79, 92, 121, 142, 143
Toller: 99, 170
Tolliver: 76, 77, 113, 170
Tolman: 67, 130
Tolover: 56
Tolver: 81, 92, 127, 162
Tomlin: 86, 130
Tompkins: 93, 113, 132, 145
Tompson: 84, 127
Toomes: 26
Torrell: 70
Torvin: 48
Totwell: 113
Trace: 102, 141
Tracy: 71
Traverse: 49, 50, 52
Travis: 55, 60
Trent: 30, 31, 46, 48, 109, 142
Tress?: 31
Tribb: 45
Triss: 30
Trotman: 17
Trower: 81, 82, 170
Trusty: 92, 141
Tucker: 23, 33, 46, 50, 53, 89, 147
Turlington: 10
Turner: 28, 31, 38, 65-67, 80, 83, 84, 100, 113, 120, 148, 150, 170
Turpin: 50, 51
Twine: 87-89, 171
Tyler: 2, 13, 43, 77, 95, 102, 171, 179
Tynes: 86, 176, 178

Unknown: 1, 2, 28, 34-37, 39, 40, 44, 46, 47, 53, 55, 62-67, 71, 74, 75, 90, 116, 117, 119, 121-124, 127-129, 131, 133-135, 137, 139, 141-146, 148-150, 152, 153, 155, 156, 158-160, 162-164, 166, 167, 169-172, 174, 177, 180
Upcher: 104, 171
Upher: 97, 157
Upshur: 11
Upshure: 82, 171
Upture: 79, 82, 96, 142, 147, 172
Valentine: 12, 14, 28, 29, 41-44, 109, 153
Vaughn: 80, 87-89, 105, 107, 110, 116, 170, 172
Venen: 47
Vest: 66, 156
Volentine: 55, 56, 58
Vonn: 25
Waddleton: 58
Wade: 25
Waden: 54
Wadkins: 38
Wafe: 11
Wagensworth: 172
Wainack: 44
Waine: 31
Wainock: 45
Wake: 50, 52, 53
Waldron: 73, 172
Walke: 1, 6
Walkens: 44

197

SURNAME INDEX - FREEDMEN

Walker: 1, 6, 11, 19, 20, 38, 45-47, 56, 57, 65, 66, 68, 69, 82, 91, 92, 96, 102, 111, 115, 130, 134, 141, 150, 172
Walkins: 70
Wallace: 47, 67, 68, 70, 71, 85, 87-89, 111, 122, 146, 149, 151, 154, 172
Walthall: 25
Walton: 15, 19
Ward: 98, 114, 172
Warden: 16, 57, 94, 156, 172
Wardy?: 80, 177
Ware: 65, 127
Waren: 94, 173
Warnder: 1
Warner: 6, 17, 18, 84, 114, 115, 133
Warren: 17, 53, 61, 71, 78, 80, 84, 91, 94, 100, 106, 107, 136, 146, 149, 167, 173
Was: 115
Washington: 1, 4, 5, 16, 18, 21, 23, 26, 31, 32, 36, 38, 40, 49, 53, 57-59, 62, 65, 67, 68, 70, 72, 75, 77, 79, 80, 87, 88, 90, 92-97, 102-104, 106, 108, 109, 113-115, 117-119, 121, 122, 125, 126, 128, 130, 133, 135, 137, 141, 144, 153, 162, 166, 169, 171, 173, 175, 178
Wason: 10
Watkins: 15, 30, 31, 41, 48, 56, 59, 60, 87, 101, 109, 110, 142, 173
Watson: 6, 28, 44, 56, 64, 74, 123
Wattes: 107, 173
Watts: 6, 87, 104, 155, 170, 173
Weather: 70
Weaver: 28
Webb: 6, 81, 98, 99, 107, 109, 115, 139, 172-174
Webster: 89, 112, 157, 174
Weed: 98, 174
Weich: 54
Weldon: 14, 57
Weleams: 58
Wells: 17, 30, 36
Wescott: 11, 82, 174
Weslawn: 47
Wess: 30
West: 1, 9-11, 23, 24, 30, 115, 155
Westen: 97, 161
Wharton: 11
Wheeler: 56, 77, 174
Whels: 31
Whigand: 30
White: 4, 6, 8, 13, 15, 18, 20, 29, 42, 43, 46, 47, 50, 51, 56, 63, 65, 66, 70, 76, 81-85, 90, 93, 105, 110, 111, 115, 116, 130, 134, 138, 159, 168, 171, 174, 175
Whitefield: 22
Whitehouse: 15
Whitehurst: 2, 6, 7, 9
Whiten: 89, 175
Whiting: 72, 87, 89, 113, 114, 169, 175
Whitmore: 55
Whitney: 95, 99, 175
Whitten: 71
Wickham: 111, 175
Wigg: 70
Wiggins: 4
Wight: 8, 15, 18, 19, 41, 43, 85, 108, 115, 117, 118, 122, 126, 128, 130, 133, 139, 140, 145, 148, 151, 155-157, 160, 163, 166, 169, 174, 176-178
Wilcox: 88, 91, 96, 97, 102, 175
Wild: 103, 175
Wiley: 6, 35, 102, 105, 160, 175
Wilkeson: 71
Wilkins: 4, 7, 22, 23, 29, 41, 49, 52, 70, 82, 90, 92, 120, 171, 176
Wilkinson: 28, 41, 56
Willey: 7, 9, 16, 17
Williams: 2, 7, 9, 11, 12, 20, 22, 33, 34, 41-44, 47, 53, 55-58, 60, 67, 68, 70-72, 76, 78, 81, 84, 86-88, 94, 97, 98, 101, 109, 111, 113, 115, 116, 122, 125, 127, 131, 132, 141, 142, 144, 153, 155, 163, 166, 168, 173, 175, 176, 178, 179

SURNAME INDEX - FREEDMEN

Williams?: 43
Williamson: 49, 76, 116
Willis: 3, 4, 8, 16, 18, 19, 24, 36, 46, 64-66, 68, 70, 71, 86, 91, 94, 100-102, 120, 121, 137, 145, 175, 176, 179
Wills: 7, 40
Wilson: 2, 4, 6-9, 11-13, 16, 18, 23, 30, 31, 35, 41, 44, 48, 51, 52, 55, 65, 68, 70, 80, 81, 83, 85-88, 95, 97, 98, 100, 101, 103, 109, 110, 113, 114, 122, 125, 142, 151, 155, 163, 166, 174-176, 179
Wimbush: 26
Winbush: 37
Winder: 11, 82, 88, 107, 151, 176, 177
Winfield: 40
Winfree: 31
Wingfield: 33
Winn: 52, 65, 97, 115, 177
Winney: 64, 70, 137
Winston: 35, 56, 62, 77, 84, 177
Wise: 4, 11, 15, 17, 31, 97, 113, 131
Wital: 113
Wobb: 90, 177
Woden: 45
Wodey: 27
Womack: 23
Wondow: 9
Wood: 7, 23-26, 65, 89, 114, 177
Wooden: 46
Woodford: 47
Woodhouse: 14, 20
Woodland: 21, 81, 179
Woodroffe: 57
Woodson: 46-48, 58, 66, 109, 142, 177
Woody: 30
Wooldridge: 35
Woolrich: 60
World: 8
Wormley: 113, 115
Wren: 68, 80, 85, 86, 177
Wright: 7, 10, 11, 13, 17, 22, 32, 64, 85, 86, 110, 111, 151, 177, 178, 180
Wuher: 30
Wyatt: 10, 30
Yancy: 56
Yates: 100, 178
Yearby: 97, 150
Young: 1, 7, 10, 12, 41, 46, 55, 70, 78, 85, 86, 92, 111, 113, 128, 130, 139, 176, 178
Younger: 22

INDEX OF FORMER SLAVE OWNERS

Acket, James 101
Adams, John 66, 86, 115
Adams, William 98
Addison, John 81
Allen, Hudson 110
Allen, John 103
Allen, William 76, 77, 81
Allen, Williamson 76
Anams, Alexander 82, 117
Anderson, F. 82, 111
Anderson, Fitchett, 135
Anderson, George 86
Andrews, George W. 81
Armistead, Robert 108
Armstead, Francis 93, 94
Armstead, Frank 93
Armstead, John 93
Armstead Lockey 88, 117
Askey, John 106
Atkins, (Dr.) J. 109
Atkins, Archie 86
Atkinson, H. 86
Augurn, Martha 95
Bacon, George 108
Badden, Daniel 86
Bailey, Richard 84, 95, 103
Ballard, Augustus 86
Barley, Jessie 100
Barley, Richard 95
Barn, Theodore 84

Barrow, Nancy 80
Bates, George 87
Baylor, Richard 85
Bean, Hezekiah 112
Beans, John 88
Bearch, Peater 91
Bell, Alexander 102
Bell, James 45, 89
Benisonk, John 101
Billups, Robert 93
Billups, Susan 93
Bird, Dr. 78
Bishoff, William 92
Bisker, Walter 104
Blackman, Oscar 99
Blake, Benjamin 83, 84
Blake, James 93
Bland, George 91
Bland, Maj. 79
Bland, Randall (Maj.) 79
Bland, Reddick 79
Bland, Robert 79
Bland, Rodrick 79
Bland, Rodward 79
Blare, John 90
Blend, John 105
Blunt, Thomas 92
Booker, A. 107
Booker, George 89
Booker, Richard 88
Booker, Virginia 87
Boyd, Dr. 110
Boyden, A. (Dr.) 95
Boykin, Dr. 85
Boykin, John 104
Boynton, Frank 86
Brady, Thomas 112

Braks, William 93
Bright, John 112
Brighten, Ann 90
Brokenburg, Austin 85
Bromley, Marshall 94
Brooks, George 67, 93
Brountey, Mary 110
Brown, Andrew 93
Brown, Christian J. 93
Brown, Christopher 93
Brown, John 87
Bryant, William 106
Bucket, William 101
Buckner, B. (Dr.) 111
Bullock, Granville 102
Bunkley, Edwin 95
Burk, John 94
Burkley, John 95
Burnham, William 109
Burr, Henry 100
Burrows, T. 112
Calrit, Fred 111
Carey, Dr. 78
Carey, John 89
Carrington, Thomas 99
Carrol, Henry 104
Carter, Hill 95-97
Carter, Mrs. 96
Casey, William 85, 86
Cassey, William 89
Chapman, Fletcher (Mrs.) 86
Chauncy, Cary 109
Cheesman, Samuel 88
Christian, Bat 98
Christian, Benjamin 95
Christian, David 105
Christian, R. 109

INDEX OF FORMER SLAVE OWNERS

Christian, William C. 99
Clark, Glotcher 78 108,
Clark, Mr. 78
Clayburn, John D. (Maj.) 94
Clayton, Jasper 80
Clement, Mr. 84
Clements, Ira 84
Clemont, Judge 83
Clemonts, Phero 81
Cleyborn, J.D. 98
Coe, Thomas 79
Cole, William 80
Colton, Henry 84
Conter, Charles 91
Cooper, Fred 108
Cooper, Henry 94
Copeland, John 94
Cord, William 104
Cotten, John 92
Covington, Thomas 95
Cox, Edward 77
Cox, Harrison 91, 92
Cox, Henry 107, 108
Cox, James B. 91, 92
Cox, James 91
Cox, Virginia 83
Craig, Charles 105
Crandall, Thomas 89
Crawken, Carey 108
Crenshaw, Agness 96
Crocker, James 106
Crocker, John 104
Crockett, W. 98
Crockett, Wilet 97
Crockston, Richard 84
Cross, William 105
Crump, Harrison 99
Crump, John 104
Crump, L. (Dr.) 107
Crump, Leonard (Dr.) 99
Crustine, James 82
Cuder, Mills 110
Custer, George (Maj.) 104
Custer, Joseph 86
Custer, Joseph M. 86
Custine, Robert 82
Custis, Maj. 99, 111
Custis, William 79
Custis, William H. 97
Dabney, William 84
Davis, Lewis 88
Davis, Marshall 97
Davis, Parlss 83
Davis, R.B. 102
Davis, Rheuben 84
Dawson, William 88
Dennis, Capt. John 88
Dennis, John 88, 97
Dexter, Jocklin 98
Difen, Dempsy 100
Diggs, John 93
Dillard, Jerry 106
Dillard, William 80
Dip, Albert 94
Dix, Albert 94
Dobson, Joseph 78
Dorbson, William 78
Dorson, John 102
Dougherty, Jacob 110
Downey, J.W. 107
Downman, John 92
Dukes, Abram 100
Dukes, Isaac 105
Dundan, Edwin 109
Dunn, Howard 97, 98
Dunn, Thomas 98
Edmunds, Washington 79, 80
Edwards, Butler 83
Edwards, David 86
Edwards, George 83, 84
Edwards, Warner 84
Elliott, George (Capt.) 88, 89
Ellio , John 89
Elliott, Logan 99
Ellio , Temple 77
Eppes, John 110
Eppes, Richard 91
Epps, Dr. 90, 95, 99, 100
Epps, Edward 81
Epps, R. (Dr.) 91
Epps, Richard 90, 91, 96, 101
Epps, Richard (Dr.) 90
Epsey, Dr. 102
Epson, Dr. 90
Ercott, James 112
Everett, Jassett 100
Farren, Lyons 98
Felter, Jasher 105
Felton, Richard 89
Fenny, John 103
Ferguson, Austin 110
Fitchett, J.H. 82
Foster, John 103
Foster, Warren 94
Fox, John 78, 82
Franklin, J.N. 110

INDEX OF FORMER SLAVE OWNERS

Free born, 65, 72, 78, 80, 81, 84-88, 94-97, 99-103, 107, 108, 110, 178, 180
Freeman, Joseph 102
Friend, Charles 90
Gadrey, Samuel 79
Gaines, Dr. 77
Gaines, William (Dr.) 77
Gaines, William G. (Dr.) 77
Gallen, Thomas 103
Gallie, Braxton 98
Gamerell, Nat 88
Gamott, Richard 107
Ganie, Madisen 101
Garden, George 94
Garey, William 83
Garlic, Braxton 98, 99
Garly, William 83
Garnett, James 93
Garrett, George 88
Gaskin, Capt. 100
Gatlin, Reddick 105
Gatlin, Redick 105
Gay, Dr. 84
Gett, Geret 87
Gidjet, William 81
Gilham, Maurice 90
Glover, Jackson 105
Gofican, Edward 82
Going, Edward 109
Golden, James 78
Golding, Simon 111
Gombley, Robert 83
Goodall, 139
Goodson, Thomas 86
Gothican, Susan 82
Gougin, Susan 82
Graham, John 102
Grasham, James 97
Graves, Ben C. 109
Green, Benjamin 76
Gregory, William 101, 102
Grey, Dr. 83
Grey, Peater 79
Grooms, J. 111
Hall, J. 108
Hall, James 108
Hall, John 85, 95
Harold, Moses 108
Harold, Sam 105
Harold, Samuel 112
Harris, Robert 102
Harrison, George E. 90, 92
Harrison, George 91, 92
Harrison, John H. 109
Harrison, Richard 90-92
Harrison, William B. 90
Harrison, William M. 109
Harrison, Windfield 91, 92
Hart, Henry H. 79
Haskins, William 79
Hawkins, John H. 80
Hawkins, John 104
Hayes, Joseph (Col.) 110
Haynes, Richard 80
Henly, Richard 77
Hennican, Roland 80
Herbert, John 89
Herbert, Thomas 88
Hew, Fitts 82, 135
Hickman, Charles 87
Hickman, William 89
Hill, James 104
Hill, Lucy 103
Hill, William 83, 84
Hinebark, Richard 84
Hoag, Thomas 108
Hobdy, William 78
Hoget, Sherno 81
Hogg, Richard 78
Hogg, Thomas 81
Holland, Edward 101
Holland, J.H. 111
Holland, Thomas 78
Holt, F. 98
Hoop, George 89
Hopkins, Charles 97
Howard, Dr. 86
Howdy, Thomas 101
Howler, Thomas 101
Howlet, James 101
Hubang, Richard 82
Hudgins, Archer 93
Hudgins, Delia 107
Hudgins, Elleck 94
Hudgins, Holden 93, 94
Hudgins, Jessie 94
Hudgins, R. 107
Hudgins, Robert 87, 89, 94
Hunt, William 103
Hunter, Robert 79, 84, 85

INDEX OF FORMER SLAVE OWNERS

Huntley, Thomas 84
Huntly, Richard 77
Hynes, Richard 80
Ivey, William 89
Jackson, Andrew 82, 110, 130
Jacobs, Robert 82
Jarget, Henry 92
Jeffers, (Dr.) 85
Jerdan, James 81
Jerdan, John 81
Jerdan, Samuel P. 95
Jerdon, William 100
Jessie, Lee 106
Johnson, Ann 99
Johnson, James 84
Johnson, Mary J. 80
Johnson, Thomas 109, 110
Jones, Burden 87
Jones, Caleb (Dr.) 104
Jones, Carey 88, 89
Jones, Cleyborn 80
Jones, George 108
Jones, Henry 80
Jones, John 109
Jones, John D.W. 109
Jones, John P. 89
Jones, Lewis 111
Jones, Richard 92
Jones, Sarah 79
Jones, Thomas 85
Jones, Warren 78
Jones, William 80, 101
Jones, Wilmot 99
Joseph, Susan 98
Kape, Jerry 89
Keetan, John 111

Kelley, Sylvestor 89
Kelly, M.H. 107
Kemp, Austin 110
Kemp, H. 111
Kenny, Baldwin 97
King, Edwin 100
King, Ned 89
King, Robert 83
Knappe, Victor 82
Knight, Joseph 93
Knox, Lewis 86
Lamb, John 80
Lancaster, A. 111
Lane, Keziah 108
Langly, Waller 104
Lariby, Charles 97
Lawson, Barnes 79
Lee, Henry 112
Lee, Thomas 104
Lee, William 89
Leonard, Parce 88
Lewellyn, J. 109
Lewis, Hands 104
Lipscae, John 83
Lipscomb, Capt. 83
Lipscon, John 83
Livingston, Martha 101
Livingston, Walter 100
Locke, W.H. 112
London, Thomas 78
Looker, Thomas 104
Lowry, Thomas 107
Madery, Eldridge 80
Madway, Eldridge 88
Maggett, Chestine 101
Major, George 96, 109
Malcott, Sylvester 87
Marshall, Valentine 109

Martin, (Dr.) 74, 75, 94
Mason, Miles 103
Mathews, James 92
McGill, Benedict 104
Middleton, James 105
Miller, Locken 94
Minster, Martha 93
Mitchell, James 79
Mocks, Julas 91
Monks, Edward 91
Moody, Mr. 102
Moore, John 107
Morral, William 88
Morrison, Edmund 86
Munday, Robert 83
Murphy, Josiah 110, 111
Murphy, Thomas 103
Murry, (Dr.) 94
Myers, Gilbert 89
Myers, William 88
Neal, Leonard 104
Nelson, Joseph 100
Newman, Sarah 85
Nodingham, Leonard 82
Norlet, Elisha 100
Norrill, William 87
Oldhern, Leroy 111
Organ, Mary 104
Osborn, Montgomery 90
Osborne, (Dr.) 91
Oulds, William 81
Outland, Augustus 108
Paden, Jerome 95
Page, Charles 96
Page, Edward 83
Parish, John 89

INDEX OF FORMER SLAVE OWNERS

Parker, George 87
Parker, George W. 97
Parker, H.D. 112
Parker, James 108
Parker, John 82
Parker, John W. 110
Parker, William 101
Parris, Jackson 87
Payton, Henry 97
Penn, John 112
Percil, Boardman 83
Phetty, William 77
Phillips, James 96
Phillips, Jefferson 88
Phillips, Thomas 88
Picket, Nathaniel 100
Pierson, Richard 90
Pinia, Fanny 83
Pollard, James 46, 83, 84
Pollard, Thomas 83, 84
Pollard, William 83
Pondexter, Dabne 104
Pressey, Calvin 108
Pretty, William 77
Price, John 99
Pritchett, David 105, 106
Rand, Charles 108
Randle, William 103
Reddick, Alvin 112
Reddick, Jeptha 110
Reddick, Richard 111
Reddick, Widow 112
Reddick, Wiley 105
Reduck, William 105
Reed, Hawkins 98

Riddick, William H. 105
Robinson, John 73, 76
Rodringham, Josaphene 97
Ronett, John P. 97
Rowe, Benjamin 78
Rowe, Edward 78
Rowell, Widow 108
Roy, John P. 96
Ruffin, Edmon 90
Ruffin, Edmund 90, 92
Ruffin, Maj. 110
Ruffin, Thomas 80, 81
Ruffin, William 80, 81
Savage, Edward 89
Savage, Fanny 87
Savage, Jesse 111
Savage, Mr. 93
Scott, John 85
Searber, Charles H. 90
Seasber, George 97
Selden, John 96, 97
Seldon, Robert 78
Shelley, Frank 86
Shepard, Ellie 93
Sherman, Ballard 98
Sherman, Benjamin 98
Sherman, Headley 99
Sherman, Mastin 98
Sherman, Mr. 98
Shields, S. (Dr.) 107
Simonds, Joshua 100
Simonds, William 103
Sinclair, John 78
Sinclare, Jefferson 87
Skinner, Joseph 106
Slocum, John 99

Smith, Frank 97
Smith, George 98
Smith, Henry 108
Smith, John 95, 105, 109
Smith, Mortimore 79
Smith, Mr. 102
Smith, Owen 88
Smith, Samuel 94
Smith, Sand 93
Smith, Tom 108
Smith, W.S. 88
Smith, William S. 95
Smith, William 78, 87, 91, 104
Snell, Henry 104
Southhould, Stephen 85
Southold, William H. 97
Spradley, Punch 81
Spradley, Thomas 81
Spradly, Richard 80
Spratley, Thomas 80
Spruell, Hesekiah 105
Stedgt, Merrit 108
Stephens, John 84
Stock, Petan 91
Stock/Stocks, (Dr.) 89, 97
Stocks, P. 95
Stocks, Potan 96
Stokeley, Franklin 107
Stovel, W. 108
Sulivan, Christian 102
Sutton, Catharine 105
Syke, Benjamin 106
Sykes, Michael 111
Symons, John 106

INDEX OF FORMER SLAVE OWNERS

Tabb, John 78
Tabb, William (Mrs.) 108
Talley, Sam 111
Taylor, Curren 78
Taylor, David 92
Taylor, George 83, 84
Taylor, John 97
Taylor, R. 108
Taylor, W.P. 97
Taylor, William P. 97
Taylor, William 78
Temple, James 110
Tennis, John 98
Thomas, Billy 112
Thomas, John E. 86
Thomas, John 109
Thomas, Richard 86
Thompson, C. 87
Thompson, Taswell 78
Thornton, Richard 80
Thurston, James 79
Todd, Robinson 95
Toland, William 77
Toller, Henry 99
Tolliver, John 76, 77
Trower, John 81, 82
Turner, John 100
Twine, M. 88
Twine, Sarah 89
Twine, Thomas 87, 89
Tyler, Hiram 95
Tyler, John 77, 95
Tyler, Thomas 77
Upcher, Ann 104
Upshure, William 82
Vanten, Robert 96
Vaughn, (Dr.) 88

Vaughn, Jacob 87, 88
Vaughn, Robert 107
Vaughn, Thomas 105
Walker, W.B. 96
Wallace, A. 111
Ward, Georgeana 98
Waren, Moses 94
Warren, Edwin P. 91
Warren, Michael 100
Warren, Mr. 80
Warren, Thomas 53, 106
Watkins, E.O. 110
Watkins, Edward 101
Watkins, Henry 87
Wattes, Catherine 107
Watts, Thomas 87
Webb, Henry 99
Webb, Mr. 81
Webb, S. (Dr.) 107
Webb, Samuel (Dr.) 95, 98
Webb, Samuel 98, 99
Webster, L. 112
Weed, Joseph 98
Wescott, William 82
Weston, Armstead, 117
Wheeler, Robert 77
White, Ambrose 83
White, Edwin 81
White, Samuel 85
White, William 93
Whiten, Canon 89
Whiting, Canen 87
Whiting, Henry 89
Whitney, Carter 99
Whitney, Sterrit 95
Wilcox, (Dr.) 96

Wilcox, Jackson 91
Wilcox, Jacob 91, 102
Wilcox, Westmore 96
Wilcox, William (Dr.) 97
Wild, Richard 103
Wiley, Thomas 102
Williams, Billy 93
Wilson, Ashby 100
Wilson, Ashfille 100
Wilson, Henry 103
Wilson, James 81, 98
Wilson, James S. 80
Wilson, John (Dr.) 95, 109
Wilson, John P. 110
Wilson, Mr. 103
Wilson, R. (Dr.) 85
Wilson, Robert 85 -87
Wilson, Willis 86
Winder, John 82, 88
Winder, Lewis 107
Winn, Edmond 97
Winston, Mackin 84
Winston, Phillip 77
Winston, William 77
Wobb, John 90
Wood, William 89
Wren, Albert 85
Wren, Thomas 80, 86
Wright, Sylvester 111
Wright, William 85
Yates, John 100
Young, Nathan 86

www.ingramcontent.com/pod-product-compliance
Lightning Source LLC
Chambersburg PA
CBHW050145170426
43197CB00011B/1968